Padre Martini's Closed and Enigmatic Canons with Solutions
by Luigi Cherubini: A 19th-Century Guide into Renaissance Music Riddles

Studies on Italian Music History

Edendum Curavit
Fulvia Morabito

Volume 19

Publications of the Centro Studi Opera Omnia Luigi Boccherini
Pubblicazioni del Centro Studi Opera Omnia Luigi Boccherini
Publications du Centro Studi Opera Omnia Luigi Boccherini
Veröffentlichungen des Centro Studi Opera Omnia Luigi Boccherini
Publicaciones del Centro Studi Opera Omnia Luigi Boccherini
Lucca

Padre Martini's Closed and Enigmatic Canons with Solutions by Luigi Cherubini

A 19ᵀᴴ-Century Guide into Renaissance Music Riddles

Luciane Beduschi

❋

BREPOLS
TURNHOUT
MMXXIII

The present volume has been made possibile by the friendly support of the

FONDATION INTERNATIONALE LUIGI CHERUBINI /
DEN INTERNATIONALE LUIGI CHERUBINI-FOND
DENMARK

© BREPOLS 2023

All rights reserved. No part of this publication may be reproduced,
stored in a retrieval system, or transmitted, in any form or by any means,
electronic, mechanical, photocopying, recording, or otherwise, without
the prior permission of the publisher.

D/2023/0095/256

ISBN 978-2-503-60847-1

Printed in Italy

Contents

Acknowledgements ... ix
Introduction ... xi

The 72 Enigmatic Canons of
Padre Martini's *Storia della Musica* ... 1

Luigi Cherubini's Solutions: A Pedagogical Work ... 5

A Table of Enigmatic Expressions ... 7

Renaissance Sources for
Padre Martini's List of *Motti o Enigmi* ... 11

    Pietro Aaron, *Libri tres de institutione harmonica*, Bologna, 1516 ... 13
    Heinrich Glarean, *Dodecachordon*, Basel, 1547 ... 14
    Hermann Finck, *Practica musica*, Wittenberg, 1556 ... 15
    Pietro Cerone, *El melopeo y maestro*, Naples, 1613 ... 22
    Giovanni Battista Rossi, *Organo de cantori...*, Venice, 1618 ... 34
    Camillo Angleria, *La regola del contraponto...*, Milan, 1622 ... 42
    Giovanni Andrea Angelini Bontempi, *Historia Musica*, Perugia, 1695 ... 43

Reception of Martini's and Cherubini's Works in the 19th Century ... 47

    Pierre-Louis Ginguené, *Encyclopédie méthodique*, Paris, 1791 ... 47
    François-Joseph Fétis, *Traité du contrepoint et de la fugue*, Paris, 1824 ... 52

Padre Martini's List of *Motti o Enigmi*
(Reproduced in Cherubini's Collection)
and the Understanding of the Renaissance Practice
of (Puzzle) Canons during the 19th Century ... 59

COMPARATIVE TABLES — 65

Table 1. Luigi Cherubini's *Table des mots latins, que les anciens compositeurs plaçaient souvent en tête des canons, avec l'explication du sens énigmatique qu'ils renferment, afin d'obtenir plus aisément la véritable solution d'un canon fermé* — 67

Table 2. Cherubini's *Table des mots latins* vs. Martini's Lists of *Motti o Enigmi* and *Vocaboli Italiani, Latini e Greci* — 75

Table 3. Padre Martini's Sources for his *Motti o Enigmi* — 85

Table 4. Martini's *Esemplare* vs. Finck's *Practica musica* — 105

Table 5. Finck's Expressions not Cited by Martini — 111

Table 6. Cherubini's and Ginguené's Translations of Martini's List of *Motti o Enigmi* — 117

Table 7. François Joseph Fétis's *Table des Devises ou Inscriptions des Canons Énigmatiques avec leur Explication* — 123

PADRE MARTINI'S CLOSED AND ENIGMATIC CANONS WITH SOLUTIONS BY LUIGI CHERUBINI — 129

LIST OF CANONS IN CHERUBINI'S COLLECTION — 303

LETTER SENT BY THE FRENCH MUSICOLOGIST HENRY EXPERT (1863-1952) TO THE ADMINISTRATOR OF THE NATIONAL LIBRARY IN PARIS ON 10 JUNE 1924 — 315

PLATES — 319

CRITICAL NOTES — 323

BIBLIOGRAPHY — 327

INDEX OF NAMES — 333

For Chiara and Sophie

Acknowledgements

I would like to express my profound gratitude to:

Helena Jank and Richard Hester, for their wise advice and unfailing support;

Nicolas Meeùs, who provided English translations for Finck, Aaron and Glarean, and solved theory-related translation problems in Cherubini, Rossi and Cerone;

Marc Vanscheeuwijck, for his very helpful assistance with revisions of old Italian, old Spanish, old French, and Latin translations. Also for his help with essential negotiations with the Museo Internazionale e Biblioteca della musica di Bologna;

Anne Smith, who generously revised scores;

Bonnie Blackburn, who kindly agreed to discuss the sources of the mottoes with me. Without her *Catalogue of enigmatic canonic inscriptions*, published in Katelijne Schiltz's *Music and Riddle Culture in the Renaissance*, my work would have taken a few more years to be finished;

Winnie Smith, whose proofreading magically transformed my shaky English into sturdy English;

Andrew Melson, for being the first to believe in this work;

Henry Cox, a Skidmore College Music Major who started working on the scores in Photoshop;

Skidmore College, for two grants: the Faculty and Student Summer Research Grant and a Student Assistant Grant;

I Tatti: Thanks to the Wallace residential fellowship received in 2019 from the Harvard University Center for Italian Renaissance Studies, Villa I Tatti, I was able to undertake in-depth research into this collection, examining Padre Martini and Luigi Cherubini's understanding of the Renaissance practice of (puzzle) canons;

NYU Paris, for the research support accorded to professors of their Global program in Paris.

Moreover, I wish to express my gratitude to the Fondation Internationale Luigi Cherubini / Den Internationale Luigi Cherubini-Fond (Denmark), which generously sponsored the publication of the volume, and in particular to Leif V. S. Balthzersen.

Finally, I am also indebted to Roberto Illiano, Fulvia Morabito and Massimiliano Sala (Centro Studi Opera Omnia Luigi Boccherini), who contributed important editorial work on the book.

Introduction

THIS WORK BEGAN when, while researching for my thesis, I came across Cherubini's collection of solutions for Padre Martini's canons quite by chance. I was in fact looking for the solution to an enigma by Sigismund Neukomm, with whom Luigi Cherubini exchanged enigmatic canons. Cherubini dedicated an enigmatic canon to Neukomm, based on the words *Non impedias musicam* (Do not impede music) and accompanied by the motto *Intendami chi può che m'intend'io* (Petrarch – Let anyone who can understand me, for I understand myself). Neukomm responded to Cherubini with another canon, with the words *Pater, dimite illis, non enim sciunt quid faciunt* (Father, forgive them, for they know not what they do)[1]. Enigmatic canons were very fashionable in the 19th century. Composers used to exchange riddles in the form of challenges. The riddles were published in newspapers, or written in albums, or on the front cover of score books, or engraved on tribute plaques inside churches, or even on tombstones.

I only had the enigma part of the canon Neukomm dedicated to Cherubini, not the solution. I went looking for it in the Music Department of the Bibliothèque nationale de France (BnF), where nearly all of Sigismund Neukomm's work is preserved. At the time, virtually none of the Paris Conservatoire collection, which had been transferred to BnF in the 1960s, was listed in the library's electronic catalogue. In order to find material pertaining to the Conservatoire's collection, one had to go to the reading room of the Music Department, then in rue Louvois (it shut its doors almost two years ago), and search through the paper catalogues (which also are no longer available). Today, without those dusty old paper catalogues, I would probably never have found Cherubini's collection.

The manuscript of Cherubini's collection is accompanied by a letter from a former librarian of the Conservatoire national de Musique et de Déclamation, Henry Expert[2]. The letter, dated 1924, is addressed to the General Administrator of the BnF, recommending the purchase of Cherubini's collection. Expert's letter fascinated me for several reasons: the story he told about the collection, found by chance around 1911-1912 at an auction of the furniture of one of Cherubini's granddaughters; the fact that Cherubini had found solutions to all of Martini's riddles, solutions that Cherubini would have liked to show off but which he had

---

[1]. See BEDUSCHI 2007.
[2]. See the letter by Henry Expert in this volume, pp. 315ff.

always refused to publish, «jealously keeping them to himself». Expert's letter was an initial gateway, providing a great deal of information about Cherubini's manuscript.

As I was having great difficulty at the time in finding solutions to Neukomm's riddles, finding those proposed by Cherubini for 72 of Padre Martini's puzzle canons was like stumbling upon a gold mine. Everything was there: not just the solutions, but also explanations of how to solve the riddles. The relationship between the riddle and the solutions (carefully written down by Cherubini) was always obvious, thanks to Cherubini's chosen presentation. But then another enigma reared its head: understanding Cherubini's explanations for his solutions also required understanding a «Table of Latin Words» to which each of the solutions referred. I, along with a number of 19th-century specialists, didn't really understand the document we now had access to. This table became the heart of the present work.

Understanding the origins of this «Table of Latin words» has been a long journey. Cherubini gives no indication of the authorship of his table. However, reading the explanations he gives for his proposed solutions, makes it clear on several occasions that this table predated Cherubini — as he himself indicates. I began to consider that Cherubini might not be the true author of the table and that he might have copied it directly from Martini without mentioning it. A similar table did indeed appear in Martini's writings. But more than half of Cherubini's table was missing from them. The logical next step was to wonder whether Martini himself might also have drawn from another source.

Although Martini is a little less mysterious than Cherubini about the origins of his table, he is not very explicit in indicating his sources. All he provides is a footnote with a list of authors and composers active from the middle of the 15th to the end of the 17th century. I had to get out of the rut of 19th-century musicological research to understand that a 15th-century canon has absolutely nothing to do with what a canon means in the 21st century. Over this period, spanning almost five centuries, we have gone from 'canon' referring to a precept in the form of an enigmatic literary text, a rule on the basis of which a musical composition is to be established, to 'canon' designating the musical composition itself, and, further still, a composition that makes use of strict imitation. So, what were those texts, which we would now call 'verbal canons', that set out rules in the form of riddles? What if the Latin words on Cherubini's and Martini's tables were nothing more than the Renaissance verbal canons? Could that be the case?

Bonnie Blackburn's 'Catalogue of enigmatic canonic inscriptions', in Katelijne Schiltz's *Music and Riddle Culture in the Renaissance*[3], has been fundamental in answering that question. Blackburn's catalogue provides a list of enigmas, or verbal canons, drawn from theoretical works and compositions of the Renaissance. It also contained most of the Latin phrases in Cherubini's and Martini's tables! Another catalogue of canons, compiled by

---

[3]. See SCHILTZ 2015, pp. 367-477.

Introduction

Michael Lamla[4], has been equally indispensable. While devoted entirely to Italian sources, it covers a later period than Blackburn's catalogue. At the same time, these Renaissance and Baroque specialists could not see a single source from these periods from which Martini might have extracted his table in its entirety. After the excitement of finding the Latin phrases of Martini's and Cherubini's tables in Blackburn's catalogue, I wondered why Martini had not included all the phrases which had made it into Blackburn's catalogue, and what, then, might have driven the selection he made.

In what follows, I attempt to answer all these questions. First, I will discuss the 72 canons by Padre Martini, which formed part of engravings that illustrated each chapter in each of the three published volumes of his *Storia della Musica*. Next, I will show how Cherubini's work, a pedagogical collection, differs from the work of the other composers who proposed solutions to Martini's riddles, including Martini himself. I will then explain the origins of the table of enigmatic expressions which lies at the heart of Cherubini's work, firstly by discussing the origins of Cherubini's table, and then, and most importantly, covering the Renaissance origins of Martini's list of *Motti o Enigmi*. I analyse the origins of each of the mottoes in Martini's list exhaustively, reviewing each of his sources. I then follow the spread of Martini's list across Europe via works published by Ginguené and Fétis, which have their origins in Cherubini's collection. From end to end, the journey is very long — from Josquin to Fétis — and witnesses the birth of enigmatic canons as a concept. Like us, Cherubini was trying to understand Martini, and Martini in turn was trying to explain the theorists and composers who had worked before him.

Following my conclusions, I present seven Tables: first, Cherubini's original table, which accompanies the manuscript in the collection preserved in Paris. Cherubini's explanations of the Latin expressions are given in the original French and in an English translation. It is to this Table that the reader should refer to understand the explanations of the solutions given by Cherubini. This is followed by a comparison that places Cherubini's table side by side with the list of *Motti o Enigmi* that appears in Martini's *Esemplare*[5]. A third Table then lays out the origins of each of Martini's *Motti o Enigmi*. Each motto (accompanied by the explanations given by each author who uses the motto) is given in the original language along with an English translation and details of its sources. The high number of potential practical sources of Padre Martini's list of *Motti o Enigmi* meant that I limited myself to looking systematically at his theoretical sources only; his practical sources could not be covered in as much detail. It may be that the only motto for which I was unable to find sources, *Fuge morulas*, will soon be found in one of his practical sources («opere pratiche»). The Renaissance and Baroque specialists I have consulted know of no source for this motto.

---

[4]. See LAMLA 2003.
[5]. MARTINI 1774/1775.

Luciane Beduschi

This third Table enables a fundamental understanding of the Renaissance origins of each 'verbal canon' in Martini's list of *Motti o Enigmi*. A huge part of his list is drawn from Finck; a concordance of Martini's *Esemplare* vs. Finck's *Practica musica*[6] is presented succinctly in the fourth Table. Table 5 gives the expressions quoted by Finck which Martini did not include. This shows how Martini's choice influenced the development of the concept of 'enigmatic canons' itself. The sixth Table compares Martini's list, published in France by Ginguené, with Cherubini's table (whose publication Cherubini's work may have preceded). The seventh and last Table is that by Fétis. We shall see in my last chapter that Fétis played a fundamental role in the dissemination of the concept of enigmatic canons in the 19th century and that all the inspiration for his work came directly from Cherubini's collection.

These Tables are followed by transcriptions of Cherubini's proposed solutions for Martini's 72 canons. All Cherubini's explanations for the solutions appear here in the original French, accompanied by English translations. Cherubini's second-language French is far from perfect. We have tried to ensure that the English translations are as close as possible to Cherubini's original, even if this means they are sometimes awkwardly phrased. In his manuscript, Cherubini transcribed the enigmas from the prints and engravings they were embedded in. I have chosen to reproduce the images of the riddles as they appear in the *Storia della musica*, rather than transcribing the riddles as Cherubini did. For the scores of the solutions, I chose to preserve the very particular way in which Cherubini wrote his solutions to Padre Martini's canons as far as possible, since Cherubini's system had a pedagogical purpose. I have followed this objective rather than privileging a performing edition[7].

Last and sadly not least, I have had to decide against publishing here the comparative study between Cherubini's solutions and those proposed by Martini for his own canons. In the critical notes, I have inserted a few comments on the solutions proposed by Martini, but only when Cherubini makes remarks about Martini's work, or about his own research into finding the solutions.

---

[6]. FINCK 1556.

[7]. It should be noted that Martini presented his solutions in a format very similar to Cherubini's. This format has not been reproduced in the 2018 edition.

The 72 Enigmatic Canons of Padre Martini's *Storia della Musica*

Giovanni Battista Martini (Bologna 1706-1784), one of the most famous figures in 18th-century music, professor of more than one hundred composers, remains also well known for his *Storia della musica*. He was able to publish three of the five volumes initially planned. These did not go beyond Ancient Greek music. A fourth volume about medieval music survives in a manuscript. The first volume, published in 1757, has eleven chapters followed by three *Dissertazioni*. Volume II (1770), also has three *Dissertazioni*, preceded by nine chapters; the last published volume, volume III (1781), contains eight chapters and one *Dissertazione*[1]. Each of these sections is headed, and most are concluded, with an illustration of an enigmatic canon[2]. In volume I, most of the vignettes at the ends of sections have small cherubs playing among the enigmas. In volume II, all the illustrations depicting enigmas reference poets of classical antiquity: Theocritus, Anacreon, Hesiod, Pratinas, Homer, Sophocles, Virgil, and Carcinus. The third volume is less systematic, since not all the sages are poets: figures mentioned in chapter headings include Plato, Plutarch, and even Pythagoras. In all, the collection contains 72 puzzle canons, which formed the subject of debate in the 18th- and 19th centuries. A number of musicians and composers proposed solutions for the entire or a part of the collection, and some even sent their solutions to Padre Martini asking him to verify their accuracy[3]. Martini

---

[1]. Martini 1757, 1770, 1781.

[2]. The three volumes were published in the 18th century in two different editions: one in «carta comune» and a second one referred to as an «edizione magnifica in gran foglio». This last one has thick frames filled with an ornamental drawing pattern in every page; these frames are absent from the «carta comune» edition whereas the canons are still part of this edition.

[3]. Alberto Zanotelli indicates that at least twenty proposals of solutions exist, some complete, others partial, practically none published, with the exception of a few canons separately published in choral anthologies. The bulk of the names that constitute Zanotelli's list of authors who proposed solutions have been identified in the summary of letters written to or by Padre Martini and published by Anne Schnoebelen (Pendragon, 1979). These individuals proposing solutions, wrote to Padre Martini asking him to provide corrections for their solutions, or simply to indicate that they had undertaken the defy of finding solutions for his canons. Zanotelli cites solutions by Andrea Basili (1705-1777), Charles Antoine Champion (1720-1788), Francesco Capalti (1701-?), Andrea Memo, Luigi Antonio Sabbatini (1732-1809), Johann Georg Albrechtsberger (1736-1809), Carlo Zuccari (1704-1792), Giuseppe Cervellini (1744-1824), Joseph Schuster (1748-1812), Paul Wranitzky (1756-1808), Giuseppe Baini

himself ended up providing his own solutions — though not for all the canons contained in the three volumes, merely for the puzzles in the first two[4].

In 1891, Leonida Busi mentions «the richest and most interesting collection of autograph music scores by Fr. Martini to be found outside of Italy»[5]; she is referring to Franz Xaver Haberl's private library, today in the Regensburg Bischöflichen Zentralbibliothek, which keeps an autograph manuscript with Martini's own solutions for the canons of two volumes of his Music History: 29 canons of volume I (BH 6466) and 27 canons of volume II (BH 6466a)[6]. In March 1761, Andrea Basili (1705-1777) had written to Padre Martini asking him to provide solutions for the enigmas of his Music History, explaining that «History is supposed to be the enemy of the mysterious», and that «canons» need to be fully explained[7]. In his answer to Andrea Basili, Martini said that the canons of his Music History and its text have no connection, and that when he inserted the canons into the volumes, he had intended to encourage young composers to give some attention to the almost lost practice of canons. Nevertheless, Martini indicated in the same letter that he had the intention to publish the solutions as an individual collection[8].

Martini didn't have the chance to see his own solutions published. The first edition of his collection dates to 2018 when Alberto Zanotelli published Martini's solutions, transcribed

---

(1775-1844), François-Joseph Fétis (1784-1871), Giuseppe Busi (1808-1871), Wolfgang Amadeus Mozart (1756-1791), Giuseppe M. Paolucci (1726-1776), Girolamo Chiti Carletti (1679-1759), Giuseppe Morosini (1732-1805).

[4]. The reason for that is probably that Padre Martini did not consider the canons of volume III to be genuinely enigmatic (meaning that their presentations requiring the solution of an enigma in order to get the complete score), but merely closed (meaning the entire composition is summarized in an abbreviated form).

[5]. «La raccolta più ricca ed interessante di partiture musicale autografe del p. Martini, che si trovi all'estero». BUSI 1891, p. 469.

[6]. See HABERL 2000, p. 173.

[7]. «Una supplica deve farsi a V. R.za che tutti i canoni che Ella hà sparso in un Libro d'istoria, che deve essere inimica di misterij siano in qualche libro, o quando tratta di far canoni, siano dessi tutti spiegati, altrimenti i dottissimi, collo studio, li raggiungeranno, i semidotti poi, e gli ignoranti li passaranno come i fogliami che li circondano». SCHNOEBELEN 1979, letter #0485, pp. 55-56. The original of the letter is preserved at the Museo internazionale e biblioteca della musica di Bologna, Collocazione I.17.122: <http://www.bibliotecamusica.it/cmbm/viewschedal.asp?path=/cmbm/images/ripro/lettereb/I17/I17_122-123/>, accessed December 2023. Transcription according to Alberto Zanotelli in MARTINI 2018, p. xii.

[8]. «I canoni di questo tomo non anno vera relazione all'Istoria, se non che in qualche modo per le parole, e niente per l'arte pratica del contrapunto, così ho pensato diversamente, cioè di dare qualche stimolo ai giovani compositori de' nostri tempi di risvegliare e rinnovare lo studio de canoni quasi affatto perduto. [...] Se a Dio piacerà di darmi vita e forza per proseguire l'opera, ne formerò una serie compita, la quale in fini sarà stampata a parte, con lo scioglimento e li opportuni artificij per formarli». SCHNOEBELEN 1979, letter #0486, p. 56. The original of the letter is preserved at the Museo internazionale e biblioteca della musica di Bologna, Collocazione I.17.123: <http://www.bibliotecamusica.it/cmbm/viewschedal.asp?path=/cmbm/images/ripro/lettereb/I17/I17_122-123/>, accessed December 2023.

in modern notation, along with solutions proposed by two other composers: August Julius Ferdinand Böhme[9] (1815-1883) and Francesco Maria Zuccàri[10] (1725-1726, 1750-1788)[11]. Martini and Zuccàri proposed solutions for the canons of the first two volumes; Böhme proposed solutions for the whole collection, the three volumes of Martini's Music History. According to Zanotelli, besides Böhme, the only one to have provided solutions for the totality of canons in the three volumes would have been Luigi Cherubini. Zanotelli says however that, even if Cherubini's collection is mentioned several times in the literature, it has never been found — thus casting doubt on its very existence[12]. It is Leonida Busi who in 1891 raised doubt about the existence of Cherubini's solutions. In her *Padre G. B. Martini musicista-letterato del sec. XVIII*[13], she says having consulted a list of Cherubini's works[14] she found in it no mention to solutions of Padre Martini's canons. Likewise, she says that in Cherubini's catalogue, written by Cherubini himself[15], while his canons are listed, there is no mention to the solutions he would have proposed for Martini's canons. What Leonida Busi didn't realise is that Cherubini would not have inserted the solutions he proposed for Martini's canons in the list of his own works. Cherubini's solutions for Martini's canons are not Cherubini's canons, but Martini's[16].

---

[9]. «Canones / ex / Storia della Musica / da / Fr. G. Martini / di Bologna. / solvit / F. Böhme. / Lipsiae 1879». Biblioteca dell'Accademia Filarmonica, I-Baf, Fondo antico, 100-101, 2 vols.

[10]. Biblioteca della Basilica di S. Francesco di Assisi, Mss. 194/1. Zuccàri 1 and Zuccàri 2.

[11]. MARTINI 2018.

[12]. *Ibidem*, pp. xiii-xiv. Cherubini's proposal is mentioned notably by FÉTIS 1835-1844, vol. VI (1837), p. 4; and by ORTIGUE 1860, cols. 188-196: 194.

[13]. BUSI 1891, pp. 448-449.

[14]. NOTICE 1845.

[15]. CATALOGUE GÉNÉRAL 1760.

[16]. Leonida Busi adds nevertheless that in the appendix to Cherubini's catalogue, Botté de Toulmon gives a list of «Musique de divers Auteurs copiée de la main de M. Cherubini», and that under number 9 of this list appears «Un cahier oblong contenant des canons du Père Martini. Avec une table-90 pag».

Luigi Cherubini's Solutions: A Pedagogical Work

The manuscript in Cherubini's hand, with his solutions for all 72 enigmatic canons of the three volumes of Padre Martini's *Storia della Musica*, was found at the beginning of the 20th century during an auction at the Hôtel Drouot in Paris, when furniture belonging to one of Cherubini's granddaughters was sold[1]. The volume is now kept in the music department of the National Library of France, Réserve VMB.MS.1 (1), In-4°, 62 ff. It has no date and is entitled *Canons Fermés et Énigmatiques Du Père Martini. Extraits des Vignettes qui ornent son Histoire de la Musique; avec les solutions de ces Canons, par L. Cherubini, suivis par d'autres Canons de différents auteurs, résolus par Fétis*. Martini's 72 enigmatic canons are followed by *Enigmatic canons by various authors solved by Fétis*, VMB.MS.1 (2). After the 72 enigmatic canons solved by Cherubini and before the 14 solved by Fétis, there is a 73rd puzzle canon, which is left unsolved. This puzzle comes not from Martini's *Storia*, but from the end of the first volume of his *Esemplare, o sia Saggio fondamentale pratico di contrappunto sopra il canto fermo*[2]. Cherubini's collection does not follow the order the canons appeared in Martini's *Storia*. The number of canonic voices in Cherubini's collection varies from 2 to 18. It includes double, triple, and quadruple canons. Two canons (Nos. 37, 40) have two different solutions and one canon (No. 3) has three different solutions.

Given that Martini's own solutions have been published recently, why publish Cherubini's? One reason is for purposes of comparison: to see whether Cherubini's solutions differ from those already published, and if so, in what ways. Some of Cherubini's solutions do indeed differ from Martini's. But the truly remarkable fact about them is that they are a pedagogical collection designed to reveal the secrets of the enigmatic canons practice to 19th-century musicians and composers. Luigi Cherubini approached Padre Martini's challenge in a consistent manner. Each of Cherubini's solutions has three shared elements: a faithful musical transcription of Martini's original canon; an explanation of the solution found (entitled *Solution*); and the solution itself (entitled *Canon ouvert*, [Open canon]).

Cherubini didn't just produce solutions for the riddles: he also explained in detail how each proposed solution was reached. These explanations clearly show the thought process of a 19th-century composer in search of solutions to puzzles dating to the century before. The scores

---

[1]. See the letter by Henry Expert in this volume, pp. 315ff.
[2]. Martini 1774, p. 256.

retain a close visual relationship to the riddle so as to clearly explain the path taken from the riddle to its solution. In Cherubini's open canons, faithfully reproduced in the present edition, the different canonic voices are never completely written out: repetition signs and directs indicate their continuation. Cherubini wrote each voice in the open canons maintaining as much as possible a visual connection to the line as it appears in the enigma. Rhythmic durations are rigorously reproduced as in the enigma: rather than using ties, dotted notes can extend over a barline. In the same way, when the canons have two or more different time signatures, rather than adapt the rhythmic durations to a single time signature, the different time signatures are kept in the different voices in the open canon, which allows different voices with different time signatures to appear in the solution with the same rhythmic note values as in the enigma. Clearly, these scores featuring the resolved puzzle canons are not intended for performance.

A Table of Enigmatic Expressions

Cherubini's solutions are all based on a table given at the beginning of the collection. In the explanation for the solution of the first canon, Cherubini writes: «One will find the Latin words placed at the head of this canon and their explanation in No. 25 of the table». The table Cherubini mentions refers to the first four pages of his collection: a «Table of Latin words that ancient composers often quoted at the head of canons, with the explanation of their enigmatic meaning in order to more easily obtain the true solution of a closed canon»[1]. This table is a list of enigmatic expressions: 91 numbered expressions in Latin in a first column on the left, aligned with music explanations for each one of them in a second column on the right (see TABLE 1). For each enigmatic expression, Cherubini gives an explanation in French detailing how the expressions must be interpreted musically in order to find the solution to the riddles that they accompany. Several of these expressions are in fact present in Martini's canons. References to the «Table of Latin words» begin practically each solution Cherubini proposed for Martini's 72 enigmatic canons.

A number of elements indicate that Cherubini's table was not prepared specifically for his collection, but that it existed previously. The table contains more Latin expressions than the ones found in the collection[2]. Also, in the preamble to several canons, e.g. No. 7, Cherubini writes: «To help me in the search for the solution, I first consulted the explanation of the Latin words written at the beginning, which I found at No. 41 in the table». This is an unambiguous indication, in his own words, that Cherubini searched a pre-existing table for a Latin expression to help solve canons.

Cherubini's Latin table is clearly divided in two parts. A first section (Nos. 1-54) consists of expressions that tend towards the cryptic, with little obvious connection to musical terms. Most of the second section (Nos. 55-end) comprises expressions easily related to music intervals. The first, more enigmatic part of Cherubini's table is taken directly from Padre Martini's writings. The second volume of Martini's *Esemplare, o sia Saggio fondamentale pratico di contrappunto sopra il canto fermo* (published in Bologna in 1775, eighteen years after the first volume of the *Storia*) opens with a section entitled 'Regole per comporre la fuga', followed by

---

[1]. «Table des mots latins que les anciens compositeurs plaçaient souvent en tête des canons, avec l'explication du sens énigmatique qu'ils renferment, afin d'obtenir plus aisément la véritable solution d'un canon fermé».

[2]. See below, p. 62.

discussions on 'Del Soggetto, o sia Proposta', 'Della Risposta', 'Della Fuga Reale', and finally a section dedicated to canons: 'Del Canone o Fuga Legata'. This section contains a list of «Motti, vocaboli Enigmatici, Enigmi» and «la loro spiegazione»[3]. Martini explains:

> Non voglio mancare di porre sotto gli occhi del Giovane Compositore alcuni *Motti*, o vocaboli *Enigmatici*, che si trovano su 'l principio delle Composizioni fatte a Canone [...]. Per liberare i Giovani Compositori dalla faticosa briga di rilevare il significato di certi *Motti* oscuri, che trovansi ne' canoni, ho pensato di esporre qui una serie dei più principali disposta in due colonne, col notare alla mano sinistra i *Motti*, o *Enigmi*, e alla mano destra la loro spiegazione[4].

Next comes a list of 56 Latin expressions («Motti, o Enigmi») with explanations in Italian («Spiegazione dei Motti, o Enigmi») for each. The «Table of Latin words» that commences Cherubini's collection is a translation of this list (see TABLE 2). Cherubini simply translated Martini's *Enigmi* explanations from Italian into French and added them at the beginning of his own table — the table that became the core of his deciphering work. Of the 56 expressions in Martini, 54 appear in Cherubini's table. The two expressions excluded from Cherubini's table are in fact not «Latin words»: the first excluded expression is in French, the second one is in Italian. The two tables are identical up to number 49. Martini then gives the first expression that does not appear in Cherubini: «Vous jejuneres le quttr temps». Cherubini may have skipped this expression considering that its meaning was obvious to French readers; the expression thus did not need to be reproduced in his table. The correspondence between the two tables restarts on the next expression: number 50 in Cherubini's table is the same as number 51 in Martini's. The tables match for five more expressions. Martini's table ends on number 56 with the expression «Intendami chi può, che m'intend'io», which is also absent from Cherubini's table. Martini comments that «The attached Example will serve as an explanation of this last Enigma»[5]. The example he refers to is a canon presented in its closed and open forms, with no accompanying explanation. Since Cherubini could not provide a translation for an explanation in Martini's table that did not in fact exist, he probably preferred not to include the Italian expression in his «Table of Latin words»[6].

It may be that the second part of Cherubini's table, from No. 55 until the end, was compiled by Cherubini himself as a result of deciphering Martini's canons. All the expressions from this point onwards occur in Martini's canons, which was not the case for expressions

---

[3]. MARTINI 1775, pp. xxv-xxvi.

[4]. *Ibidem*, pp. xiv-xxv.

[5]. «L'annesso Esempio servirà di spiegazione a quest'ultimo Enigma».

[6]. It is interesting to note that Ginguené did provide a translation for this last Martini's expression. «M'entendra qui pourra, moi je m'entends», he writes. See below, pp. 47-52.

A Table of Enigmatic Expressions

1-54. A portion of the later expressions also appear in Martini's counterpoint treatise (mostly in volume II, pp. xxiii-xxiv), but are not related by him to (what he termed) enigmatic canons. Martini considered the expressions taken over in the second part of Cherubini's table to be simple musical instructions, not riddles. The expressions are single Greek and Latin words, which refer straightforward to transposition intervals or rhythmic delay. For Cherubini, these words were enigmatic, indicating a clear difference in the two men's understanding of the term.

The second part of Cherubini's table also includes fifteen expressions that do not appear in Martini's counterpoint treatise at all; all, however, are used in his enigmatic canons:

C.63. *Crescit eundo*, canon No. 21[7]
C.64. *Decrescit eundo*, canon No. 26
C.70. *Ad Equisonum*, canon No. 25
C.72. *Ad Diapente expensum*, canon No. 28
C.74. *Ter terni canite vocibus*, canon No. 32
C.75. *Congenita haec tria sunt*, canon No. 33
C.77. *Ter voci ciemus*, canon No. 38
C.78. *Voce ter insonuit*, canon No. 38
C.81. *Ibit, redibit*, canon No. 42
C.83. *Six* [sic] *Vocum*, canon No. 49
C.84. *Ad Diapason, et Unissonum Vicissim*, canon No. 51
C.85. *Tot tempora, tot sunt voces*, canon No. 51
C.86. *Ad Diapason intensum*, canon No. 55
C.87. *Ad Diapason espensum* [sic], canon No. 55
C.88. *Ad Sub-Sesquiditonum*, canon No. 59

---

[7]. From this point on, the indication «C.» followed by a number corresponds to the number in Cherubini's table. The indication «M.» followed by a number corresponds to the number in Martini's list of *Motti o Enigmi*.

Renaissance Sources for Padre Martini's List of *Motti o Enigmi*

Virtually all the enigmatic expressions of Martini's list of *Motti o Enigmi* published in his *Esemplare* can be traced back to treatises belonging to the long Renaissance (see Table 3). During the Renaissance, a 'canon' was a formula for finding the solution to an enigmatic composition, and several treatises present these formulas, which now we tend to call 'verbal canons'. Nowadays, we understand a canon to be a polyphonic composition involving strict imitation. However, at least until the first half of the 16th century, a canon (from the Greek 'kanōn', meaning 'rule', 'precept') was a rule, formula, or instruction that musicians would put into action to create one or more parts of music, using previously notated material — the 'canon' was just the rule and not the music itself. Even less was it a polyphonic composition based in strict imitation.

In what became known as one of the first dictionaries of musical terms, the *Terminorum musicae diffinitorium* (Treviso, 1475), Johannes Tinctoris defined canon as «a rule showing the purpose of the composer behind a certain obscurity». Almost one century later, in *Le istitutioni harmoniche* (Venice, 1558), Gioseffo Zarlino still relates the term 'canon' to its meaning as a rule[1]. In fact, in most Renaissance music treatises, 'canon' was the formula used to create a piece of music. By the end of the period, one starts seeing definitions of 'canon' as a musical composition obtained using a puzzle formula. Only from the 18th century on did an additional sense of 'canon' start to emerge, as a polyphonic piece making use of imitative procedures.

From the Renaissance to the Baroque period, the meaning of the word 'canon' shifted, from an enigmatic formula used to obtain a piece of music to the piece itself, which eventually lost all enigmatic features. At the same time, we see the so-called 'enigmatic canons' appear. An enigmatic canon is normally interpreted as a piece of music, accompanied by a cryptic inscription, which must be decoded before the entire musical composition can be unlocked. The piece may or may not involve imitation. We will see below that the enigmatic formulas that were the Renaissance canons constitute the basis of Cherubini's deciphering work of Padre Martini's enigmatic canons.

In his *Esemplare*, Martini does not specify from which treatise each of the expressions that make up his table of «Motti, o Enigmi» is taken. In a footnote he simply lists the authors of

---

[1]. Mann – Wilson – Urquhart 2001.

«theoretical» and «practical» works from which he claims to have taken the puzzles. Martini does not attribute each expression to a particular source, nor does he give the full references, either for the treatises or for the «Opere Pratiche»:

> Sono estratti gli esposti Enigmi, con le loro Spiegazioni dalle Opere Pratiche di Jusquin del Prato, Gio: Mouton, Enrico Isaas, Alfonso Lobo, P. Emanuel Cardoso Carmelitano, e dai Trattati di Pietro Aron, Ermano Finck, Enrico Glareano, D. Pedro Cerone, P. D. Gio. Battista Rossi, P. Camillo Angleria, Andrea Angelini Bontempi[2].

Six of the seven authors mentioned by Martini published treatises between the early 16th and early 17th centuries, pertaining thus to the long Renaissance. Only one of these authors (Bontempi) published a treatise at the end of the 17th century:

Pietro Aaron, *Libri tres de institutione harmonica*, Bologna, 1516;
Hermann Finck, *Practica musica*, Wittenberg, 1556;
Heinrich Glarean, *Dodecachordon*, Basel, 1547;
Pietro Cerone, *El Melopeo y maestro*, Naples, 1613;
Giovanni Battista Rossi, *Organo de cantori per intendere da se stesso ogni passo difficile che si trova nella musica, et anco per imparare contrapunto*, Venice, 1618;
Camillo Angleria & Cima, G., *La regola del contraponto, e della musical compositione,* Milan, 1622;
Angelini Bontempi, *Historia mvsica, nella quale si ha piena cognitione della teorica, e della pratica antica della mvsica harmonica; secondo la dottrina de' Greci … e come dalla teorica, e dalla pratica antica sia poi nata la pratica moderna, che contiene la scientia del contrapunto*, Perugia, 1695.

Martini seems to be the true author of the first part of Cherubini's table. Martini did not copy his list entirely from another source, instead, he collected and chose the verbal canons he wanted to put together for a publication in his counterpoint manual, intended to teach composition to a new generation of musicians and composers. The origins of this table and the meaning of the Latin tags it contains bear further investigation. The «Table of Latin words» which Cherubini used as the basis for his proposed solutions circulated widely during the 19th century, always accompanying attempts to explain enigmatic canons in practice. Everything points to this table playing a central role in the creation of the notion of 'enigmatic canons'. Luigi Cherubini's collection of solutions to Padre Martini's enigmatic canons illustrates this long and complex journey — the one enigmatic expressions took as they travelled from the Renaissance into the 19th century. Cherubini's collection is fundamental to understanding the reception of enigmatic canons during the 19th century, allowing us to understand how the composers of Cherubini's and Martini's generation studied an originally Renaissance practice, interpreted it, and transposed it into their time.

---

[2]. MARTINI 1775, vol. II, p. xxv, fn. 3.

Renaissance Sources for Padre Martini's List of *Motti o Enigmi*

In what follows, I propose a detailed analysis of each of Martini's sources. This will enable us to determine the provenance of each motto on his list. I look at how Martini did or did not modify the explanations that each motto had in its original sources. I then look at how Martini made his choice of expressions to be reproduced in his list. This analysis provides a very clear picture of how the switch between 'canons' as literary expressions and 'canons' as musical pieces came about. In a second time, I analyse the dissemination of Martini's list during the 19th century, studying two authors in particular: Pierre-Louis Ginguené, who worked with Cherubini and was responsible for publishing the first French translation of Martini's table; and François-Joseph Fétis, who published a very extensive table, most certainly not taken from Martini's table, but rather from the work that Cherubini had done to compile his collection of solutions for Martini's canons. This analysis shows how this particular category of canons — the enigmatic canon — came to be established in the 19th century.

Pietro Aaron, *Libri tres de institutione harmonica*, Bologna, 1516

The expressions which Martini borrowed from Pietro Aaron come from Chapter 15 of Book 2 (ff. 25r-26r) of Aaron's *Libri tres de institutione harmonica*, which was published in Bologna in 1516 and dedicated to the Bolognese patrician Girolamo San Pietro. The book was probably written in Imola, where, by 1516, Pietro Aaron was a priest[3]. It was translated into Latin by Giovanni Antonio Flaminio.

In chapter 15, *QVOD Sunt duo modi necessarii non arbitarii*, four enigmatic expressions appear:

Dum lucem habetis credite in lucem, f. 26r (M.54 C.53)[4]

Clama ne cesses, f. 26r (M.1 C.1)[5]

Qui quaerit, invenit, f. 25v

Omnia probate, quod bonum est tenete, f. 25v

In the copy of Aaron's treatise preserved in Bologna[6], all four mottoes are handwritten in the margins of ff. 25v and 26r. The handwritten mottoes are underlined and above them, one can read «Jusquini». Aaron is Martini's only source for *Dum lucem habetis credite in lucem*[7].

---

[3]. BLACKBURN 2001.

[4]. See BLACKBURN 2012, pp. 182-203. From this point on, the number following 'M.' indicates the number of the expression in Martini's table; the number following 'C.' indicates the number of the expression in Cherubini's table.

[5]. *Ibidem*.

[6]. Museo internazionale e biblioteca della musica di Bologna, Collocazione B.8.

[7]. Unidentified composer.

Clama ne cesses also appears in Finck[8], Cerone[9] and Bontempi[10]. *Qui quaerit, invenit* is not part of Martini's table, but is used in his canon number 10. The motto is also mentioned by Rossi[11]. *Qui quaerit, invenit* (He that seeketh, findeth) is open to all sorts of interpretations, which may explain why Martini did not find it possible to insert this motto in his table, perhaps because he was unable to give a comprehensive explanation for all the canons where it is used. This may also be the reason why Martini also omitted *Omnia probate, quod bonum est tenete* (Prove all things; hold fast what is good): as with *Qui quaerit, invenit*, this motto leaves room for multiple interpretations.

Writing about chapter 15 of Aaron's work on enigmatic expressions, Katelijne Schiltz has observed that Aaron «must have considered himself the decipherer of enigmas for the benefit of the readers»[12]. When publishing his list of mottoes, Martini further clarifies that this is precisely his intention: «In order to liberate young composers from the tiring task of revealing the meaning of certain obscure mottoes found in the canons, I thought of revealing here a series of the most important ones»[13].

Heinrich Glarean, *Dodecachordon*, Basel, 1547

Among the theoreticians mentioned by Martini, the only source for the motto *Duo adversi adverse in unum* (M.45 C.45) appears to be Heinrich Glarean's *Dodecachordon*, published in Basel by Heinrich Petri in 1547. Glarean uses the expression in an example on pages 464-465 (Liber III) taken from a *Salve mater salvatoris* by Jean Mouton. In the copy of the treatise preserved in Bologna[14], attached to page 464 there is a piece of music paper with Mouton's *Salve mater salvatoris* written in score[15]. Glarean gives the work in separate parts. Martini wrote it down in score. Another motto in Martini's list, *Omne trinum perfectum*[16] (M.22 C.22), also appears in the *Dodecachordon*, p. 444, and occurs in Finck's list, *Practica musica* (1566), Cc 1r / Ff 3v.

---

[8]. Book 3, Bb 4v / Cc 3v.
[9]. *Enigma com outra differente Cruz*, Num. xxxxiii, p. 1130.
[10]. P. 232.
[11]. See below, pp. 34-42.
[12]. Schiltz 2015, p. 228.
[13]. «Per liberare i Giovani Compositori dalla faticosa briga di rilevare il significato di certi Motti oscuri, che trovansi ne' Canoni, ho pensato di esporre qui una serie de' piu principali». Martini 1775, p. xxv.
[14]. Museo internazionale e biblioteca della musica di Bologna, Collocazione B.87.
[15]. One reads on the recto: «Aut. Martini. Partitura del canone di Mouton, Glareano, B.87. Foglio sciolto a p. 464 di B.87».
[16]. See *New Senfl edition* 2023.

Renaissance Sources for Padre Martini's List of *Motti o Enigmi*

Hermann Finck, *Practica musica*, Wittenberg, 1556

Practica musica... exempla variorum signorum, proportionum et canonum, iudicium de tonis, ac quaedam de arte suaviter et artificiose cantandi continens, published in Wittenberg in 1556, is Hermann Finck's (Pirna, 1527 – Wittenberg, 1558) most important work. Divided into five books, it presents the rudiments of music. Its third book, *Liber Tertius. De Canonibus,* is entirely devoted to verbal canons.

The chapter starts with a definition of 'canon': «Canon is an imaged prescription, eliciting an unwritten part of the cantilena from those written; or it is a rule ingeniously revealing the secrets of the chant»[17]. It is interesting that here Finck comes back to the Greek etymology relating canon to a rule ('praeceptio' - 'regula'). He then continues: «We make use of canons for the sake of subtlety, of brevity, or of experiment. Their number is infinite, at the will of any master, because new ones are devised every day. I will nevertheless give a few special ones by the most prominent ancient and recent musicians, and explain them»[18]. This is followed by a list of enigmatic expressions accompanied by explanations.

One could very easily imagine that Finck's list constitutes Martini's main source of inspiration for his own list of mottoes, since more than 67% of Martini's expressions are also found in Finck's treatise (see TABLE 4). This amounts to thirty-eight of the fifty-six expressions on Martini's list:

M.1. *Clama ne cesses* (Bb 4v / Cc 3v)[19]
M.2. *Otia dant vitia* (Bb 4v)
M.3. *Dii faciant sine me non moriar ego* (Bb 4v)
M.4. *Omnia si perdas famam servare memento, qua semel emissa: postea nullus eris* (Bb 4v)
M.5. *Sperare et praestolari multos facit morari* (Bb 4v)
M.6. *Otia securis insidiosa nocent* (Bb 4v)
M.7. *Tarda solet magnis rebus inesse fides* (Bb 4v)
M.9. *Misericordias et veritas obviaverunt sibi* (Bb 4v / Dd 3r)
M.10. *Justitia et pax se osculatae sunt* (Bb 4v / Dd 3r)
M.11. *Nescit vos missa reverti* (Bb 4v)
M.12. *Semper contrarius esto* (Bb 4v)
M.13. *Signa te signa temere me tangis et angis, Romae tibi subito motibus ibit amor* (Bb 4v)
M.14. *Frangenti fidem fides frangatur eidem* (Bb 4v)

---

[17]. «Canon est imaginaria praeceptio, ex positis non positam cantilenae partem eliciens: Vel, est regula argute reuelans secreta cantus».

[18]. «Utimur autem Canonibus, aut subtilitatis, breuitatis, aut tentationis gratia, eorumque infinitus est numerus, pro arbitrio cuiusque artificis, quia quotidie noui excogitantur. Addam tamen aliquos praecipuos praestantissimorum ueterum et recentium Musicorum, eosque explicabo».

[19]. These indications correspond to the folios on Finck's treatise.

M.15. *Roma caput mundi si verteris, omnia vincit* (Bb 4v)
M.16. *Mitto tibi metulas, erige si dubitas* (Cc 1r)
M.17. *Cancrizat* (Cc 1r / Ee r)
M.18. *Retrograditur* (Cc 1r)
M.22. *Omne trinum perfectum* (Cc 1r / Ff 3v)
M.23. *Trinitas et unitas* (Cc 1r / Ff 3v)
M.24. *Trinitate in unitate veneremur* (Cc 1r / Ff 4v)
M.25. *Sit trium series una* (Cc 1r / Ff 4r)
M.26. *Vidi tres viri qui erant laesi homonem* (Cc 1r)
M.27. *Manet alta mente repostum* (Cc 1r-v / Gg r)
M.28. *De ponte non cadit, qui cum sapientia vadit* (Cc 1v)
M.30. *Non qui inceperit, sed qui perseveraverit* (Cc 1r / Mm 2r)
M.31. *Itque, reditque frequens* (Cc 1r)
M.32. *Crescitin Duplo, Triplo, &c.* (Cc 1v / Gg v)
M.33. *Decrescit* (Cc 1v)
M.34. *Digniora sunt priora* (Cc 1v / Gg 4r)
M.35. *Descende gradatim* (Cc 1v / Hh 2v)
M.37. *Et sic de singulis* (Cc 1v / Hh 4v)
M.38. *Nigra sum sed formosa* (Cc 1r)
M.40. *Qui se exaltat humiliabitur* (Cc 2v)
M.41. *Qui se humiliat exaltabitur* (Cc 2v / Nn 1v)
M.42. *Plutonico subiit regna* (Cc 2v)
M.43. *Contraria contrariis curantur* (Cc 2v / Mm 3v)
M.52. *Cantus duarum facierum* (Cc 1r / Ii 3v)
M.53. *Tolle moras placido maneant suspiria cantu* (Cc 1r / Ii 3v)

However, Martini does not replicate Finck's entire list. In addition to the expressions indicating intervals (*Hiper- vel Epi-Diatessaron / Diapente / Diapason et Hypo- vel Sub-Diatessaron / Diapente / Diapason* [Cc 3r])[20], thirteen enigmatic expressions explained by Finck are not part of Martini's list:

Gaude cum gaudentibus (Cc 1r / Dd 3v)
Celsa canens imis commuta quadruplicando (Cc 1v)
In gradus undenos descendant multiplicantes, Consimilique modo crescant antipodes uno (Cc 1v / Hh 3v)
Vae tibi ridenti, nam mox post gaudia flebis (Cc 1v)
I prae, sequar: inquit cancer (Cc 2r)
Undecies canito pausas linquendo priores (Cc 2r / Ii 1v)
Dormivi & soporatus sum (Cc 2r)
Ranam agit Seriphiam (Cc 2r)
Vox faucibus haesit (Cc 2r)

---

[20]. Martini actually mentions these expressions on the previous page, number xxiv, where he refers to Finck in footnote number 2.

Da mihi dimidiam lunam, solem, & canis iram (Cc 2r)
Dimidium spherae, spheram, cum principe romae, Postulat a nobis totius conditor orbis (Cc 2r)
Quamlibet inspicias notulam qua clave locetur, Tunc denique socios in eadem concine tentos (Cc 2r / Kk v): /
Sed vere prolationes non petunt pausationes, sed sunt signa generis (Cc 2r)
Desiderium crescit cum spe (Cc 3r / Nn 2v)

How would Martini have made his choice? Finck first lists expressions (Bb 4v / Cc 3r), followed by examples (Cc 3v / Oo 2r). The examples form a separate part of his third book. Not all expressions in Finck's list are provided with examples. In addition, Finck never states his sources: the authors of his examples are not cited. Bonnie Blackburn has indicated a series of expressions from Finck's list for which she could not find the corresponding compositions. She adduces the hypothesis that Finck may have invented some of the expressions on his list: «one suspects that in some cases he happily proposed or made up apposite tags that might inspire composers»[21].

One might be tempted to believe that Martini would have taken from Finck's list only the expressions for which Finck gave an example. But this is not the case. Of the thirty-eight expressions taken up by Martini, twenty are not accompanied by an example in Finck's treatise[22]:

Ocia dant vitia (Bb 4v)
Dii faciant sine me non moriatur ego (Bb 4v)
Omnia si perdas famam servare memento, Qua semel amissa, postea nullus eris (Bb 4v)
Sperare & praestolari multos facit morari (Bb 4v)
Ocia securis insidiosa nocent (Bb 4v)
Tarda solet magnis rebus inesse fides (Bb 4v)
Nescit vos missa reverti (Bb 4v)
Semper contrarius esto (Bb 4v)
Signa te signa temere me tangis et angis, Romae tibi subito motibus ibit amor (Bb 4v)
Frangenti fidem fides frangatur eidem (Bb 4v)
Roma caput mundi si verteris, omnia vincit (Bb 4v)
Mitto tibi metulas, erige si dubitas (Cc 1r)
Retrograditur (Cc 1r)
Vidi tres viri qui erant laesi homonem (Cc 1r)
Nigra sum, sed formosa (Cc 1r)
Itque, reditque frequens (Cc 1r)
De ponte non cadit, qui cum sapientia vadit (Cc 1v)

---

[21]. BLACKBURN – HOLFORD-STREVENS 2002, p. 161.

[22]. Bonnie Blackburn was able to find a source of composition for *Itque, reditque frequens* (Cc 1r): Cristóbal de Morales, *Tu es Petrus et super hanc petram*. See SCHILTZ 2015, p. 472. Among these expressions without examples in Finck but quoted by Martini, *Nigra sum, sed formosa* is also quoted by BONTEMPI 1695 (p. 232) and *Qui se exaltat humiliabitur* is quoted by Cerone (*Enigma de los tres caminos*, Num. XXI).

Decrescit in Duplo, Triplo, &c. (Cc 1v)
Qui se exaltat humiliabitur (Cc 2v)
Plutonica subiit regna (Cc 2v)

Martini not only listed expressions for which Finck does not give examples, but also left off expressions for which Finck does give examples. Among the thirteen expressions that were not included by Martini, four are equipped with examples: *Gaude cum gaudentibus* (Cc 1r / Dd 3v)[23]; *In gradus undenos descendant multiplicantes, Consimilique modo crescant antipodes uno* (Cc 1v / Hh 3v)[24]; *Undecies canito pausas linquendo priores* (Cc 2r / Ii 1v); *Quamlibet inspicias notulam qua clave locetur, Tunc denique socios in eadem concine tentos* (Cc 2r / Kk v); *Sed vere prolationes non petunt pausationes, sed sunt signa generis*. The first three expressions come from Josquin, the last from Ockeghem[25].

Four mottoes without examples in Finck, and not included in Martini, have an identified composition or composer — which means that Martini could have known these works, but preferred not to include the expressions in his list: *Celsa canens imis commuta quadruplicando* (Cc 1v), Josquin, *Missa fortunata desperata*, Agnus I, also mentionned by Glarean (*Dodecachordon*, 1547, p. 389); *Vae tibi ridenti, nam mox post gaudia flebis* (Cc 1v), Brumel (?), *Magnificat octavi toni*, Sicut erat a 8; *I prae, sequar: inquit cancer* (Cc 2r) in Marbriano de Orto, *Missa ad fugam*, and Johannes Martini, *J'ay pris amours a ma devise*; *Dormivi & soporatus sum* (Cc 2r), Josquin, *Domine quid multiplicati sunt* (? lost)[26].

From the thirteen expressions in Finck's list not taken up by Martini, only four are both example-less in Finck and unidentified to date: *Ranam agit Seriphiam* (Cc 2r); *Vox faucibus haesit* (Cc 2r); *Da mihi dimidiam lunam, solem, & canis iram* (Cc 2r); *Dimidium spherae, spheram, cum principe romae, Postulat a nobis totius conditor orbis* (Cc 2r).

What the expressions that Martini left aside share is that they do not express a general rule that can be easily applied in the same way in a different context (see TABLE 5). Rather than rules, they are essentially explanations about a particular context (possibly, but not necessarily, associated with a particular example). For example:

[23]. *Gaudete cum gaudentibus* is also present in ROSSI 1618, p. 13.
[24]. Also in GLAREAN 1547, p. 389.
[25]. *Gaude cum gaudentibus*: Josquin, *Missa l'Homme armé super voces musicales*, Osanna / *In gradus undenos descendant multiplicantes, Consimilique modo crescant antipodes uno*: Josquin, *Missa Fortuna desperata*, Agnus I / *Undecies canito pausas linquendo priores*: Josquin, *Missa Gaudeamus*, Et in terra / *Quamlibet inspicias notulam qua clave locetur, Tunc denique socios in eadem concine tentos. Sed vere prolationes non petunt pausationes, sed sunt signa generis*: Ockeghem, *Ut heremita solus*. B. Blackburn clarifies: «ex. In Finck, sig. Kk 1v, but instead of 3rd-4th lines has "*Pro qualibet litera duo tu tempora pausa*" with solution». See SCHILTZ 2015, p. 428.
[26]. See Blackburn's catalogue in SCHILTZ 2015, pp. 367-477.

Renaissance Sources for Padre Martini's List of Motti o Enigmi

Celsa canens imis commuta quadruplicando.
In gradus undenos descendant multiplicantes.
Consimilique modo crescant antipodes uno. (Cc 1v)

That is, count [descending] from this note which is notated in the Discantus as Ffaut to the eleventh degree which will be Cfaut, place in this degree (*clave*) the first note and make these notes of the solution ascend, which in the canon are descending. Then you will also note that each note must be multiplicated by four[27].

Dormiui et soporatus sum. (Cc 2r)

That is, when the work is of many parts, and something notable happens in the last part, then while in the preceding parts there were only four or five voices, another voice is added, or a conventional sign in one of the voices signifies that some other must follow from this one. It is so that Josquin composed a Psalm in which this text is given[28].

Desiderium crescit cum spe. (Cc 3r)

This song likewise has been composed for four voices. But in addition a fifth is produced from the one to which the canon has been appended, and indeed is performed with text, and the sentence is this: *desiderium crescit cum spe*: the first starts, and begins the whole song in order; the second emerges, rests four, and begins the eleventh below it, which it then follows again for as long as it takes to catch up with this text, *Le desir croist quant et quant l'esperance*. There the voice that follows sings all the notes slowly and dwells on them twice as long, until it reaches the point where they cease together[29].

In other cases, Finck's instructions are too vague:

Vae tibi ridenti, nam mox post gaudia flebis. (Cc 1v)

In this verse are contained all eight parts of the discourse, by what they want to signify that the chant notated with this canon can be accommodated to any of the eight tones [modes][30].

I prae, sequar: inquit cancer. (Cc 2r)

That is, when from the last part of the cantilena two voices follow each other after a few rests[31].

---

[27]. For the list of Finck's expressions not used by Martini (original in Latin, and English translation), see Table 5.

[28]. «Id est, quando cantus plurium est partium, et postea in postrema parte aliquid notabile incidit, ibi cum antea praecedentes partes tantum quatuor aut quinque uocum fuerint, tunc adhuc alia uox additur: aut per signum conuenientiae in aliqua uoce significatur, aliquam aliam ex illa sequi debere: Sic Iosquinus composuit Psalmum, in quo iste textus ponitur».

[29]. «Haec itidem cantilena quatuor uocibus composita est. Sed insuper ex illa, cui Canon appositus est, quinta propagatur, et quidem cum textu profertur, estque haec sententia: desiderium crescit cum spe: prima inchoans, cantum ordine pertexit: altera emergens, quatuor pausat: et undecimam infra hanc orditur, quam deinceps tantisper sequitur, donec textum hunc assequatur, le desir croist quant et quant lesperance: Ibi uox illa, quae sequitur, omnes notas tractim et duplo maiori cum mora canit, donec progrediatur eo ubi simul desinant».

[30]. «In hoc uersiculo continentur omnes octo partes orationis, indeque significare uolunt, cantum notatum hoc Canone, ad quemlibet octo tonorum accommodari posse».

[31]. «Id est, quando ex postrema cantilenae parte duae uoces se post aliquot pausas sequuntur».

Ranam agit Seriphiam.
Vox faucibus haesit. (Cc 2r)

This canon is often used in masses, on the text *Benedictus qui venit in nomine domini* and it notes that one should be silent, even though a voice is written[32].

In other cases still, the instructions refer to solmisation (see TABLE 5 for Finck's original explanations and translations):

Dimidium spherae, spheram, cum principe Romae,
Postulat a nobis totius conditor orbis.
Quamlibet inspicias notulam qua claue locetur,
Tunc denique socios in eadem concine tentos:
Sed uere prolationes non petunt pausationes, sed sunt signa generis. (Cc 2r)

or to mensural notation (see TABLE 5 for Finck's original explanations and translations):

Gaude cum gaudentibus. (Cc 1r)
Da mihi dimidiam lunam, solem, et canis iram. (Cc 2r)

All these expressions are assembled in the second part of the *Liber Tertius* (Cc 1v ff.), with the exception of *Gaude cum gaudentibus*, which appears at the beginning. From this second part, Martini's table retains only five expressions, all of which indicate a precise rule: *Et sic de singulis*; *Qui se exaltat humiliabitur*; *Contraria contrariis curantur*; *Plutonico subiit regna*; *Qui se humiliat exaltabitur*.

If the order of the expressions in Finck's list is not exactly the same as Martini's, Finck's and Martini's explanations agree completely, with a few minor exceptions (see TABLE 4). Any differences are not true divergences, but rather clarifications added by one of the two authors:

Crescit in Duplo, Triplo, &c. et Decrescit in Duplo, Triplo, &c. (M.32, 33; F. Cc1v/Ggv)
Finck is quite laconic in his explanation for these two expressions («These canons are extremely common, they are used at the discretion of the symphonistae»[33]) while Martini explains them thoroughly («The consequent must double or triple, etc., the value of the figures; or decrease it by half or two thirds»[34]).

Digniora sunt priora (M.34; F. Cc1v/Gg 4r)
The explanations of the two authors relate to the way in which the consequent must be sung by following the rhythmic values from the longest to the shortest («In the consequent, the note values must be sung in the order

---

[32]. «Hunc Canonem plaerunque usurpant in Missis, in textu: Benedictus qui uenit in nomine domini: Et notat silendum esse, etiamsi uox adscripta sit».

[33]. «Isti Canones admodum uulgares sunt, ijsque pro arbitrio symphonistae utuntur».

[34]. «Il Conseguente deve radoppiare, o tripliare, &c. il valore delle Figure; o diminuirlo la metà, o due terzi».

of their magnitude, i.e. first the maxims, then the longs, followed by the breves, the semibreves, the minims, the semiminims, etc.»[35]). Finck specifies that this rule also applies to silences («This is to say that the notes of longer value must be sung first, then the ones with shorter value; so that a long note precedes a breve, a breve a semibreve, a semibreve a minim, and the rests must be judged in the same way»[36]).

Descende gradatim (M.35; F. Cc1v/Hh2v)

Martini associates this with the expression number 36 «Ascende gradatim» and explains: «If a part forms a small Cantilena, this must be repeated until the composition is finished; when repeating, it should ascend or descend a tone»[37]. Finck mentions only the first expression, «Descende gradatim»: «When some phrase (clausula), in a cantilena of several voices, appears more often in one single voice, then this must be lowered by a second in each single repetition». One might be tempted to wonder if Martini would not have created the expression «Ascende gradatim» himself, without having identified it in a composition[38].

Qui se humiliat exaltabitur (M.41; F. Cc2v/Nn1v)

Martini associates this expression with «Qui se exaltat humiliabitur» and explains that for both mottoes «the response must be sung to the contrary, in such a way that if the antecedent ascends, the consequent descends, and if the antecedent descends, the consequent ascends»[39]. Finck gives an identical explanation for «Qui se exaltat humiliabitur»: «That is, by how much a note ascends, by that much you will imagine it to descend, and the reverse»[40]. Nevertheless, Finck adds a further explanation about «Qui se humiliat exaltabitur»: «Although I find this canon in a slightly different form in the French chanson *Languir me fais*, in which I have established that not only should the descending notes be sung at high pitch, but the chanson itself, although it appears to be for only four voices, and is one of those over which is written the canon *Qui se humiliate exaltabitur*. Yet out of the four written voices a fifth emerges as well by artifice, as follows: the four voices begin the song, each at that pitch which the signed clef requires; the fifth voice rests for two ordinary tactus, and begins at the interval of a fifth below that voice from which is derived. For example: the preceding voice begins on Ffaut: the other that has two rests is sung on b-fa-bquadrum-mi, a fifth below it; then too whenever a rest occurs, the following voice does not keep up the same sound, but after observing the rest is always raised in sound by a second, and observes the rule right to the end»[41].

---

[35]. «Si devono cantar dal Conseguente le Figure per ordine del loro maggior valore, cioè prima le Massime, indi le Longhe, poscia le Brevi, le Semibrevi, le Minime, le Semiminime, &c.».

[36]. «Id est, notae quae maiorem habent ualorem, primum cantandae sunt, deinde illae quae minus ualent: ut longa breuem superat ualore, breuis semibreuem, semibreuis minimam, et caetera simili modo de pausis iudicandum est».

[37]. «Se una Parte forma una piccola Cantilena, questa deve repplicarsi fin tanto che sia teminata la Composizione; e nel repplicarsi deve alzarsi, o abbassarsi un Tuono».

[38]. See below: CERONE 1613.

[39]. «La risposta deve cantarsi al contrario in maniera tale, che se l'Antecedente ascende, il Conseguente discenda, e se l'Antecedente discende, il Conseguente ascende».

[40]. «Hoc est, quantum ascendit nota, tantum descendere illam imagineris, et econtra».

[41]. «Quamuis hunc canonem in Gallica cantilena, *Languir me fais*, paulo aliter deprehendo, in qua inuestigaui, quod non solum descendentes notae uoce sublata cani debent, sed ipsa quoque cantio etsi tantum quatuor uocum apparet, ex illarumque numero est, quibus supra scriptus est canon, *Qui se humiliat exaltabitur*: Tamen ex quatuor

Cantus duarum facierum (M.52; F. Cc1r/Ii 3v)
To this expression, Martini adds «Tolle moras placido maneant suspiria cantu», and numbers it 53, as if it were a separate expression. He gives the same explanation for both: «The consequent can be sung with pauses, or without pauses, always maintaining however the crotchet rest, i.e. the quarter of a *battuta*, if it is written in the antecedent, so that the *battuta* remains complete»[42]. In Finck, on the other hand, «Tolle moras placido maneant suspiria cantu» appears not as an enigmatic expression in its own but as a proverb in the middle of the explanation given for «Cantus duarum facierum»: «i.e. that which can be sung with or without pauses, but retaining the suspiria that serve the integrity of the tactus according to the verse *Tolle moras placido maneant suspiria cantu* (Take the delays away, let your breath remain calmly in the song)»[43].

Pietro Cerone, *El melopeo y maestro*, Naples, 1613

El melopeo y maestro: tractado de música theorica y pratica; en que se pone por extenso; lo que uno para hazerse perfecto musico ha menester saber is the most important work of the Italian theorist, singer and priest Pietro Cerone (Bergamo, 1566 - Naples, 1625). Published in Naples in 1613 by Juan Bautista Gargano and Lucrecio Nucci, in two massive volumes (849 chapters, 1160 pages), this treatise appears to be Martini's second main source for his list of *motti enigmatici*[44]. It is written in Spanish and dedicated to King Philip III. Cerone was in fact associated with the Spanish-owned Kingdom of Naples, becoming a singer at the church of Ss. Annunziata in Naples in 1603, then in 1610 a singer of the royal chapel, a position he kept until the end of his life.

The final book of the *Melopeo*, *Libro veyntidoseno. En el qual se ponen unos enigmas musicales, para sutilizar el ingenio de los estudiosos*, is a collection of forty-five enigmatic canons. Numbering sixty-nine-pages (pp. 1073-1141), this 22nd book is self-contained, a sort of appendix to the main body of the *Melopeo*, which is organised in order of increasing complexity. For Michael Lamla, the puzzles appear at the end of the treatise because they represent the most difficult form of counterpoint to approach. As the canons became more and more obscure, finding their solutions required more and more experience, reflection and experimentation[45].

---

positis insuper quinta artificiose promanat, hoc modo: quatuor uoces ordiuntur cantum, singulae quidem eo sono, quem clauis signata postulat. quinta uero uox pausat duos uulgares tactus, et quinto interuallo infra illam uocem, ex qua deriuatur, oritur. Exempli gratia: praecedens uox oritur in Ffaut: altera uero quae duas pausas habet in bfa♮mi, quinta infra illam canitur, deinde etiam quoties occurrit pausa, sequens non eundem retinet sonum, sed post obseruatam pausam illam, attollitur in sono semper per secundam, idque obseruat ad finem usque».

[42]. «Si può cantare il Conseguente con le Pause, o senza le Pause, ritenendo però sempre il sospiro, o sia quarto di Battuta, se trovasi scritto nell'Antecedente, affinchè resti compiuta la Battuta».

[43]. «Id est, qui potest cum et sine pausis cantari, attamen ut suspiria tantum maneant quae tactus incolumitati inseruiunt, iuxta uersum: *Tolle moras placido maneant suspiria cantu*».

[44]. The chapter presenting the enigmas in the copy of the treatise preserved in Bologna (Collocazione: C.128) is very little annotated.

[45]. Lamla 2003, vol. II, p. 310.

Renaissance Sources for Padre Martini's List of Motti o Enigmi

The riddles are taken from compositions by Franco-Flemish, Roman, Spanish or Neapolitan composers, including Josquin, Palestrina, Nanino, Rovello, Rodio, Mensa, Suave, Cerreto, Ingegneri, Vaet, Metallo, de Rore, Ghiselin, Montanos, and Cerone himself. There are two identified composers who have examples in Cerone's 22nd book and mottoes in Martini's table: Giovanni Nanino (*Clama ne cesses*; *Misericordias & veritas obviaverunt sibi*; *Justitia et pax se osculatae sunt*; *Ascendo ad Patrem meum*; *Qui non est mecum, contra me est*); and Cerone himself (*Respice in me: Ostende mihi faciem tuam* and *Qui sequitur me non ambulat in tenebris* are secure; possibly also *Qui venit post me, ante me factus est* and *Me oportet minui, illum autem crescere*). Four of the mottoes featured both in Cerone and in Martini's list do not have identified composers: *Vado. oineV*; *Qui se exaltat, humiliabitur*; *Qui se humiliat, exaltabitur*; *Praetor de minimis non curat*.

The riddles in Cerone's treatise are consistently presented: the kind of enigma is identified first, followed by the *declaracion*, a very detailed explanation about the example and how to find the solution to the riddle. This is completely in line with the idea behind *El Melopeo y maestro*: Cerone is the master who explains to the student how to solve enigmas step by step[46]. In the same way that Finck seems to have been the main source for Martini's list of mottoes, Cerone may have similarly inspired Cherubini's work, since Cherubini clearly had pedagogical purposes in mind when developing his collection of solutions for Padre Martini's canons[47].

Unlike Finck, who only gives a list of canons accompanied by explanations for each motto, Cerone does not present the riddles as a list of expressions; instead, he always provides musical examples. Many of the puzzles are a combination of music, text and images (a snake, an elephant, a ladder, a balance, crosses, a key, a chessboard, the sun and the moon, the four elements, etc.). In many cases, all of these elements — music, text, and image — are fundamental for the solution of the enigma. For that reason, Cerone does not give a definition for every expression, but places each into context, matching it to a specific example and explaining how to solve the puzzle. Neither does he provide a universal explanation for each motto, preferring to interpret each according to the specific context of the riddle in which it appears. He explains his decision as follows: «To this way of singing, one cannot give a rule, for everything is founded in obscure and secrete invention: as the grammarians have no rule for their enigmas, so the musicians don't have them for theirs»[48]. Even though Martini's ideas match up with this perfectly, he does not refer to Cerone but to Sebald Heyden[49] (*De Arte Canendi*, Lib. 2, p. 135) when he points

---

[46]. ARIAS 1989, pp. 85-114.

[47]. See BEDUSCHI 2021, pp. 325-350.

[48]. «A esta manera de Cantos no se le puede dar regla, pues todo esta fundado en invencion obscura, y secreta: que assi como los Gramaticos no tienen reglas para sus Enigmas, assi tampoco las tienen los Musicos para los suyos». CERONE 1613, p. 1074.

[49]. HEYDEN 1540.

out that «non si può assignare niuna regola certa» to the «vocaboli enigmatici»: «About enigmatic canons, which are frequently added to songs, no definite rule can be given»[50].

El Melopeo y maestro seems to have been Martini's second main source, just after Finck. Of the fifty-six expressions on Martini's list, at least eleven[51] (c. 19%) appear in Cerone's treatise (see TABLE 3). Five of these eleven also appear in Finck: *Clama ne cesses*; *Misericordias & veritas obviaverunt sibi*; *Justitia et pax se osculatae sunt*; *Qui se exaltat, humiliabitur*; *Qui se humiliat, exaltabitur*. The motto *Qui non est mecum, contra me est*, is also mentioned by Rossi; *Qui sequitur me non ambulat in tenebris* is mentioned by Bontempi; and *Pretore de minimis non curat* is quoted in both Rossi and Bontempi. Cerone must have been Martini's only theoretical source for five expressions: *Vado. oineV*; *Ascendo ad Patrem meum*; *Me oportet minui, illum autem crescere*; *Qui venit post me, ante me factus est*; *Respice in me: Ostende mihi faciem tuam*.

Again, this raises the question of how Martini made his choices. Cerone's book 22 contains forty-five examples of riddles and at least as many mottoes; Martini transmits fifteen of these at most. Cerone can also be excluded as the source for between two and four expressions: *Duo in unum*; *Tres in unum*; and very probably also *Vado. oineV*, and *Ascendo ad Patrem meum*. Glarean, not Cerone, is clearly Martini's source for *Duo in unum adversi in unum*: in Cerone, the expression appears in a reduced form *Duo in unum*, i.e. without the sense of inversion intended by Martini. *Tres in unum* appears only in Cherubini. It is associated with Martini's expression *Sit trium series una*, for which Martini's source is Finck. The motto *Vado. oineV* has the same meaning in Martini as it does in Cerone's example: retrograde motion. But in Martini, the motto is *Vadam et veniam ad vos*. This version of the phrase does not appear in any of Martini's theoretical sources, but in a Mass composed by Alonso Lobo, who is one of the musicians mentioned by Martini in the list of his *Opere Pratiche* sources for the mottoes list. The same applies to *Ascendo ad Patrem meum*, which is paralleled by *Ascende gradatim* in Martini. The meaning of the two expressions is practically the same. But nothing excludes the possibility that Martini may have invented *Ascende gradatim* in opposition to *Descende gradatim*, for which his sources are Finck and Bontempi.

The authorship of Cerone's riddles seem to have been a decisive factor for Martini. All of the unattributed enigmas which appear in both Cerone and Martini (with the exception of *Vado. oineV*) also appear in one or more of Martini's other sources: Finck, Rossi, or Bontempi. Martini seems to have singled out two named composers from Cerone's work for inclusion in his own: Giovanni Nanino and Cerone himself. Martini took all of Nanino's examples quoted in Cerone, and all those composed by Cerone unless the solution to the riddle required more than

---

[50]. «De Canonibus aenigmatici, qui plaerunque cantibus adscribi solent, nulla certa regula dari potest». Quoted by MARTINI 1775, p. xxiv, fn. 5.

[51]. It could be fifteen expressions, if one counts *Duo in Unum, Tres in unum, Vado. oineV*, and *Ascendo ad Patrem meum*. See below.

the accompanying motto. For example, Riddle 28 (*Enigma adonde las Notas blancas, se cantan por negras; y las negras, por blancas. Duo: in Diapente, Post duo Tempora*), written by Cerone, is about an elephant. The image of the elephant is necessary to understand the riddle. The same applies to Riddle 34 (*Enigma que se declara con la senal de la Cruz*), and Riddle 42 (*Enigma de la escala*): in these cases, the image is key to solving the puzzle. The solution of Riddle 35 (*Enigma del Cantor pobre*) involves a poem, and Riddle 32 (*Enigma que forma Ut re mi fa sol la; Duo in unum. Syllaba Guidonis dant tibi vitam*) requires knowledge of solmisation problems.

Cerone's Mottoes Quoted by Martini

C.1 M.1. *Clama ne cesses*
Giovanni Maria Nanino[52]
CERONE (*Melopeo*, 1613): *Enigma con otra differente Cruz*[53]. Num. XXXXIII, ff. 1130-1
FINCK (*Practica Musica*, 1556), Bb 4v / Cc 3v

C.9 M.9. *Misericordias & veritas obviaverunt sibi*
Giovanni Maria Nanino
CERONE (*Melopeo*, 1613): *Enigma con otra differente Cruz*. Num. XXXXIII, ff. 1130-1
FINCK (*Practica Musica*, 1556), Bb 4v / Dd 3r

C.10 M.10. *Justitia et pax se osculatae sunt*
Giovanni Maria Nanino
CERONE (*Melopeo*, 1613): *Enigma con otra differente Cruz*. Num. XXXXIII, ff. 1130-1
FINCK (*Practica Musica*, 1556), Bb 4v / Dd 3r

These three puzzles appear together in a single example, No. 43. Cerone's explanation is minimal: «And because there is nothing difficult or secret in it, we will continue without wasting time in making a particular *declaracion*, and only give the beginning of the solution»[54].

All three expressions also appear in Finck.

C.19 M.19. *Vado. oineV*
CERONE (*Melopeo*, 1613): *Enigma de la Cruz*[55]. Num. XX, f. 1095

The second word of this riddle should be read from right to left, starting with its last letter: «Venio». In Cherubini and Martini, the expression is slightly different: «Vadam et veniam ad vos». Cerone's version of the expression does not appear in Martini's theoretical sources. Cherubini explains that these words «indicate that two other parts are formed from the consequent: one that begins from the first note of the antecedent and

---

[52]. For author names indicated for Cerone's enigmas, see LAMLA 2003, vol. III, pp. 304-309.
[53]. (Enigma with another different Cross). Giovanni Maria Nanino, see *ibidem*, vol. III, p. 248 and LAMLA 1997, pp. 479-510.
[54]. «Y porque en ella no ay cosa dificultosa ni secreta, passaremos adelande, sin perder tempo en hazer su particular declaracion, solo ponremos el principio de la Resolucion».
[55]. (Riddle of the cross). Without author information.

continues until the last, and another that begins with the last note of the antecedent and proceeds by retrograde back to the first»[56]. Like Cherubini and Martini, Cerone also refers to retrograde motion: «Here there is not so much a need for an explanation as for a solution: for it is quite clear that the bass and the tenor begin differently, from the foot of the cross, and join each other at the tree, singing the notes each from his side, that is, the one contrary to the other [...]. And the contralto sings its part on the arm of the cross, once going, then returning: This is why on one side it has the inscription *Vado*, showing the way to the right, and on the other *oineV* which tells us that it sings in the reverse»[57].

Looking at Cerone's image (see ILL. 1, p. 27), it becomes very clear that, in the case of the alto voice, «to sing to the contrary» means retrograde motion. In the case of the bass and the tenor lines, when Cerone writes that from the point where they «join each other at the tree (*arbol*)» and start «singing the notes each from his side», he means that at that point both voices start singing from the same written line, but each one reads the same line with the page reversed (the tenor with the page turned to the left, the bassus with the page turned to the right), so that «to the contrary» also means contrary motion. From the place Cerone called «arbol», both tenor and bass lines have contrary and retrograde motion.

The motto in the version given by Martini, *Vadam et veniam ad vos*, appears in one of his *Opere Pratiche* sources: Alonso [Alphonsi] Lobo de Borja, «O Rex gloriae Quatuor vocibus», Agnus Dei I, *Liber Primus Missarum*, Madrid, 1602[58]. In a letter addressed to Girolamo Chiti in April 1748, Martini mentions Alonso Lobo's work and explains that this motto indicates retrograde motion[59].

C.25 M.25. *Tres in unum*
Josquin, *Missa L'Homme armé*, Agnus Dei.
CERONE (*Melopeo*, 1613): *Enigma con tres Tiempos*[60]. Num. 1, f. 1075

Cerone's explanation of how to solve the example corresponds roughly to Cherubini's and Martini's: «Two consequents are formed from the antecedent, producing a three-part canon, most often at the unison or octave»[61]. Indeed, in the example given by Cerone, one voice ends up making three. However, the example taken from Josquin adds a lot of complexity: all the voices start together, there are transpositions of fourth and fifth, and, on top of that, rhythmic relations are established according to different metres indicated in the closed canon. This is in fact what the title of Cerone's enigma refers to: «Enigma con tres Tiempos». «Josquin composed a *Tercio*

---

[56]. «Les mots [...] signifient que du conséquent il doit se former deux autres parties, l'une qui commence par la première note de l'antécédent en suivant jusqu'à la dernière, et l'autre commençant par la dernière note de l'antécédent revient en rétrogradant à la première».

[57]. «Aqui no ay tanta necessidad de declaracion, come de Resolucion: pues harto claro se conoce, que el *Baxo y el Tenor començan differentemente, desde el pie de la Cruz, y ayuntanse en el arbol*: cantando las notas cada uno por su verso; que viene aser; el uno contrario al otro [...]. Mas el contralto canta su parte sobre del braço de la Cruz, *andando una vez, y otra bolviendo*: que por esto de una parte tiene escrito, *Vado*; que muestra camino derecho; y de otra, *oineV*: con que nos avisa que canta al contrario».

[58]. See LAMLA 2003, vol. II, p. 552.

[59]. SCHNOEBELEN 1979, Letter No. 1393. The letter is dated Bologna, April 17, 1748. Bologna, Collocazione: I.012.013.

[60]. (Enigma with three Metre).

[61]. «Que de l'antécédent on forme deux conséquents, dont il résulte un canon à 3 parties, lequel canon le plus souvent est à l'unisson ou à l'octave».

Renaissance Sources for Padre Martini's List of *Motti o Enigmi*

Ill. 1: Pietro Cerone, *El melopeo y maestro*, book 22, f. 1096.

for the second *Agnus Dei* of the Missa L'homme armé *super voces musicales* for 4 voices, with three different metres, but very dry in its expression, because it does not say more than *Tres in unum*. In this canon all three parts begin together, but with different values, and in different voices [...]»[62].

Cherubini is the only one to write «Sit trium series una. Tres in unum»; Martini and Finck only have «Sit trium series una», or the first part of the phrase. Cerone, on the other hand, lists only the second part: «Tres in unum». This clearly implies that Finck is Martini's source here, rather than Cerone.

Tres in unum also appears in another example quoted by Cerone: *Enigma de los tres caminos*. Num. XXI, f. 1098. Another variation «Cum tribus vocibus», appears in ff. 1093-1094, *Enigma de las Sierpes*, Num. XVII; and f. 1095, *Enigma de la Cruz*, Num. XX.

C.36 M.36. *Ascendo ad Patrem meum*
Giovanni Maria Nanino
CERONE (*Melopeo*, 1613): *Enigma, que en la Repeticion sube un punto*[63], Num. VIII, f. 1081

Cherubini and Martini write «Ascende gradatim» instead, and specify that it is only a portion of the canonic melody that must be sung one tone higher: «There may be in one part a passage that is repeated as many times as is necessary to match the duration of the main voice. These repetitions should be raised or lowered by a whole tone»[64]. Cerone, however, specifies that it is the whole part that must be sung «un punto» higher at the repetition: «In addition, the mystery of that text, *Ascendo ad Patrem meum*, is that arriving at the repetition, the cantus must go up one degree: that is that the fugue starts again, Re fa sol la &c., but it is sung one voice higher than where it was sung the first time [...]»[65]. From his example, one can infer that «un punto» means «one tone», and the «canto» is the canonic line.

Cerone provides «Sol post vesperas declinat» as *Ascendo*'s musical opposite: *Sol* [...] *declinat* indicates that the part descends one tone at the repetition. The equivalent motto in Cherubini and Martini for this descending version is «Descende gradatim» (C.35 M.35).

C.40 M.40. *Qui se exaltat, humiliabitur*
CERONE (*Melopeo*, 1613): *Enigma de los tres caminhos*[66], Num XXI, f. 1098
FINCK (*Practica Musica*, 1556), Cc 2v

Cerone's explanation of the example that contains this motto is similar to Cherubini's and Martini's. Cherubini says that «The response must be the opposite of the antecedent, meaning that if the antecedent ascends,

---

[62]. «Iusquin hizo un Tercio en el *Agnus Dei* segundo, de la Missa Lomme arme *super voces musicales* à 4 vozes, formado con tres differentes Tiempos, pero muy seco en el letrero, pues no dize mas de assi: Tres in unum. En este Canon todas tres partes comiençan juntamente, pero com diferentes valores, y en diversas vozes [...]».

[63]. (Enigma that moves one *punto* higher in the repetition). Giovanni Maria Nanino. See LAMLA 2003, vol. III, p. 248 and LOWINSKY 1989, pp. 316-320.

[64]. «Il peut y avoir dans une partie un passage de nature à être répété autant de fois qu'il faut pour remplir la durée du chant principal, et qu'en le répétant il soit haussé ou baissé d'un ton».

[65]. «Mas el mysterio de aquel letrero, *Ascendo ad Patrem meum*, es que en llegando à la Repeticion, se ha de subir el Canto un punto mas en alto: esto es, que comiença de nuevo la Fuga, *Re fa sol la, &c.* pero cantase una boz mas subido de lo se cantò la primera vez [...]».

[66]. (Enigma of the three paths). Without identified author.

Ill. 2: Pietro Cerone, *El melopeo y maestro*, book 22, f. 1098.

the consequent must descend and vice versa»[67], while Cerone writes: «The first treble (because it has no pause) starts first; which, taking the upper part, goes up and down: that is why it has the expression that says *Qui se exaltat, humiliabitur*»[68].

The same example in Cerone is also used for *Qui se humiliat, exaltabitur* (which follows *Qui se exaltat, humiliabitur* in Cherubini and Martini's tables). Cerone's explanation is again apparently similar to Cherubini and Martini's: «Then, after four bars, the second treble enters, which goes down and up; and to warn about this, there is the sign *Qui se humiliat, exaltabitur*»[69].

The expression *Qui se humiliat, exaltabitur* is used in Cherubini Canon No. 7 where Cherubini (and Martini) uses contrary motion in the consequent parts. Cerone's example, however, does not relate to (musical) contrary motion. It relates to contrary motion when reading the enigma's visual layout. The enigma is presented in pieces of staves displaced in four levels. (See Ill. 2.) Each level has different pieces of music in it. The three (voice) parts start the enigma on the same middle level. The first voice moves one level up, then another level up (arriving

---

[67]. «La réponse doit être l'opposé de l'antécédent, c'est-à-dire, que si celui-ci monte, le conséquent doit descendre et vice-versa».

[68]. «Adonde el prim. Tiple (pues no tiene pausa) comiença primero; el qual, tomando-se à la parte alta, sube y baxa: que por esto tiene su lettra, que dize *Qui se exaltat, humiliabitur*».

[69]. «Luego despues de quatro Compasses, entra el segundo Tiple, el qual abaxa y sube; y para los advertir desto, tiene el letrero: *Qui se humiliat, exaltabitur*».

on the highest level), then goes one level down, and another, finishing in the middle level, where it had started. The second voice starts on the same middle level, but then goes to the opposite direction to the first voice: down one level, and then down again to the lowest level, before moving back up one level, and then another. In other words, the two voices move in opposite directions through different staves, each of which contains a different melodic line. In any case these two voices do not read the same melodic line in contrary motion. The contrary motion does not refer to the same canonic line, but to the direction each voice is supposed to read the *image* where the pieces of staves are displaced.

C.41 M.41. *Qui se humiliat, exaltabitur*
CERONE (*Melopeo*, 1613): *Enigma de los três caminhos*, Num XXI, f. 1098
FINCK (*Practica Musica*, 1556), Cc 2v / Nn 1v
See the explanation of the previous riddle.

C.44 M.44. *Qui non est mecum, contra me est*
Giovanni Maria Nanino
CERONE (*Melopeo*, 1613): *Enigma adonde dos partes proceden al contrario de las dos principales*[70]. Num. VI, f. 1080
ROSSI (*Organo*, 1618), pp. 13, 18
Cherubini and Martini's explanation for this riddle is the same as for the previous two riddles: it indicates contrary motion. Their explanation coincides with Cerone's enigma No. 6: «[...] but the other two [voices] (which is the first and the third) [...] proceed in contrary [motion]: this operation is notified stating *Qui non est mecum contra me est*»[71]. Cerone's example No. 6 does truly have musical contrary motion, because the same canonic line is sung in contrary motion by voices 1 and 3.

C.45 M.45. *Duo in unum*
The expression «Duo in unum» appears in several examples given by Cerone, always accompanying another expression. However, «duo in unum» and that other expression never combine to make the phrase found in Cherubini and Martini, «Duo adversi adverse in unum». This long form has a precise meaning related to inversion, whereas Cerone's shorter «Duo in unum», only indicates that two parts are involved — not necessarily that they are related by inversion. The various expressions «Duo in unum» combines with in Cerone each add a different element to the puzzle.

Duo in unum, Respice in me: Ostende mihi faciem tuam, Enigma che para conocerle, se han de poner los Cantores enfrente, Num. IX, f. 1082

Duo in unum, Canon: Bis canendum. Contrarium tenet iter, Enigma, que se canta de dos differentes maneras, Num. X, f. 1083

Duo in unum, non voce sed tempore, Enigma de la Sol fa, Num. XVIII, f. 1091

Duo in unum, Communis media est via, Enigma de la division, Num. XXX, f. 1109

Duo in unum, Post duo Tempora incipe in Subdiapason [...], Enigma, que se guia de la letra, Num. XXXI, f. 1110

---

[70]. (Enigma where two parts proceed in contrary [motion] to the two main ones). Giovanni Maria Nanino, see LAMLA 2003, vol. III, p. 248.

[71]. «[...] mas los otros dos (que es el primero y el tercero) sin que la letra lo diga, *cantan un punto mas baxo del Principal, y proceden al contrario*: la qual operacion se avisa con dezir: *Qui non est mecum contra me est*».

Renaissance Sources for Padre Martini's List of Motti o Enigmi

Duo in unum, Syllabae Guidonis dant tibi vitam, Enigma, que forma Vt re mi fa sol la, Num. xxxii, f. 1111
Due parti in una, Canto primo, e Canto secondo [...], Enigma del espejo, Num. xxxx, f. 1121
A motto identical to Martini's and Cherubini's can be found in Glarean, *Dodecachordon*, 1547, pp. 464-465. Glarean may therefore be Martini's source.

C.46 M.46. *Praetor de minimis non curat*
Cerone (*Melopeo*, 1613): *Enigma del espejo*[72]. Num. xxxx (Tenore, e Alto), f. 1123
Rossi (*Organo*, 1618), p. 13
Bontempi (*Historia*, 1695), p. 232
Cherubini's and Martini's explanations are similar to Cerone's: «The consequent must include neither the half notes nor the quarter notes, even if they are notated in the antecedent»[73]. Cerone says: «And of the two parts that are contained in this song, none sings the notes in order; for the tenor (which serves as bass) is extracting and singing only the notes and pauses of breve and semibreve, leaving aside all the others of lesser value, as the minima, etc. To warn us of this, the motto says *De minimis non curat Praetor*»[74].

C.47 M.47. *Me oportet minui, illum autem crescere*
Pietro Cerone?
Cerone (*Melopeo*, 1613): *Enigma que diminuye y aumenta el valor de las notas*[75]. Num. xxviiii, f. 1108
Cerone seems to be Martini's only theoretical source for this motto.

Cerone's *declaracion* says: «In this canon there are two parts, both secret, although of opposite effect, because one part decreases the values of the notes and the other increases them, so that none of them sings with the values shown by the time signature which is ₵, which means that the breve counts two bars, the semibreve one, the minim half and the semiminim a fourth. Because of the inscription *Me oportet minui*, the one who sings the principal part alters this value and diminishes its natural quantity, singing the breve as a semibreve, the semibreve as a minim, the minim as a semiminim and the semiminim as a quaver, as if the cantus sang *per dimidium* and took this other time signature ₵. But the part that follows works totally in opposition, since it augments the value of the notes because of the text which says ...*illum autem crescere*, that is that it sings the semibreve as a breve, the minim as a semibreve and the semiminim as a minim»[76].

---

[72]. (Mirror riddle.) Without specified author.
[73]. «Le conséquent ne doit chanter ni les <u>blanches</u>, ni les <u>noires</u>, quoiqu'elles soient notées dans l'antécédent».
[74]. «Mas de las dos partes, que aqui en este Canto estan encerradas, ninguna dellas cantan los puntos seguidos; porque el Tenor (que sirve de Baxo) va sacando, y cantando solamente las notas y pausas de Breve y Semibreve, dexando à parte todas las demas, que son de menor valia; como es la Minima, &c. y para avisarmos desto, dize el mote; De minimis non curat Praetor».
[75]. (Enigma that decreases and increases the value of the notes). Pietro Cerone?
[76]. «En este Canon ay dos partes ambas secretas, aunque contrarias en el effecto, por quanto una parte diminuye el valor de las notas, y la otra lo aumenta: de modo que ninguna dellas canta con el valor, que muestra la señal indicial del tiempo q es este ₵; el qual dize, que la Breve vale dos Compases, la Semibreve uno, la Minima medio, y la Semiminima la quarta parte. Que por causa del letrero, *Me oportet minui*, altera este valor el que canta la parte principal, y diminuye su natural cantidad; cantando la Breve en consideracion de Semibreve, la Semibreve de Minima, la Minima de Semiminima, y la Semiminima de Corchea; come si el Canto cantara *per dimidium*, y tuviera estotra señal ₵. Mas la parte Consiguiente obra todo al côtrario, pues aumenta el valor à las notas à causa de la letra

Martini's text for this expression is translated by Cherubini and by Ginguené[77] in two different ways:

– Martini: «L'Antecedente diminuisce per metà il valor delle Figure, e il Conseguente lo accresce in quadruplo».

– Cherubini: «L'antécédent diminue de moitié la valeur des notes que le conséquent a quadruplées».

– Ginguené[78]: «L'antécédent, ou partie proposante, diminue de la moitié la valeur des notes, & la partie répondante les augmente du quadruple».

In practice, Cherubini's and Ginguené's translations indicate two fundamentally different things. One can see that Ginguené, like Martini, refer to the given canonic line (the part to which the antecedent should respond by halving the values of the notes), while the consequent should quadruple the values of that same line: the given canonic line. In the antecedent, a minim in the given line would therefore become a semiminim. In the consequent, the same minim of the given line would be quadrupled, producing a breve. Cherubini translates Martini writing: «The antecedent halves the duration of the notes that the consequent quadrupled»[79]. One could understand Cherubini means the consequent must quadruple not the values of the given line, but the values of the antecedent — and only after the antecedent has halved the values of the given line. A minim of the given line thus becomes a breve in the consequent, and then this breve in the consequent becomes a semibreve in the antecedent. None of these explanations matches to what Cerone says in his riddle number 29. Cerone seems to refer to the given canonic line: its values should be halved in one part and doubled in the other part.

C.48 M.48. *Qui venit post me, ante me factus est*
Pietro Cerone?
CERONE (*Melopeo*, 1613): *Enigma que diminuye y aumenta el valor de las notas*. Num. XXVIIII, f. 1108

Cerone seems to be Martini's only source for this motto, which translates as «He who comes after me was made before me». The explanation given by Martini for this motto is: «Il Conseguente è stato composto prima dell'Antecedente». Cerone's Enigma 27 is inscribed with two mottos listed separately in Cherubini (No. 47, *Me opportet minui, illum autem crescere*; and No. 48, *Qui venit post me, ante me factus est*). Cerone explains the first motto (discussed above), but not the second.

C.50 M.51. *Respice in me: Ostende mihi faciem tuam*
Pietro Cerone
CERONE (*Melopeo*, 1613): *Enigma, que para conocerle, se han de poner los Cantores enfrente*[80]. Num. IX, f. 1082
Cerone seems to be Martini's only source for this motto.

Cerone starts his *declaracion* explaining: «There is no doubt that this canon similarly goes singing in contrary motion. [...] To make known the effect of contrary motion, and also for the greater ease of the second singer, it has the text *Respice in me; Ostende mihi faciem tuam*»[81]. Then he adds: «With this saying, it shows that

---

que dize... *illum autem crescere*: y es que canta la Semibreve en consideracion de Breve, la Minima de Semibreve, y la Semiminima de Minima».

[77]. About Ginguené, see below, pp. 47-52.
[78]. FRAMERY – GINGUENÉ 1791, p. 201.
[79]. «L'antécédent diminue de moitié la valeur des notes que le conséquent a quadruplées».
[80]. (Enigma, that to know it, the singers have to put themselves in front of [each other]). Pietro Cerone.
[81]. «No ay duda, que este Canon assi mesmo no vaya cantando al contrario [...]. Y porque se conozca el effecto contrario que haze, y juntamente para mayor facilidad del segundo Cantante, tiene el letrero: *Respice in me; Ostende mihi faciem tuam*».

those who sing must face each other, looking the one toward the other who holds the book in hand, but in such a way that both can see the chant»[82].

Martini seems to have more or less kept this notion of singers looking at each other for the performance of the canon: «Che il Conseguente canta l'istesse Note dell'Antecedente, ma al contrario voltando la faccia l'uno verso dell'altro». However, from the wording it is not entirely clear whether he means that consequent and antecedent voices should look to each other *metaphorically*, or whether the singers should look at each other literally: «Faccia» could refer either to the facets of the antecedent and the consequent, or to the singers' faces. Cherubini, on the other hand, overlooked the notion of the canon being performed by singers using a single score. He understood Martini's explanation to mean that it is the vocal lines that look at each other and not the singers: «The consequent has the same notes of the antecedent, but in reverse order, as if each was looking at the other»[83]. If both singers read from the same score but one facing the score and one facing the first singer, as in Cerone's example, the parts would be in contrary and retrograde motion.

C.54 M.55. *Qui ambulat in tenebris nescit quo vadat / Qui sequitur me non ambulat in tenebris*
Pietro Cerone, Mass
CERONE (*Melopeo*, 1613): *Enigma adonde una voz canta solamente las notas blancas*[84]. Num. XXVII, f. 1105
BONTEMPI (*Historia*, 1695), p. 232

Cherubini and Martini use different wording (*Qui sequitur me non ambulat in tenebris*), but give the same explanation given by Cerone for his example: «The explanation of this canon is that the consequent part omits the black notes and sings only the white ones»[85]. Cerone's example is taken from one of his own masses. Further on, in f. 1106, Cerone provides a third example of «Enigma adonde una voz canta solamente las notas blancas» and this time he uses the same expression as Cherubini and Martini, *Qui sequitur me non ambulat in tenebris*, adding «These principles suffice for our teaching for they all say the same thing»[86].

Apart from mentioning Cerone as a theoretical source for his list of mottoes, Martini also refers to him in footnote 3 on p. XXIV, where he mentions Cerone's riddle number V, «Enigma que anade una pausa»[87], ff. 1079ff. This riddle is marked *post duo tempora*. Martini explains: «Sometimes, however, in addition to the words indicating in which *Corda* or *Voce* any consequent must respond, other words are found, indicating the distance of time that each consequent must use in responding, and these words are equivalent to the *Guida* or *Presa*.

---

[82]. «Con esto digo, viene à mostrar *que los que cantan han de estar hueltos con las caras*, mirando el uno hazia el otro, que tiene el libro en mano; pero de manera, que entrambos puedan ver el Canto».

[83]. «Le conséquent exécute les mêmes notes de l'antécédent, mais dans le sens inverse comme si l'un et l'autre se regardaient». Ginguené's translation is again closer to Martini's original: «La partie répondante chante les mêmes notes que celle qui propose, mais en sens contraire ; de façon que l'une est toujours tournée vers l'autre». FRAMERY – GINGUENÉ 1791, p. 201. See below, TABLE 6, pp. 117-122.

[84]. (Enigma where a voice sings only the white notes.) Pietro Cerone, Mass.

[85]. «La declaracion deste Canon es, que la parte Consiguiente dexa las notas negras, y canta solamente las blancas».

[86]. «Estos principios bastam para nuestro enseñamiento: pues todos dizen una mesma cosa».

[87]. (Enigma that adds a pause).

These are *Fuga* or *Canon post unum Tempus, post duo Tempora* etc., which indicate that the consequent must respond after the pause of one or two *tempi*»[88].

Giovanni Battista Rossi, *Organo de cantori per intendere da se stesso ogni passo difficile che si trova nella musica, et anco per imparare contrapunto*, Venice, 1618

The Organo de cantori per intendere da se stesso ogni passo difficile che si trova nella musica, et anco per imparare contrapunto, a treatise by Giovanni Battista Rossi published in Venice in 1618 and designed for self-instruction (*per intendere da se stesso*), seems to be among Martini's major sources of inspiration for his introduction to the *Esemplare*. Chapter 14 of Rossi's treatise, *Della fuga detta volgarmente Canon, & de' motti che vi si pongono*, pp. 12-17, is entirely dedicated to canons. In the copy of the treatise preserved in Bologna[89], practically all the mottoes quoted in chapter 14 are highlighted.

Rossi's treatise inspired Martini not just in terms of its mottoes, but throughout the parts of the *Esemplare* dedicated to canons. Martini quotes a passage from the beginning of Rossi's Chapter 14 in its entirety, placing the quote centre stage in his introduction to his list of mottoes: «And because in making these chants his mottos are placed there, it is necessary to make sure that they are clear and intelligible, because the singers are not necromancers, nor soothsayers, nor indeed prophets, to divine the thoughts, or rather the unfounded caprice, of another»[90]. Martini uses this quote to justify the need to explain these mottoes to the «Giovane Compositore» who, without Martini's explanations, would run the risk of not understanding the compositions of the past or, worse, having his own compositions misunderstood by singers, who, being unable to "divine" the meaning of the mottoes, would be unable to sing them.

Rossi's Chapter 14 starts by associating the word canon with «regola»: «But to come back to the subject, let's say that canon means rule […] almost a rule of what must be sung»[91]. Martini's opinion, on the contrary, is closer to Cerone's: quoting Sebaldo Heyden, he affirms

---

[88]. «Alcuna volta però, oltre i vocaboli descritti indicanti in qual Corda, o Voce debba rispondere qualunque *Conseguente*, si trovano notati altri vocaboli, che indicano la distanza del tempo, che deve usare ogni *Conseguente* nel rispondere, e questi vocaboli equivalgono ai vocaboli della *Guida*, o *Presa*. Sono questi *Fuga*, o *Canon post unum Tempus*, post *duo Tempora* &c., i quali indicano, che il *Conseguente* deve rispondere dopo la Pausa di uno, o di due *Tempi*».

[89]. Museo internazionale e biblioteca della musica di Bologna, Collocazione: E.30

[90]. «Et perche facendo di queste cantilene vi si pongono li suoi Motti, bisogna avertire che siano chiari & intelligibili, perche li cantori ne sono negromanti, ne indovini, ne meno profeti, per indovinare il pensiere d'un altro, ò per dir meglio il suo non fondato capriccio». Martini 1775, p. xxv. Rossi 1618, p. 13.

[91]. «Ma per tornar à noi, diciamo che canon vuol dir regola […] quasi regola di quello che si deve cantare».

Renaissance Sources for Padre Martini's List of Motti o Enigmi

that no rule can be established for the «mottoes or enigmatic words found at the beginning of the compositions in canon, to which [...] no certain rule can be assigned»[92]. What Martini means by quoting Heyden is that it is impossible to lay down rules as clear as those given for the expressions he discussed just before (on pages xxiii and xxiv) when it comes to the *Motti, o Enigmi*, which he is about to list (pp. xxv-xxvi). Unlike the earlier expressions, these *Motti, o Enigmi* do not indicate intervals of transposition, rhythmic shifts and delays, or repetitions in an immediately understandable way. Rather, the *Motti, o Enigmi* are expressions that must be analysed, understood and applied according to the particular context of each composition with which they are associated.

Like Rossi, Martini[93] gives definitions for *Guida*, *Corona*, and *Ritornello*[94]. However, he does not cite Rossi in them, but rather five other sources, four of which predate Rossi: *Prattica musica* (Scipione Cerreto, Naples, 1601)[95]; *Scintille di musica* (Gio. Maria Lanfranco, Brescia, 1533)[96]; *Il compendio della musica* (Oratio Tigrini, Venice, 1588)[97]; *Compendium musicae Latino-Germanicum* (Adam Gumpelzhaimer, Valentini Schoenigij, 1611)[98]; *Musico Prattico* (Gio. Maria Bononcini, Bologna, 1673)[99]. Compared to Martini's, Rossi's explanations are indeed quite rudimentary and confusing: «The *guida* is placed at the beginning of the *cantilena* where one wants the other part to begin. The *corona* is placed above the figure where the other part begins to sing after the first. If there are more parts, more *guide* and *corone* are placed»[100]. As well as providing a much fuller explanation, Martini relates these three signs to the «canoni chiusi», which Rossi does not[101]. In Rossi, the designation *canoni chiusi*

---

[92]. «Motti, o vocaboli enigmatici che si trovano su 'l principio delle Composizioni fatte a Canone, de' quali [...] non si può assignare niuna regola certa». MARTINI 1775, p. xxiv.

[93]. *Ibidem*, pp. xxii and xxiii.

[94]. «Vi si trovano alle volte in questi canoni, tre caratteri cioè, guida, corona, è ritornello». ROSSI 1618, p. 13.

[95]. CERRETO 1601, Lib. 3, Cap. 16, p. 219. In fact, the passage to which Martini refers is found rather at p. 220. Museo internazionale e biblioteca della musica di Bologna, Collocazione: C.129.

[96]. LANFRANCO 1533, p. 127. A copy of the work is preserved in Bologna. Collocazione: B.108. The page in question is not annotated.

[97]. TIGRINI 1588. A copy is in Bologna, Collocazione: C.25. Martini indicates that the passage is on page 104, chapter 2, Book 4: «Delle Fughe, Conseguenze, overo Reditte, & prima della Fughe legate». MARTINI 1775, p. xxii.

[98]. Martini says that Gumpelzhaimer's observations on *Presa*, *Ritornello* and *Corona* are on p. 11. This work is also in Bologna, Collocazione: B.100.

[99]. BONONCINI 1673, p. 2. Cap. 12, pp. 100-101. Bologna, Collocazione: C.101.

[100]. «La guida si mette nel principio della cantilena dove si vuole che comminci l'altra parte. La corona si pone sopra la figura dove hà da fornire l'altra parte che comminicia à cantare dopò il primo: & se sono più parti si formano più guide, & più corone».

[101]. Martini, however, does not yet make an explicit difference between enigmatic canons and *canoni chiusi*.

simply does not appear. Martini specifies that *Guida*, *Corona* and *Ritornello* are used on the «proposta» of the «canoni chiusi», to give indications about the «risposte», and adds that the three signs are often used interchangeably:

> Some signs are noted in the *Canoni chiusi* above the part that forms the *Proposta*; these serve to let the singers know where to repeat the *Risposte*. Three are the most frequent: the *Guida* or *Presa*, the *Corona*, and the *Ritornello*. The *Guida* (or *Presa*) is needed to indicate to the parts which respond where the *Risposte* must begin. The *Corona* serves to indicate where the responding parts must end; sometimes, however, to indicate the end of the *Risposta*, some have used the *Guida* (or *Presa*). In the *Canoni Infiniti* (or *Circular*), the *Ritornello* serves to indicate that, once the *Cantilena* is finished, it must be resumed from the beginning both by the part that led the canon, and by the parts that respond; however, some use the sign called *Presa* instead of the *Ritornello*[102].

Rossi's treatise contains five expressions on Martini's list (see TABLE 3): *Exurge in adjutorium mihi*; *Vous ieiuneres les quatr'temps*; *De minimis non curat pretor*; *Qui non est mecum contra me est*; and *Symphonizabis*. For three of them, *Vous ieiuneres le quattr'temps*, *Exurge in adjutorium mihi*, and *Symphonizabis*, Rossi is Martini's only source. On the other hand, as with Finck's and Cerone's treatises, Martini did not take up all the expressions quoted by Rossi. Seven of Rossi's expressions are not in Martini's list. The first of these, *Le primier và devaint*; *Le derain va primier*, seems to be related to a specific example, without expressing a clear rule valid in any context. *Gaudete cum gaudentibus* (which also appears in Finck) relates to mensural notation problems (see above, pp. 16-20). *Missa sine pausis*; *Missa cuiusuis toni* is too general in its reference, as is *Nobis datum*: they lack detail. *Diversi diversa orant* does not seem to refer to a composition involving imitation. Finally, the expression *Qui querit invenit*, quoted by Rossi and Aaron, is not part of Martini's list of expressions, although it is employed in his canon number 10.

---

[102]. «Alcuni segni ritrovansi notati ne' *Canoni chiusi* sopra la Parte, che forma la *Proposta*, i quali segni servono ai Cantanti per sapere ove devono ripligiare le *Risposte*. Tre sono i più frequenti, e sono la *Guida*, o sia *Presa*, la *Corona*, e il *Ritornello*. Serve la *Guida*, o *Presa* per indicare alle Parti, che rispondono, ove devono cominciare le *Risposte*. La *Corona* serve per indicare ove devono terminare le Parti, che rispondono; alle volte però per indicare il termine della *Risposta*, alcuni si sono serviti dell'istesso segno della *Guida*, o *Presa*. Il *Ritornello* serve per indicare nei *Canoni Infiniti*, o *Circolari*, che terminata che sia la Cantilena, deve ripligliarsi da capo tanto dalla Parte, che ha proposto il Canone, quanto dalle Parti, che rispondono; alcuni però in vece del *Ritornello* si servono del segno chiamato *Presa*».

Renaissance Sources for Padre Martini's List of *Motti o Enigmi*

Mottoes cited by Rossi

M.49. C.49. *Exurge in adjutorium mihi* (Rossi, p. 13)[103]

«Gio. Mouton, in the bass part of an Agnus Dei[104], says: *exurge in adiutorium mihi*; call another bass to do the same fugue. The motto is clear»[105].

When Rossi writes «call another bass do the same fugue», he seems to indicate that this second bass would sing exactly the same line as the first bass. One could understand it as an indication of an answer in unison. If this is the case, Martini, like Cherubini, agrees with Rossi, who indicates that «the answer (or *il conseguente*) is in unison». Rossi is Martini's only theoretical source to present this motto.

M.50. *Vous jejuneres le quattr temps* (Rossi, p. 13)

«Josquin in his Messa della Madonna[106] uses this motto in French, *Vous jejuneres le quattr' temps*, that is, you will fast the four seasons of the year, a charming motto, which means that in that *cantilena* or fugue the singer waits four *tempi* which will be eight *tatti* or *battute*»[107].

Martini modernises Rossi's rhythmic indications: «The consequent must respond after the value of four *tempi*, i.e. of four *brevi*»[108]. Rossi seems to be Martini's only theoretical source for this motto, which is not taken up by Cherubini.

Le primier và devaint (Rossi, p. 13)
Le derain va primier (Rossi, p. 13)

«And in the tenor of the same Mass[109], in the Credo, he says: *le primier và deviant* [*le premier va devant*], as if to say that the first goes ahead; understanding by "the first" the one who sings in the clef, that is the one who had sung the tenor up to then; and the one who sings a fifth lower he understands "from behind" ["from the back"].

---

[103]. See Bonnie Blackburn (in SCHILTZ – BLACKBURN 2007), p. 372: «Pipelare, *Missa L'homme armé*, Agnus III, B (Vatican CS 41, Liber 15 missarum; Jena 22) cited by Rossi (*Organo*, 1618), p. 13, but crediting the unnamed mass to Gio. Mouton; he says that he omits the name because the notebook in which he had all these examples was stolen in 1585». Schiltz thinks that authors used to collect «inscriptions and their exempla in notebooks», and she mentions Rossi to exemplify her reasoning: for her, the book that Rossi claims to have lost containing the inscription that he considers to be by Mouton, is indeed a notebook where the composer collected mottoes. SCHILTZ 2015, p. 131.

[104]. Pipelare, *Missa L'Homme armé*, Agnus III. See SCHILTZ 2007, p. 372. For the precise sources of each motto, see TABLE 3, pp. 85-104.

[105]. «Gio. Mouton in un'Agnus Dei nella parte del Basso, dice: *exurge in adiutorium mihi*: chiama un'altro Basso che faccia l'istessa fuga il motto è chiaro».

[106]. *Missa de Beata Virgine*, Sanctus, Agnus I, Agnus III.

[107]. «Iusquino nella Messa della Madonna dice questo motto in lingua francesca, *Vous jejuneres le quattr' temps*, cioè voi degiunerete le quattro tempora dell'anno, motto gratioso: che vuol dire che il cantore in quella cantilena ò fuga, uno aspetti quattro tempi che faranno otto tatti ò battute».

[108]. «Il Conseguente deve rispondere dopo il valore di quattro Tempi, cioè di quattro Brevi».

[109]. Rossi refers to Josquin's *Messa della Madonna*, quoted as reference for the motto which precedes it. «*Le devant va derriere*: Josquin, Missa de Beata Virgine, Et in spiritum. *Le premier va devant*: Josquin, Missa de Beata Virgine, Patrem».

And in the part *Et in Spiritum Sanctum* he says 'the reverse', that is le *derain và primier* [*le dernier va premier*], which means that the last sings first; by *il derier* [*le dernier*, the last] he means the one who sings a fifth lower»[110]. These two mottoes are not taken up by either Martini or Cherubini.

Gaudete cum gaudentibus

«And in the Tenor part of the Osanna, in the Mass L'homme armé[111], he says *gaudete cum gaudentibus*, because the other parts sing in proportion. And since the proportion seems to be one voice more joyous than the other, and since the Tenor has always sung in prolation but in equal measure, then he means that with its prolation the tenor should conform with the others and sing, considering that he sings the real prolation, i.e. in inequal measure»[112].

This motto is not in Martini or Cherubini, but it appears in Finck (Cc 1r / Dd 3v) who, like Rossi, goes back to notions of mensural notation[113]: «This canon is found when some sign (and particularly the sign of the *prolatio maior*) is added to one voice; the other voices must be put in *proportione tripla*, and can nevertheless be sung according to the requirement of either sign»[114]. It seems to have been a clear decision on Martini's part not to include in his list the mottoes related to mensural notation, a system not current in Martini's (or Cherubini's) time.

M.46. C.46. *De minimis non curat pretor* (Rossi, p. 13)
CERONE (*Melopeo*, 1613): Praetor de minimis non curat, *Enigma del espejo*, Num. XXXX
BONTEMPI (*Historia*, 1695), p. 232

«The same [Josquin] in the Messa Mal'heur[115] says *De minimis non curat pretor*, i.e. that the judge does not value trifling things, or petty sins. This means that all the major figures must be sung except the minims, and therefore anything smaller, and this is how we must understand the minim rests»[116]. Martini does not mention rests, nor does Cherubini: «Neither minims nor semiminims are sung in the consequent, although written in the antecedent»[117].

---

[110]. «Et nell'Tenore dell'istessa Messa, nel Credo, dice: *le primier và devaint*, come se dir volesse che il primo vada innanzi, per il primo intende quello che canta sù la chiave, cioè, quello che hà fatto il Tenore sin'all'hora: & quello che canta una quinta più basso, intende per il deriero, & nella parte, & in Spiritum Sanctum dice allo rovercio cioè, le derain và primier, che vuol dire, che l'ultimo canta primo, per *il derier* intende quello che canta una quinta più basso».

[111]. Josquin, *Missa L'Homme armé super voces musicales*, Osanna.

[112]. «Et nella parte del Tenore, nella Messa l'homme armé, nell'Osanna, dice, *gaudete cum gaudentibus*: perche l'altre parti cantano in proportione: & essendo che la proportione pare un canto più lieto dell'altro, & havendo il Tenore cantato sempre con la prolatione ma sotto il tatto equale, hora vuol dire che con la sua Prolatione si conformi con gli altri, & canti, secondo che va cantata la Prolatione reale, cioè sotto il tatto inequale».

[113]. About this canon cited by Rossi and Finck, see in particular FINCK 2008, pp. 8, 40-42.

[114]. «Hic canon reperitur, quando uni uoci aliquod signum, (et praesertim signum prolationis maioris) additur: reliquae uero uoces in proportione tripla ponuntur, quae tamen iuxta utriusque signi exigentiam cantari possunt».

[115]. Josquin, *Missa Malheur me bat*, Agnus I.

[116]. «L'istesso [Josquin] nella Messa mal'heur; dice: *De minimis non curat pretor*: che vuol dire, che il giudice non fà stima delle cose leggiere, ò de' peccati piccioli: dando ad intendere che si devon cantare tutte le figure maggiori eccetto che le minime, & per consequenza le altre inferiori: & cosi si deve intendere delle Pause minime».

[117]. «Non si cantano dal Conseguente, benché scritte nell'Antecedente, né le Minime, né le Semiminime».

Renaissance Sources for Padre Martini's List of Motti o Enigmi

M.44. C.44. *Qui non est mecum contra me est* (Rossi, pp. 13, 18)

CERONE (*Melopeo*, 1613): *Enigma adonde dos partes proceden al contrario de las dos principales*, Num. VI

«Don Tomasso Sanguineto, a Genovese canon of Sturla, famous in his day for this knowledge, made this *rovercio*, saying in this way *Qui non est mecum contra me est*»[118].

Cherubini and Martini interpret this motto as relating to contrary motion: «The response must be sung in contrary [motion] in such a way that if the antecedent ascends, the consequent descends, and if the antecedent descends, the consequent ascends»[119]. From Rossi's example, given without solution on page 18, it is not possible to understand if «rovercio» means contrary and/or retrograde motion. The example in Rossi is not the same as the one in Cerone. Cerone's example relates to contrary motion, not retrograde motion.

Missa sine pausis (Rossi, p. 13)
Missa cuiusuis toni (Rossi, p. 13)

«And Pietro di Molù composed a Mass[120] that says *Missa sine pausis*, which can be sung with pauses and without pauses. The same has been done by Constanzo Porta in one of his motets[121]. OKghen composed another that says *Missa cuiusuis toni*[122], which can be sung in all tones. The Mass is in the Pope's Chapel»[123]. Neither of these two mottoes are taken up by Martini or by Cherubini.

M.21. C.21. *Symphonizabis* (Rossi, p. 13)

«Palestrina in the Missa Brevis[124] says *Symphonizabis*, which means to sing the same notes, with the same voice»[125].

Rossi's explanation seems to indicate singing in unison, and coincides with Martini and Cherubini's interpretations: «The consequent answers in unison»[126]. Rossi appears to be Martini's only source for this motto among the theoreticians that he cites.

Qui querit invenit (Rossi, p. 14)
Aaron (*Libri tres de institutione harmonica*), f. 25v
«We then have the motto as *qui querit invenit*: an easy motto»[127].

---

[118]. «Don Tomasso Sanguineto Genovese canonico di Sturla, famoso à suoi tempi in questa scienza, fà questo roverscio, dicendo à questo modo: *Qui non est mecum contra me est*». ROSSI 1618, p. 18.

[119]. «La risposta deve cantarsi al contrario in maniera tale, che se l'Antecedente ascende, il Conseguente discenda, e se l'Antecedente discende, il Conseguente ascende».

[120]. Rossi refers probably to the same example quoted by Finck: Moulu, *Missa Alma redemptoris mater / A deux visages*. But the expression given by Finck to indicate the omission of rests is *Cantus duarum facierum*.

[121]. *Sapientia ubi invenitur*, 1580. See LAMLA 2003, vol. III, p. 378.

[122]. Ockeghem, *Missa Cuiusvis toni*. Kyrie I has the expressions *Nemo me condemnat* (S) and *Nec te condemn* (B), without imitation involved.

[123]. «Et Pietro di Molù, fece una Messa, che dice: *Missa sine pausis*, che si puote cantare con le Pause & senza Pause: questo istesso hà fatto Constanzo Porta in uno de' suoi motetti. / OKghen, ne fece un'altra che dice: *Missa cuiusuis toni*, che si puote cantare di tutti li toni, la qual Messa si ritrova nella Capella del Papa».

[124]. Palestrina, *Magnificat sexti toni a 4*, Sicut erat (Vatican CG XII, 2, fols. 214ᵛ-220ʳ)

[125]. «Il Palestrina nella Messa, Brevis, dice, *Symphonizabis*, che vuol dire cantar l'istesse note, con l'istessa voce».

[126]. «Il Conseguente risponde all'Unissono».

[127]. «Noi poi habbiamo il motto in questo modo, *qui querit invenit*: motto facile».

This motto appears in Martini's canon number 10, but not in his table. It also does not feature in Cherubini's, probably because no precise rule can be established for it.

Nobis datum (Rossi, p. 18)

«Constanzo Porta composed a motet for four voices that says *Nobis* [sic] *datum*[128], where the second time one sings, turning the cards, the soprano becomes bass, the alto tenor, the tenor alto, and the bass soprano. To compose such *cantilene*, it is necessary to make sure that the canto does not make a fourth with the alto, and that the soprano does not make thick sixths [that would conflict] with the other parts; that the parts do not make cadences within them, things that make the *cantilene* insipid»[129]. This motto is not reproduced by Martini or Cherubini.

Diversi diversa orant (Rossi, p. 18)

«Nicolò Gombert[130], excellent in this science, in the second book of the motets à 4[131], gives this motto which says *Diversi diversa orant*. This is because the bass sings *Alma redemptoris* in the manner of the cantus firmus, the soprano sings *Salve regina* on the course of the cantus firmus, the alto sings *Ave regina celorum* also in the manner of the cantus firmus, and the tenor sings *Inviolata* in the manner in which it stands in the *Motetto della corona*[132]. In addition, the soprano imitates the cantus firmus which is in b quadro, and the other parts are in b molle because the antiphons are in b molle, an artifice that indeed is not as easy as some think»[133]. This motto is not taken up by Martini or Cherubini. Martini may not have considered this kind of composition, which did not involve imitation, to be canons.

Once the mottoes announced, Rossi gives then a series of «termini» indicating intervals of transposition[134]. «E perche in questi canoni vi sono termini non cosi intesi da tutti, sia bene in dicchiararli»:

---

[128]. Costanzo Porta, 4-part Motet, Vobis datum est.

[129]. «Constanzo Porta fa un mottetto à quattro voci che dice, *Nobis datum*, dove che la seconda volta che si canta voltando le carte il soprano diviene basso: il contr'alto Tenore, & il Tenore contr'alto, et il Basso soprano. Per comporre tali cantilene, bisogna guardare che il canto non faccia quarta con l'Alto, & che il soprano non faccia seste che siano grosse con l'altre parti; che non facciano cadenze le parti fra di loro, cose che rendono le cantilene insipidi».

[130]. Nicolas Gombert, Salve Regina.

[131]. Venice, 1541. See LAMLA 2003, vol. III, p. 379.

[132]. *Motetti della corona*, Petrucci, 1514-1519.

[133]. «Nicolò Gombert eccellentissimo in questa scienza nel secondo libro de' motetti à quattro fa questo motto in uno che dice, *Diversi diversa orant* è questo perche il basso dice Alma redemptoris, su la maniera del canto fermo: il canto dice, Salve regina sul'andata del canto fermo, l'alto dice "Ave regina celorum" pure sopra il modo del "canto fermo" & il tenore dice, "Inviolata" in quella maniera che stà il motetto della corona. Di più il soprano, imita il canto fermo, che è per b quadro: & l'altre, parti sono per b molle, perche anco, l'antifone loro sono per b molle, artificio invero non cosi facilè come alcuni pensano».

[134]. ROSSI 1618, p. 13. It is interesting to notice that the expression *Symphonizabis* (M.21. C.21.) appears in Rossi's along with the other expressions («termini») providing intervals of transposition indications.

All'unifono, vuol dire che si canta nell'istessa voce.
Ad tertiam, s'intende tre voci sopra.
In Diatessaron, vuol dire una quarta più alto.
In Diapente, una quinta più sopra.
In Diapason, un'ottava più alto.
Exacordon, vuol dire una sesta che sono sei chorde.
Eptacordon, una settima.
Maggiore, ò Minore.
Dittono, vuol dire terza maggiore.
Semidittono, terza minore[135].
Diapente col dittono, una settima maggiore.
Diapente col semidittono, una settima minore[136].
Diapason diapente, una duodecima.
Disdiapason, una quintadecima.
Disdiapason col dittono, una decima settima[137]. *Ad nonam.*

Several terms from this list also appear in Martini[138], but Rossi is not cited as his source. Martini refers to Rossi only for the prefix 'sub' which, added to Diapason and Diapente, makes them mean an octave lower and a fifth lower, respectively[139]. Martini also refers to Rossi in his explanation of the rhythmic delays between the canonic voices, which are indicated through the use of a rhythmic durational value, or «Figura»: «At other times, to indicate the distance of time, they used a *Figura*, the value of which indicated how much later the consequent had to answer»[140]. Examples taken directly from Rossi, pp. 15ff., follow this quote[141].

---

[135]. Martini indicates that «Semiditonum» in Latin means a minor second. This is undoubtedly a mistake. There are obviously errors related to the naming of the minor second and minor third intervals in the table on p. xxiii of MARTINI 1775, which should read as follows: Alla Seconda minore = Ad Semitonum = Ad Hemitonium / Alla Terza minore = Ad Semiditonum = Ad Hemiditonium, vel Trihemitonium.

[136]. Martini indicates that a minor seventh in Greek is also indicated as a «Diapente cum Trihemitonio».

[137]. Not in Martini.

[138]. MARTINI 1775, p. xxiii.

[139]. (They have also practiced adding to these words two particles, Sub and Supra, e.g. ad Sub-Diapason, ad Sub-Diapente etc., the particle Sub indicates that the consequent or consequents must respond an octave below, or a fifth below). «Praticarono in oltre di aggiungere a questi vocaboli due particole, l'una Sub, e l'altra Supra v.g. ad Sub-Diapason, ad Sub-Diapente &c., la particola Sub indica, che il Conseguente, o i Conseguenti devono rispondere all'Ottava sotto, o alla Quinta sotto». *Ibidem*, p. xxiii, fn. 2.

[140]. Altre volte per indicare la distanza del Tempo, si servirono d'una *Figura*, il valor della quale indicava quanto tempo dopo doveva rispondere il *Conseguente*.

[141]. On the other hand, one of Rossi's examples concerns the expression «post duo tempora», ROSSI, p. 15. Martini explains this expression and adds «post unum Tempus», but, instead of quoting Rossi, he cites Cerone as his source. CERONE 1613, Num. v, ff. 1079ff.

The similarities between the chapters dedicated to the canon in Martini's *Esemplare* and Rossi's *Organo de Cantori* are so great that one might easily believe that Rossi was Martini's main source of inspiration, even if little mentioned. Martini no doubt wanted to produce a more extensive, more modern text, especially in terms of anything related to mensural notation. Martini also started outlining (nevertheless without clearly stating) the difference between 'closed' and 'enigmatic' canons, which Rossi did not do at all; Rossi not event mention *canoni chiusi*. Martini organised Rossi's text into two distinctly separated lists: one for expressions that he considered truly enigmatic[142] (corresponding to the ones Rossi called *motti*), the other for expressions that were more easily understood (corresponding what Rossi called *termini*)[143]. Martini did indeed manage to produce lists which were much more sought after and far more comprehensive than Rossi's, thanks in particular to also drawing from Finck and Cerone. Martini's lists are much more systematic than Rossi's: they are presented as true lists, rather than being diluted by the discourse. Martini's explanations are intended be read without being accompanied by examples. However, the entire structure and foundation of Martini's discussion on canons is already very clearly present in Rossi's text, which predates his by more than a century and a half.

Camillo Angleria, *La regola del contraponto, e della musical compositione...*, Milan, 1622

Camillo Angleria's *Regola del Contrapunto, e della musical Compositione*, published in Milan by Giorgio Rolla in 1622[144], includes two mottoes on Martini's list: *Cæcus non judicat de colore* and *Intendami chi può, che m'intend'io*. They are taken by Angleria from two examples by Paolo Cima given at the end (pp. 111ff.) of his treatise: «Ricercare et Canoni a due, tre et quattro voci da cantarsi in vari modi con differente armonia del Signor Giovan Paolo Cima, organista nella Chiesa di Nostra Signora presso à Santo Celso di Milano». The mottoes appear in two examples given on p. 121, both canons. The first, *Canon à quattro*, is accompanied by *Intendami chi può, che m'intend'io*; *Cæcus non judicat de colore* accompanies the second, *Canon à 3 & 4*. Neither example is provided with explanations or solutions. Angleria is the only theoretical source cited by Martini to include either motto.

---

[142]. Martini 1775, pp. xxv-xxvi
[143]. *Ibidem*, pp. xxiii-xxiv.
[144]. Angleria 1622.

Renaissance Sources for Padre Martini's List of Motti o Enigmi

M.39. C.39. *Cæcus non judicat de colore*[145] Angleria: *Regola del contraponto* (1622), p. 121
M.56. *Intendami chi può, che m'intend'io* Angleria: *Regola del contraponto* (1622), p. 121[146]
Intendami chi può, che m'intend'io is not in Cherubini's list, only in Martini's.

Angleria does not provide a solution. Martini does, just after his list, specifying: «It is so difficult to solve this enigma that I thought it would be helpful to young composers to lay out the score of the canon, in which the enigma is placed. [...] The attached example will serve as an explanation for this last enigma»[147].

Giovanni Andrea Angelini Bontempi, Historia Musica, Perugia, 1695

Giovanni Andrea Angelini Bontempi's *Historia Musica*, published in Perugia by Costantini in 1695[148] is the latest theoretical source whom Martini cites for his list of mottoes. Bontempi's work, the first history of music in Italian[149], includes, in its second part, a short chapter (less than a page and a half) dedicated to *Cantilene artificiose*[150]. Unsurprisingly, being so much shorter, this section is far less detailed than Rossi's; it also lacks examples. Bontempi does, however, define «Cantilene artificiose» by relating them to *Canone*:

> *Cantilene Artificiose* are those in which an *Ordine di Figure* is hidden at the Dia tessaron, at the Dia pente, or at the Dia pason, placed either above or below. This *Ordine* has been barbarously called *Canone* by musicians[151].

Bontempi seems to use «ordine» to refer to what Rossi had called «regola». According to Bontempi, it is this «ordine» that has been «barbaramente» called «canone» by musicians. In the passage that follows, Bontempi makes it clear that in «cantilene artificiose» only one voice is written, and that the other voices must be deduced from this single notated

---

[145]. Michael Lamla indicates a solution for this motto in a *Kanonsammlung*, D-Bds L200, p. 17v. See LAMLA 2003, vol. II, p. 354.

[146]. Laurence Wuidar quotes some well-known examples in which the motto *Intendami chi può* appears, including a Ricercar by Frescobaldi (*Fiori musicali*, Venice) from 1635, i.e. later than Angleria's treatise. Wuidar also mentions Lodovico Agostino (*Enigmi musicali [...] il primo libro, 6 voci con dialoghi a 7, 8, 10 voci*, Venice, Gardano, 1571) and Giovanni Antonio Riccieri (1679-1746), Padre Martini's professor. WUIDAR 2007, pp. 42-49.

[147]. «È così difficile lo scioglimento di questo Enigma, che ho creduto di far cosa grata ai Giovani Compositori l'esporre lo spartito del Canone, al quale è posto l'Enigma. [...] L'anesso Esempio servirà di spiegazione a quest'ultimo Enigma». MARTINI 1775, pp. xxvi, xxvii.

[148]. BONTEMPI 1695.

[149]. BRUMANA 2001.

[150]. BONTEMPI 1695, pp. 232-233.

[151]. «Le Cantilene Artificiose sono quelle nelle quali vien nascosto un'Ordine di Figure o per la Dia tessaron o per la Dia pente, o per la Dia pason collocate o sopra o sotto; il quale Ordine fu da Musici chiamato barbaramente Canone».

voice[152]. Bontempi begins by giving a list of words which indicate the intervals at which the other voices must respond to the notated voice: *Canon in Unissono, Canon in Dia tessaron, in Dia pente, in Dia pason, subdia tessaron, subdia pente, subdia pason, Altior tono (la Seconda Parte canta un Tuono piu acuto)*, and *Tono demissior (un Tuono piu grave della Prima)*. If the «ordine di figure» is more complex than these indications of transposition, Bontempi calls them «motti»: «They also used other ways of *Compositioni*, which are signified by the *Motti* expressed at the beginning of the *Cantilena*»[153]. The word «motti» appears here for the first time, as an introduction to the list of expressions that follows. Each motto is accompanied by a short explanation. Bontempi mentions eight mottoes in all (excluding those which simply indicate transposition intervals, which he does not consider *motti*); all of which are present both in Martini's list and in other theoretical sources quoted by Martini. Bontempi is therefore not Martini's sole source for any of the mottoes on Martini's list.

Mottoes cited by Bontempi

M.1. C.1. *Clama ne cesses* BONTEMPI (*Historia*, 1695), p. 232
FINCK (*Practica Musica*, 1556), Bb 4v / Cc 3v
«*Clama ne cesses* [indicates] that the Pauses are never counted, even if they are written»[154].

M.17. C.17. *Cancrizat* BONTEMPI (*Historia*, 1695), p. 232
FINCK (*Practica Musica*, 1556), Cc 1r / Ee r
«*Cancrizat* [indicates] that one should start singing from the end»[155].

M.32. C.32. *Crescit in Duplo, Triplo, &c.* BONTEMPI (*Historia*, 1695), p. 232
FINCK (*Practica Musica*, 1556), Cc 1v / Ggv
«And *Crescat in duplum* indicates that the notes and rests double»[156].

M.34. C.34. *Dignora sunt priora* BONTEMPI (*Historia*, 1695), p. 232
FINCK (*Practica Musica*, 1556), Cc 1v / Gg 4r

---

[152]. Bontempi uses and explains the terms Presa and the Coronata with the same meaning as Rossi. The beginning is always indicated by the sign called Presa. Depending on its position — with the more accentuated curve facing up or down — it indicates whether the beginning is done by the lower or the upper voice. The end is always indicated by the Coronata. The definition of *Ritornello* appears later, as Bontempi explains the motto *Descende gradatim*: «Every time you arrive at the *Ritornello*, a sign expressed with two perpendicular and parallel lines with four dots marked two on each side, you start again, but always a tone below».

[153]. «Usarono anche altre maniere di Compositioni, le quali sono significate dai Motti espressi nel principio della Cantilena».

[154]. «*Clama ne cesses*, che non si contano mai le Pause, ancorche vi sieno scritte».

[155]. «*Cancrizat*, che si devono cominciare a cantar nel fine».

[156]. «E dinotano *Crescat in duplum*, che le Note e le Pause crescono il doppio».

Renaissance Sources for Padre Martini's List of Motti o Enigmi

«*Sunt digniora priora* [indicates] that the maxims are sung first, then the longs, then the breves, and in the same way the other notes following the ranks allocated to them among many others that are written»[157].

M.35. C.35. *Descende gradatim* Bontempi (*Historia*, 1695), p. 232
Finck (*Practica Musica*, 1556), Cc 1v / Hh 2v
«*Descende gradatim* [indicates that] every time you arrive at the *Ritornello*, a sign expressed with two perpendicular and parallel lines with four dots marked two on each side, you start again, but always a tone lower»[158].

Martini explains *Descende gradatim* as: «If a part forms a small *Cantilena*, this must be repeated until the composition is finished; when repeating, the part should rise or fall a tone»[159]. For Bontempi, what Martini calls «una piccola Cantilena» would therefore be clearly indicated by the «Ritornello».

M.38. C.38. *Nigra sum sed formosa* Bontempi (*Historia*, 1695), p. 232
Finck (*Practica Musica*, 1556), Cc 1r
«*Nigra sum sed formosa* [indicates] that black notes are sung as white»[160].

M.46. C.46. *De minimis non curat Praetor* Bontempi (*Historia*, 1695), p. 232
Cerone (*Melopeo*, 1613): Enigma del espejo. Num. xxxx (Tenore, e Alto)
Rossi (*Organo*, 1618), p. 13
«*De minimis non curat Prætor* [indicates] that although written, neither minims nor semiminims are sung»[161].

M.55. C.54. *Qui sequitur me non ambulat in tenebris* Bontempi (*Historia*, 1695), p. 232
Cerone (*Melopeo*, 1613): Enigma adonde una voz canta solamente las notas blancas. Num. xxvii
«*Qui sequitur me non ambulat in tenebris* [indicates] that the second part does not sing black notes»[162].

Bontempi appears a step ahead of Rossi. He still does not make any reference to *canoni chiusi*, but he does write: «Ancorche la Compositione fosse a due o tre voci si esprimeva solamente quella che prima delle altre dava principio alle Cantilene". In addition, compared to Rossi, Bontempi's definitions of each motto are much clearer, and express general rules.

---

[157]. «*Sunt digniora priora*, che si cantano prima le Massime, poi le Lunghe, e poi le Brevi, & in simil guisa le altre Note secondo i gradi loro collocate fra molte altre che vi sono scritte».

[158]. «*Descende gradatim*, che ogni volta che si arriva al Ritornello, segno espresso con due linee perpendicolari e paralelle con quattro punti segnati due in ciaschedun lato, si ricomincia, ma sempre un Tuono piu grave».

[159]. «Se una Parte forma una piccola Cantilena, questa deve repplicarsi fin tanto che sia teminata la Composizione; e nel repplicarsi deve alzarsi, o abbassarsi un Tuono».

[160]. «*Nigra sum sed formosa*, che essendovi le Note nere si cantano per bianche».

[161]. «*De mininiis non curat Prætor*, che non si cantano benche scritte, ne le Minime ne le Semiminime».

[162]. «*Qui sequitur me non ambulat in tenebris*, che la seconda Parte non canta alcuna Nota nera».

Reception of Martini's and Cherubini's Works in the 19th Century

Pierre-Louis Ginguené, *Encyclopédie méthodique*, Paris, 1791

One of the entries for 'Canon' in the *Encyclopédie méthodique*[1] appears to be the first French translation of Martini's list of mottoes. Published seventeen years after the first edition of the *Esemplare*, this translation is quite different from those by Cherubini or Fétis (see below, pp. 52-57 and Table 6). The entry is signed by Pierre Louis Ginguené (Rennes, 1748 – Paris, 1816), a musicologist, composer, and, chiefly, a politician specialising in Italy: he served as ambassador to Turin[2]. Ginguené's collection of Italian books was one of the most remarkable since Floncel's[3]; at the time of his death, his personal library numbered some 5,000 books, 130 of which related to music history and theory. Martini's *Esemplare*[4] and the three volumes of the *Storia della Musica*[5] were both part of this collection. Ginguené knew Cherubini, the two collaborated on the preparation of the *Méthode de chant* for the very recently created Conservatoire de Paris[6]. As early as 1796, Cherubini had written to Ginguené, who was then the general director of public education, to ask him whether Napoleon's conquest of Italy might make it easier to bring Bologna's exceptional music library, the fruit of Padre Martini's labours, to the Paris Conservatoire[7].

---

[1]. Framery – Ginguené 1791, pp. 195-202. Tome I [A-Gymnopédie] edited by Framery and Ginguené; Tome II, [H-Za] edited by Framery, Ginguené and Momigny in 1818.

[2]. From 1811 till 1819, Ginguené also published a *Histoire littéraire d'Italie* in nine volumes, where we find articles related to music, Salfi, Paris.

[3]. *Catalogue des livres* 1817, p. xix.

[4]. *Ibidem*, p. 195, entry 90.

[5]. *Ibidem*, p. 194, entry 81.

[6]. *Méthode de chant* 1803, note on p. 66: «La commission chargée de la rédaction de cette méthode, fut composée de Cherubini, Garat, Gossec, Méhul, Ginguené, Langlé, Plantade et Guichard».

[7]. «Le 14 Messidor An 4e de la Republique Française, une et indivisible / Citoyen / Le Géneral Buonaparte est dans Bologne, ne seroit il pas possible que comme la peinture, la musique profitait du succès de ses armes; il existe en cette ville, la collection des œuvres du Père Martini, ensemble la plus précieuse collection des ouvrages traitant de cet art réunie par le P. Martini: cet article est dans le couvent de St. François, Bologne renferme aussi la collection complète des œuvres de Perti, maitre de chapelle de St. Petrone ou d'une autre église. / C'est peut être

The *Encyclopédie méthodique* has four entries titled 'Canon'. The first is signed «J. J. Rousseau»[8]; the second one has two signatures: Rousseau again for the first part, and «M. de Castilhon» for the second[9]; the third entry is subscribed «M. de Framery»[10]; and the fourth and last, the one presenting Martini's table, is signed «Ginguené»[11]. All four entries are more or less closely related. Sometimes, the author of one entry refers to what the author of the previous one wrote. Nevertheless, these four aligned entries disagree remarkably about the origin of the word 'canon'. Two distinctly different explanations are proposed: one by Rousseau, adducing Zarlino, and the other by Ginguené, who translates Martini's explanation.

The first entry for 'Canon' in Framéry and Ginguené *Encyclopédie*, the one signed by Rousseau alone, is an identical reproduction of the first entry for 'Canon' in Rousseau's 1768 *Dictionnaire de musique*[12]:

> CANON, This was, in the ancient music, a rule or method to determine the reference and connection of intervals. They gave also the name of Canon to the instrument, by which they discovered these connections, and Ptolemy has given this same name to the book which we have of his on the reference of all the harmonic intervals. They called in general the division of the monochord by all these intervals, sextis canonis [*sic*], and the monochord, thus divided, or the Table which represented it, Canon universalis. (Vide MONOCHORD.)
>
> CANON, In modern music, is a kind of fugue, which is called perpetual, because the parts succeeding each other, continually repeat the self-same air. Formerly, says Zarlin, there were placed at the head of the perpetual fugues, which he calls *Fughe in consequenza*, certain notes[13] which directed the method of singing those kinds of fugues, and these directions, being properly the rules of these fugues, were called Canoni-Rules-Canons. From thence, taking the title for the thing, that kind of fugue, by Metonymy, has been stilled canon[14].

---

lorsque le conservatoire de France forme sa bibliothèque que les contributions de l'ennemi doivent en faciliter les moyens et celle la est trop importante pour être négligée. / Je soumets cette note au citoyen Ginguené trop amateur du vrai beau, pour ne pas faire les démarches qui pourroient procurer à ce précieux ouvrage le voyage de France. / Salut et fraternité / Cherubini / Inspecteur de l'enseignement du Conservatoire de Musique / P.S. Le Général ne pourroit il pas être autorisé à recueillir tout ce qui est désigné par l'opinion publique?». DELLA CROCE 1986, vol. II, pp. 33-34. Letter dated 2 July 1796.

[8]. Pp. 195-196.
[9]. Pp. 196-197.
[10]. P. 197.
[11]. Pp. 197-202.
[12]. ROUSSEAU 1768, pp. 69-71.
[13]. The original word in French is «avertissemens», not «notes». «Avertissemens» clearly indicates directions given by words, not by music notes.
[14]. ROUSSEAU 1779, p. 50. «CANON, s. m. C'étoit, dans la musique ancienne une règle ou méthode pour déterminer les rapports des intervalles. L'on donnoit aussi le nom de *canon* à l'instrument par lequel on

Reception of Martini's and Cherubini's Works in the 19th Century

Ginguené, on the other hand, begins his entry by quoting Martini on the origin of the word *canon*: «The *fugue liée* or *perpétuelle*, says P. Martini, was called *Canon*, because this word in Greek means rule, and in this sort of fugue, the proposition serves as a rule for the answer, which is obliged to follow its paths exactly from the beginning to the end»[15]. Ginguené adds that Rousseau's explanation of the word canon — which appears three pages above in the *Encyclopédie* — «is a little different; but that is of little importance»[16]. In fact, Martini's and Rousseau's explanations, defining which «rule» is at the origin of the word 'canon', are not «a little different», as Ginguené claims, but rather distinctly different from each other: one associates «rule» with words, the other associates «rule» with musical signs. For Rousseau, the «rule» to which *canon* originally referred were «avertissements»: indications, in the form of a (non-musical) text, that were necessary to perform a musical composition. For Ginguené, and therefore for Martini, the word «rule» refers to a musical part, the «proposta», which, because it has to be reproduced by the other voices, serves as a rule. In his *Esemplare*, a little further the passage quoted by Ginguené, Martini is even more explicit about the meaning he gives to «rule»:

> This fugue is called *Fuga legata* because the *Risposte* must be completely identical to the *Proposta*, from the beginning to the end, in the figures, syllables and intervals. Such fugues are also called Canon, a word that comes from the Greek [...], or in Latin, *Regula*, because the *Proposta* serves as a Rule for the *Risposta* in such a way that the *Risposta* can be sung on the same notes of the *Proposta*[17].

---

trouvoit ces rapports; & Ptolomée a donné le même nom au livre que nous avons de lui sur les rapports de tous les intervalles harmoniques. En général, on appeloit *sectio canonis*, la division du monocorde par tous ces intervalles, & *canon universalis* le monocorde ainsi divisé, ou la table qui le représentoit. (Voyez Monocorde.) / CANON, en musique moderne, est une sorte de fugue qu'on appelle *perpétuelle*, parce que les parties, partant l'une après l'autre, répètent sans cesse le même chant. / Autrefois, dit Zarlin, on mettoit à la tête des fugues perpétuelles, qu'il appelle *fughe in conseguenza*, certains avertissemens qui marquoient comment il falloit chanter ces sortes de fugues; et ces avertissements, étant proprement les règles de ces fugues, s'intituloient *canoni*, règles, *canons*. De là, prenant le titre pour la chose, on a, par métonymie, nommé *canon* cette espèce de fugue».

[15]. Ginguené: «La fugue liée ou perpétuelle, dit le P. Martini, fut appellée [*sic*] Canon, parce que ce mot en grec signifie règle, & que dans cette sorte de fugue, la proposition sert de règle à la réponse, qui est obligée de suivre exactement ses traces depuis le commencement jusqu'à la fin». / Martini: «Del Canone, o Fuga legata. Questa Fuga fu denominata ancora *Canone*, perché, siccome tal vocabolo viene dal Greco, che in nostro linguaggio significa *Regola*, come si è notato alla pag. 251, perciò serve la Proposta di Regola alla Risposta, la quale viene a seguire esattamente su la traccia della Proposta dal principio fino al fine».

[16]. «L'explication que Rousseau donne du mot canon est un peu différent; mais cela est de peu d'importance». Framery – Ginguené 1791, p. 197.

[17]. «Questa Fuga vien chiamata Fuga legata, perche le Risposte devono essere dal principio fino al fine in tutto simili alla Proposta nelle Figure, nelle Sillabe, e negl'Intervalli; dicesi ancora Canone, parola che viene dal Greco

Martini therefore clearly understands «rule» as the «proposta», i.e. the notated line.

As with the first paragraph, practically all the rest of Ginguené's entry for 'Canon' in the *Encyclopédie méthodique* is a French adaptation of the introduction to Martini's *Esemplare*. However, this is never made explicit. The article is signed «Ginguené» and Martini's name is mentioned only three times: at the very beginning of the entry, at the introduction to the table of Latin words, and at the very end, when Ginguené makes some comments on canons in practice. Martini begins his explanation of canons in the *Esemplare* with an example of a closed canon[18]. Ginguené does not reproduce this first example, but does print the one that immediately follows: an example by Francesco Turini (*Messa in Canone*, Christe) on how to transform a closed canon into an open canon[19]. Ginguené uses the unattributed example to explain the terms *Presa* (*prise*), *Corona* (*couronne*) and *Ritornello* (*ritournelle*). Then, by means of a very lengthy explanation, he sets out how the transposition indications work for each part, which are given by means of the clefs placed at the beginning of the closed canon.

Ginguené's entry omits the entire paragraph which Martini dedicated to *Canone Finito* and *Infinito* (*Circolare*)[20], jumping directly to an explanation of how to indicate transposition intervals. He copies the table on page xxiii of Martini, reproducing Martini's errors: like him, Ginguené indicates that the word for a minor second in Latin is «semiditonum»[21] instead of «semitonum» (see above, p. 41, fn. 135). Similarly, Ginguené did not realise that the Latin word for minor third had slipped (most probably by mistake) into Martini's column of Greek words, where (Latin) «semiditonum» is given instead of (Greek) «hemiditonium». The entry's wholesale reproduction of Martini's text continues by translating all the explanations of *sub* and *supra*, *hypo* and *hyper*, *post unum tempus* and *post duo tempora*. In addition to reproducing Martini's examples of rhythmic figures used to indicate the delay between the canonic lines, Ginguené gives an explanation of «brève [...] la mère d'où naissoient les autres figures», referring the reader to the entry «brèves & caractères de musique» for more information. There then follows an introduction to Martini's list of *Motti, o Enigmi*:

> But these are not all the difficulties one finds in reading the old canons. These first masters seemed to want to exact revenge for the trouble they had in composing such learned pieces of music, by making them almost as difficult to understand and

---

[...] o in Latino Regula, perché la Proposta serve di Regola alla Risposta en tal modo, che su le istesse Note della Proposta può cantarsi la Risposta». MARTINI 1775, p. 251.

[18]. MARTINI 1775, p. xx. Martini makes clear that the example is from BONONCINI 1673, P. 2, Cap. 12, p. 10.

[19]. MARTINI 1775, pp. xx and xxi. On p. 198, Ginguené copies the very example, without however mentioning sources: Martini is not cited, let alone Francesco Turini. Ginguené appends the solution — the open canon — in the appendix: Pl. de musique, figure 54.

[20]. MARTINI 1775, pp. xxi and xxii.

[21]. FRAMERY – GINGUENÉ 1791, p. 198.

decipher as they were to make. In order to achieve this, they imagined enigmatic
phrases which gave the key to the canon, and without which it was impossible to
guess what their canons meant. These Latin words or phrases were usually a kind of
proverb. They indicate the note on which the answers must be started, the pauses
which must be skipped in performing of the canon, those which must be observed,
the values of the notes which must sometimes be reduced or doubled, etc. The result
is that if one does not understand this key at the beginning, the canon becomes
invincibly obscure, and impossible to solve[22].

Like Martini, Ginguené then quotes Rossi — again, however, without naming any of his sources: Aaron, who pioneered the idea that it was a musical obligation to make these old mottoes comprehensible; Rossi, whose quote he copies word by word; and Martini himself: «The authors who wrote treatises on the manner of composing fugues and canons recommended, it is true, to make these enigmatic phrases as clear and intelligible as possible; for, they said, singers are neither magicians, nor soothsayers, nor prophets, able to divine the thought of others when these are expressed only in a capricious and extravagant way»[23]. Martini is eventually mentioned again (acknowledgment two of three)[24]:

> The learned Padre Martini took the trouble of collecting almost all these
> enigmatic expressions and to explain them; I believe I am rendering a service to lovers
> of ancient music, and to those who want to know the genius of the first masters of
> the art, by placing here this explanation, thanks to which few of those enigmatic
> canons will remain for which the attentive reader cannot find the meaning[25].

---

[22]. «Mais ce ne sont pas là toutes les difficultés qu'on trouve dans la lecture des anciens canons. Ces premiers maîtres sembloient vouloir se venger de la peine qu'ils avoient à composer ces morceaux savans de musique, en les rendant presque aussi difficiles à comprendre & à déchiffrer qu'ils l'étoient à faire. Ils avoient imaginé pour cela des *mots* énigmatiques qui en donnoient la clef, & sans lesquels il étoit impossible de deviner ce que leurs *canons* vouloient dire. Ces *mots* ou phrases latines étoient ordinairement des espèces de proverbes. Ils indiquoient la note sur laquelle dévoient entrer les reponses, les pauses que l'on devoit passer dans le cours du *canon*, celles qu'il falloit observer, les valeurs des notes que l'on devoit quelquefois ou diminuer ou redoubler, &c. Ensorte que si l'on n'entendoit pas cette clef qui étoit au commencement, le *canon* devenoit d'une obscurité invincible, & d'une exécution impraticable».

[23]. «Les auteurs qui écrivoient des traités sur la manière de composer les fugues & les canons, recommandoient, il est vrai, de rendre ces mots énigmatiques le plus clairs & le plus intelligibles que faire se pourroit; car, disoient-ils, les chanteurs ne sont ni magiciens, ni devins, ni prophètes, pour deviner la pensée des autres quand elle n'est exprimée que d'une manière capricieuse & extravagante». See above, p. 34.

[24]. The first time was at the beginning of the entry: «La fugue liée ou perpétuelle, dit le P. Martini [...]».

[25]. «Le savant Père Martini s'étoit donné la peine de rassembler presque tous ces mots énigmatiques & d'en donner l'explication; je crois rendre un service aux amateurs de l'ancienne musique, & à ceux qui veulent connoître le génie des premiers maîtres de l'art, en plaçant ici cette explication, au moyen de laquelle il y aura peu de ces canons énigmatiques dont le lecteur attentif ne puisse trouver le sens». FRAMERY – GINGUENÉ 1791, p. 199.

Ginguené provides Martini's list of mottoes with a French translation of the explanations, twice adding a few comments of his own. The first comes after the explanations for expressions 9 to 20: «We can imagine how difficult such a canon must be to write, and how impossible it would be to guess its execution if we did not understand the meaning the composer assigned to one of the twelve phrases above. It is less easy to imagine the pleasure which could result from this execution, and the merit of going to so much trouble for so little pleasure»[26]. Then, after the explanation for *Digniora sunt priora*, Ginguené exclaims: «What hard work! and such painful futility!»[27].

The French definitions of *canons fermés* and *canons ouverts* are clearly established by Ginguené when he translates Martini's explanations about *canoni chiusi* and *canoni aperti*. Ginguené translates *motti o enigmi* as 'enigmatic words' (*mots énigmatiques*). We are very close here to the definition of the «enigmatic canon» that Fétis would clearly state 33 years later.

François-Joseph Fétis, *Traité du contrepoint et de la fugue*, Paris, 1824

In 1824, in the first edition of his *Traité du contrepoint et de la fugue*[28], François-Joseph Fétis published an enlarged and revised version of Cherubini's table, containing 103 numbered expressions (see Table 7). The table was reproduced without change in the second edition 1846[29]. Unlike Ginguené and Forkel[30], Fétis did not simply present a translation of Martini's table: instead, clearly having been inspired by Cherubini's work, he published a table which was very similar to Cherubini's, but with fourteen additional expressions:

In girum imus noctu ecce ut consumimur igni
Ascendo ad patrem meum
Sol post vesperas declinat

---

[26]. «On conçoit combien un tel canon doit être difficile à faire, & combien il seroit impossible d'en deviner l'exécution si l'on n'entendoit pas le sens qu'a donné le compositeur à l'un des douze mots ci-dessus. On conçoit moins aisément le plaisir qui peut resulter de cette exécution, & le mérite de se donner tant de peine pour faire si peu de plaisir». *Ibidem*, p. 200.

[27]. «Quel travail! & quelle pénible futilité!».

[28]. Fétis 1824, vol. II, pp. 163-168.

[29]. Fétis 1846, vol. II, pp. 146-148. The manuscript used for the second edition of the treatise is preserved at the KBR: Ms II 4174 Mus Fétis 6795bis (<https://opac.kbr.be/LIBRARY/doc/SYRACUSE/17297618>, accessed December 2023). The table appears at the very end of the manuscript, on pp. 134-148, and also includes 103 expressions, as in both editions.

[30]. The second translation of Martini's table appears to be by Forkel 1801, vol. II, pp. 538-539. The chronological order of publication is Ginguené's translation in 1791, then Forkel's in 1801, and finally Fétis's in 1824.

Reception of Martini's and Cherubini's Works in the 19th Century

Qui ambulat in tenebris nescit quo vadat
Qui prior canit, et canat ut ipse videt posterior vero pro nigris albas, et contra
Contrarium tenet iter
Se'l mio compagno vuol meco cantare / Per altra strada li convien andare
Vous jeunerez le quatre tems
Haec parili modulanda gradu, contraria saltu
Has gradus aequales, contra dissultus habebit
Ad hyper diapason
Ad hyper diapente
Quatuor vocum
Quinque vocum

With the exception of *Vous jeunerez le quatre tems* (which Martini lists), these fourteen phrases do not appear in either Martini or Cherubini. Among other expressions, the picture is more mixed. *Sit trium series una. Tres in unum* (the version found in Cherubini's table) is divided by Fétis into two distinct parts: *Sit trium series una* and *Tres in unum*. Only the first, *Sit trium series una*, appears in Martini. Similarly, Fétis separates *Signa te signa temere me tangis & angis* and *Romae tibi subito motibus ibit amor*, dividing what was in Cherubini and Martini a single expression. The numbering of Fétis's table is also different to Cherubini's or Martini's: the fourteen additional expressions are inserted into Fétis to accompany expressions with similar meanings, thus changing the overall order. In addition, Fétis reorders Cherubini's expressions, particularly in the second half of the table, to better fit his organisational principle of presenting expressions with similar or identical meanings together where possible. It is also clear that Fétis sought to improve Cherubini's Italian-influenced French; this may be linked to the subtle differences in the explanations which accompany the puzzle phrases: although very similar and expressing the same rules, they are not identical to Cherubini's. Two expressions present in Cherubini's table are absent from Fétis: *Ad Equisonum* and *Ad Tonum, infinit, et finit*.

Fétis's table is presented as part of an appendix to his treatises, «Des Canons énigmatiques», along with explanations of «canons par mouvement rétrograde» and «canons par mouvement rétrograde contraire». He explains his decision to «leave what remains to be said on [the] subject [of enigmatic canons] to the end of [his] book, and as a sort of *hors d'œuvre*»[31] by stating that «the art of deciphering enigmatic canons is more an object of curiosity than of real utility»[32].

Fétis seems to make no distinction between an enigmatic and a closed canon:

> In order to shorten the notation of Canons, we often write only the subject
> or antecedent, indicating by some sign, or motto [devise], the number of voices of

---

[31]. «Rejetter ce qui restoit à dire sur cette matière à la fin de [son] livre, et comme une sorte de hors-d'œuvre».
[32]. P. 158. «L'art de déchiffrer les Canons énigmatiques est plutôt un objet de curiosité que d'utilité réelle».

which the Canon is composed, and the way to solve it. A canon written in this way is called a "Closed", or "Enigmatic Canon"; when it is solved and notated, it is called an "Open Canon"[33].

Fétis continues by explaining how to interpret the «signs» (*signes*) that accompany closed canons, so as to transform them into open canons: the clefs, which indicate the number of voices as well as the transposition intervals and the order of entries; the § sign, which indicates the precise location of each new entry; the (.) sign, which denotes the point on the canonical line where the canon ends; and various measure indications (c and ¢) to signal rhythmic alterations to be added to the canonical line. After having explained these symbols, Fétis proceeds to the mottoes (*devises*) which introduce his «Table des devises ou inscriptions des canons énigmatiques, avec leur explication»:

> Finally, as I said above, composers often use "*devises*", whose meaning is allegorical, as inscriptions in the Enigmatic Canons, and which serve as keys to solve them. Here is the table, with the meaning of each[34].

The table is followed by illustrative examples, including some of the solutions that Cherubini proposed for the canons of the *Storia della Musica*. Fétis makes this very clear in his attributions: «Cherubini, who resolved all the Canons that serve as vignettes for Padre Martini's History of Music, found the solution to this one [...]»[35]. Fétis's treatise gives four such solutions for Martini's canons proposed by Cherubini (pp. 171, 172, 175, 176)[36], as well as unattributed solutions for a canon by Scipione Cerreto, p. 169, a canon by Giovanni Maria Nanino, p. 173, and a canon by Cipriano de Rore, p. 180[37].

The Bibliothèque Royale de Bruxelles, KBR, preserves a manuscript with solutions for thirty-five canons in Padre Martini's *Storia della musica*: «Trente cinq canons résolus | par Fétis ms autographe»[38]. The KBR states that the «manuscript comes from an old collection acquired

---

[33]. P. 161. «Dans le dessein d'abréger la notation des Canons, on n'écrit souvent que le sujet ou antécédent, en indiquant par quelque signe, ou devise, le nombre de voix dont le Canon se compose, et la manière de le résoudre. Un Canon écrit ainsi s'appelle "Canon fermé" ou "Énigmatique"; lorsqu'il est résolu et mis en Partition, on lui donne le nom de Canon ouvert».

[34]. «Enfin, comme je l'ai dit plus haut, ce sont souvent des devises, dont le sens est allégorique, que les Compositeurs mettent pour inscription aux Canons énigmatiques, et qui servent de clefs pour les résoudre. En voici la table, avec la signification de chacune».

[35]. P. 172.

[36]. From fn. 32 onwards, the page numbers of the treatise always refer to its first edition.

[37]. In fact, about Padre Martini's solved canons, Fétis states clearly that it was Cherubini who found the solutions for the first two published canons (pp. 171 and 172). Fétis does not mention Cherubini's name when he publishes the solutions for the other two Padre Martini's canons (pp. 175 and 176).

[38]. KBR 4957. <https://uurl.kbr.be/1985793>, accessed December 2023, RISM nr.: 700007154.

by the B Br on 28/10/1909». The library attributes the manuscript to Fétis; Cherubini's and Martini's names are not mentioned. The author of the canons for which Fétis is said to have proposed solutions therefore does not appear in the manuscript. It is clear, however, that these are Padre Martini's canons. Moreover, it seems evident that the solutions are Cherubini's, and not Fétis own. Fétis therefore appears to have simply copied Cherubini's solutions.

Up to where it stops, at canon No. 35, the Brussels manuscript is practically an identical copy of the solutions proposed by Cherubini for the first thirty-five canons in the Paris manuscript collection. As in the Paris manuscript, the order of presentation of the canons in the Brussels manuscript does not correspond to the order of presentation of the riddles in Martini's *Storia della musica*. The order of the solutions, their explanations, and the layout of how the riddles (and solutions) are presented is identical in both the Brussels and Paris manuscripts (see PLATES 1 and 2): the riddle is presented first, followed by an explanation of its solution, followed in turn by an open canon. On the other hand, the table of Latin words present in the Paris manuscript is absent from the Brussels manuscript.

The first of Cherubini's solutions which Fétis published corresponds to canon No. 19 in the Paris manuscript[39]. The second canon corresponds to No. 29 of the Paris manuscript. The Brussels manuscript offers an identical copy of the Paris manuscript in both cases. The versions Fétis published in the *Traité du contrepoint et de la fugue* are always very faithful to both manuscripts. The solution on p. 175 of Fétis' treatise corresponds to canon No. 13 in Cherubini's original. The publication in the treatise is again identical to both manuscripts, except for the indication «Resolutio ad Diatessaron», translated in the KBR manuscript and in the treatise as «Résolution à la quarte». The indication «Resolutio ad sub diatessaron», which accompanies the bass voice in Cherubini's manuscript, does not appear in the KBR manuscript or in the treatise. The solution presented on page 176 of the treatise corresponds to canon No. 40 of the Paris manuscript. This canon is absent from the Brussels manuscript.

While the version of Cherubini's solutions published in the *Traité du contrepoint et de la fugue* is identical to those in the manuscripts (Cherubini's original, preserved in Paris, and Fétis' copy, preserved in Brussels), Fétis' *published* explanations of those solutions differ from the manuscript ones. On a trivial level, the reference numbers in the table obviously correspond to the (enlarged) table as published by Fétis in his treatise, and not to the table that accompanies the Paris manuscript. More interestingly, unlike Cherubini, Fétis does not merely refer the reader to the table, but also explains in detail and contextualises each of the expressions used for the solutions.

At the end of the appendix, from p. 185 onwards, Fétis sets out ten canons for which he does not provide solutions. The authors of these canons are not indicated, but eight are taken

---

[39]. FÉTIS 1824, vol. II, p. 171.

from Martini's *Storia della musica*, the other two (canons Nos. 6 and 7) are canons by Giovanni Maria Nanino published in Cerone's *El Melopeo y Maestro*[40]:

Canon 1. *Sit trium series una. Repleatur os meum.* Corresponds to canon No. 1 in Cherubini.

Canon 2. *Canon post unum tempus. Cantate Domino omnis terra cantate. Canon 6, 7, 8. Pars si placet.* Corresponds to canon No. 3 in Cherubini.

Canon 3. *Canon Ad semiditonum. Cantabo Deo Jacobo. Canon Symphonizabis.* Corresponds to canon No. 8 in Cherubini.

Canon 4. *Clama ne cesses. Ad duodecim. Confitebor tibi Domine in gentibus.* Corresponds to canon No. 18 in Cherubini.

Canon 5. *Crescit eundo. Canon ad unissonum, et bis ad diapente. Canon ad diatessaron.* Corresponds to canon No. 21 in Cherubini.

Canon 6. *Quatuor vocibus. Qui non est mecum contra me est.* This canon by Giovanni Maria Nanino appears in Cerone's *El Melopeo y maestro* (1613), *Enigma adonde dos partes proceden al contrario de las dos principales*, Num. VI, f. 1080[41].

Canon 7. *Ascendo ad patrem meum.* This canon by Giovanni Maria Nanino appears in Cerone's *El Melopeo y maestro* (1613), *Enigma, que en la Repeticion sube un punto*, Num. VIII, f. 1081[42].

Canon 8. *Canon ad unisonum. Sumite psalmum date tympanum psalterium.* Corresponds to canon No. 31 in Cherubini.

Canon 9. *Canon ad hypo-diapason. Bis dicitur. Placent convivia et oblectant cantus. Canon ad hyper diapason. Otia dant vitia.* Corresponds to canon No. 46 in Cherubini.

Canon 10. *Hilari merum bibentis bromium patrem canamus.* Corresponds to canon No. 48 in Cherubini.

In the Paris manuscript, Cherubini's solutions for seventy-two canons by Padre Martini are followed by fourteen «Enigmatic canons by various authors solved by Fetis»[43]: Vmb. Ms. 1 (2). These fourteen canons, which occupy the last twenty-four pages, numbered 52 to 62, form a second part of the Paris manuscript, and are completely separate from the collection of solutions proposed by Cherubini for the canons of Padre Martini. In the letter accompanying the Paris manuscript that the musicologist Henry Expert sent to the administrator of the Bibliothèque Nationale, he pointed out that these last twenty-four pages are not in Cherubini's hand but Fétis's. Henry Expert thus claims to have identified Fétis's handwriting (see p. 317).

The five canons in Fétis's *Traité du contrepoint et de la fugue* which are not by Martini (whether they were solved by Cherubini or left unsolved as exercises), all appear in this appendix to the Paris manuscript. Everything in the Paris manuscript is identical to the edition of these canons in Fétis's treatise, including the text containing the explanations, which, like the music, is a faithful copy with very minor exceptions. The appendix to the Paris manuscript therefore

---

[40]. These two canons are also part of the appendix to the Paris manuscript. See below.

[41]. Paris manuscript, «Canon 2ᵉ», p. 52r.

[42]. Paris manuscript, «Canon 3ᵉ», p. 52v.

[43]. «Canons Enigmatiques de différents Auteurs résolus par Fetis».

clearly precedes the edition of the *Traité du contrepoint et de la fugue*. Though Fétis does not identify the author(s) of the solutions of the three canons published in his treatise for which the solutions are not in Cherubini's hand, they appear in Pietro Cerone's *El Melopeo y Maestro*, where they are both solved and explained:

• *Traité du contrepoint et de la fugue*, pp. 169-171: Canon. Scipione Cerreto, *S'el mio compagno vuol meco cantare, per altra strada li convien andare*. Corresponds to «Canon 7e», pages 55v-56r, of the Paris manuscript. This canon, together with its solution and explanations, is presented as enigma number XI in CERONE 1613, f. 1085.

• *Traité du contrepoint et de la fugue*, pp. 173-175: Canon. B. Nanino, *Duo, Bis Canendum. Unum post silentium, marte me sequentis adversum. Tu quoque fac simile, sic ars deluditur arte*. Corresponds to «Canon 6e», pp. 54v-55r, of the Paris manuscript. It appears on f. 1084 of CERONE 1613.

• *Traité du contrepoint et de la fugue*, pp. 180-185: 13e Canon[44], de Cipriano de Rore, *Quattro fratelli fuor d'un parto tira...* Corresponds to «Canon 13e», pp. 59v-61r, of the Paris manuscript. It appears as enigma 37 on f. 1118 of CERONE 1613.

Pietro Cerone solutions and explanations were published over two hundred years before Fétis's treatise appeared. Yet Fétis makes no mention of Cerone, nor does he indicate that the 'enigmatic' canons published unsolved as exercises are all taken from Martini's *Storia della musica*. It is clear that the main source of inspiration for the appendix on enigmatic canons in Fétis's *Traité du contrepoint et de la fugue* came from Cherubini's collection. Fétis's appendix contains only five canons which do *not* appear in Cherubini (either as proposed solutions or as the canons of Padre Martini — all from his *Storia della musica* — reproduced without a solution). Of these five, one is by Scipione Cerreto, three by Giovanni Maria Nanino (one solved and two unsolved) and one by Cipriano de Rore. All are included in the appendix to Cherubini's collection in the Paris manuscript. Fétis's expanded table was undoubtedly inspired by Cerone's *El Melopeo y maestro*, from which he also took the only three solutions not proposed by Cherubini. This does not alter the fact that Cherubini's work of compiling the table of Latin words and finding solutions for Padre Martini's canons remains at the heart of Fétis's appendix.

---

[44]. It is interesting to note that this is the only canon numbered in the treatise. This number corresponds to that of the Paris manuscript, but does not make sense in the treatise where, if the canons had been numbered, this canon would have been number 7 rather than 13. This could indicate that the Paris manuscript served somehow for the publication of these three canons in Fétis's treatise.

Padre Martini's List of *Motti o Enigmi* (Reproduced in Cherubini's Collection) and the Understanding of the Renaissance Practice of (Puzzle) Canons during the 19th Century

After analysing Martini's sources and the first disclosures of his *Motti o Enigmi*'s list, it is time to draw conclusions about the place Cherubini's collection occupied in the 19th century understanding of enigmatic canons, and also about how the 19th century understanding of (puzzle) canons can be traced back to the Renaissance. A kind of 'Chinese whispers' game radically altered the Renaissance conception of 'canons', creating in addition the category of 'enigmatic canons'. Obviously, these changes did not occur because of Cherubini, Fétis or Martini. Yet their work is central to this phenomenon. Fétis presented Cherubini's work as he understood it. Cherubini's collection of solutions and list of Latin words is Cherubini's account of what he perceived of Martini's work. Martini, for his part, took up several sources from the long Renaissance, codifying them in his own way.

While reproducing Cherubini, both his list of Latin words and proposed solutions for the canons of the *Storia della musica*, Fétis eliminated the difference between closed and enigmatic canons. Fétis considered closed canons to be all enigmatic, probably because he did not realise that Cherubini's list has two distinct parts: the expressions of its second part do not belong to Martini's category of enigmatic words. These expressions had been classified by Martini in a separate list that included only ordinary vocabulary in Italian, Latin or Greek used in closed (not necessarily enigmatic) canons. In fact, Martini only mentioned 'closed canons'; the term 'enigmatic canons' never appeared in his *Esemplare*, where Martini merely indicated that in some compositions «fatte a canone» there are a few motti or enigmatic vocabulary[1].

Martini lists seven theoretical sources (six pertaining to the long Renaissance), with a clear division by language. The first three authors, who wrote in Latin (Aaron, Glarean and Finck), span a gap of forty years, from 1516 to 1556. The remaining four are Italian sources (three in Italian and one in Spanish, but all published in Italy) with a very small gap of just nine years separating the first three: Cerone (1613), Rossi, and Angleria (1622). The fourth Italian source, Bontempi, appeared seventy-three years later, in 1695.

---

[1]. Martini 1775, p. xxiv.

Aaron	1516
Glarean	1547
Fink	1556
Cerone	1613
Rossi	1618
Angleria	1622
Bontempi	1695

Among the Latin sources, Finck's list of enigmatic expressions is clearly the most developed. More than fifty expressions appear in Finck's text, whereas Glarean and Aaron limit themselves to a few expressions each, which are not organised into lists. Not surprisingly, therefore, Finck appears to be the source from which Martini drew the greatest number of expressions. The structure of Martini's and Finck's lists is very similar: Martini simply rearranged a few of Finck's mottoes to order them better. On the other hand, Aaron is Martini's only source for *Dum lucem habetis credite in lucem*. Glarean is the only source for the motto *Duo adversi adverse in unum*.

There is a huge gap between the Latin and Italian sources: fifty-seven years separate Finck, the latest source in Latin, from Cerone, the first 'Italian' source. The number of expressions Cerone publishes (45-46 enigmas, associated with an even greater number of mottoes) is comparable to Finck. However, unlike Finck, Cerone does not present the expressions in list form. Instead, he gives musical examples containing mottoes and explains each motto in the particular context of its example. Finck's examples appear completely separated from his list of expressions; in addition, not all expressions are necessarily associated with a musical example. Neither does he explain his examples in detail, as Cerone does. Unsurprisingly, given the number of expressions published in Cerone's, he is Martini's second most cited source.

Cerone wrote in Spanish but published in Naples; there was clearly a great interest in canons in Italy in the years after his work appeared[2]. The four Italian sources cited by Martini precede him by more than a century and a half — a testament of the longevity of the tradition which culminated in his work. While undoubtedly the most accomplished, Martini's treatise is rooted in the very long and solid Italian tradition that precedes it.

In 1618, one hundred and fifty-six years before the publication of Martini's *Esemplare*, Rossi's work on enigmatic canons uses a structure which Martini reproduced wholesale in the introduction to his own treatise; the only difference is that Rossi does not present the mottoes in the form of a list. Instead, like Cerone, Rossi associates the expressions with examples,

---

[2]. See notably LAMLA 2003.

though without the detailed explanations Cerone provides. Rossi often simply contains cursory references to the titles of works, without giving the scores.

On the Italian side, Angleria (like Glarean and Aaron for Latin) seems to be only a minor source. At the end of his treatise, Angleria cites two enigmatic expressions associated with examples taken from Paolo Cima — examples that are neither commented on nor resolved. The two expressions are not even contextualised. Nevertheless, Angleria is Martini's only source for two expressions: *Cæcus non judicat de colore* and *Intendami chi può, che m'intend'io*.

Bontempi, although a minor source in terms of the number of expressions cited by Martini, provides a list of mottos associated with very precise explanations. The importance of Bontempi and Rossi as sources of inspiration for Martini's *Esemplare* thus seems crucial. It is as if the structure of Martini's text came directly from Rossi and that Martini simply added a list to it, as Bontempi also does.

But the importance of Martini's work goes far beyond that. As well as providing a selection of mottoes, he also gives clear and precise indications for each. None of the earlier works achieve this. Finck mixes analysis and prescriptions. Cerone does not draw up a list; he analyses canons. With Rossi, it is even more difficult to understand the expressions referred to than with Cerone, who at least gives examples; with Rossi one has to know the works he mentions to understand the explanations. This is not the case with Bontempi, who had already worked out the rudiments of a list.

Drawing up a list of mottoes was in vogue at the time. But the merit of Martini's work lies in choosing mottoes, creating categories, and eliminating expressions that were used in a very specific context and were difficult to reproduce in a different context. Given the analyses set out in the preceding pages, Martini's process for selecting expressions seems quite clear. Firstly, like Finck, Martini creates two separate lists, one with expressions indicating transposition intervals — whose meaning is not enigmatic — and the other with expressions whose meaning is truly enigmatic. Secondly, Martini chose not to include in his list expressions containing concepts of mensural notation. He also excluded expressions used in works that do not make use of imitation.

Martini then eliminated all mottoes for which the explanations do not announce general rules, but simply describe particular contexts (generally in the form of analyses) which are directly associated with a specific work. With Martini's list, we are moving very clearly from description (presented in the form of analysis) to prescription.

Martini's list was reproduced many times. The starting point for its popularity outside Italy was in France with Ginguené's article in Framéry's *Encyclopédie méthodique*, which was published in 1791, seventeen years after Martini's *Esemplare*. Ginguené's entry was both the first publication of Martini's list in France and essentially a copy of Martini's text translated into French. Cherubini was undoubtedly aware of Ginguené's version of Martini's list, which cannot have predated Cherubini's own manuscript by much. In fact, given the poor quality of Cherubini's French translations, it is even conceivable that his text predates Ginguené's, whose translations are of a much higher quality. Thanks to a tremor in the handwriting that he claimed to have spotted, Henry Expert imagined that Cherubini's manuscript dates from the last twenty years of his life[3]. It seems clear, however, that the manuscript at the very least predates the publication of Fétis's *Traité du contrepoint et de la fugue* in 1824.

In that treatise, Fétis published an expanded version of Cherubini's list. Both the treatise and the list are central to understanding practice surrounding the so-called enigmatic canons in the 19th century. Fétis's list of enigmatic expressions was the first to be more extensive than Martini's — and indeed the first published list to include expressions that Martini did not consider to be enigmatic. Fétis does not mention that the bulk of his text was drawn from Cherubini. It is quite clear, however, that Cherubini's work in finding solutions for the canons of Martini's *Storia della musica* is the basis for the conception of Fétis's text. Along with Forkel, Fétis was the great disseminator of Martini's list — not simply by transmitting that list, but by tacitly appropriating the work Cherubini had done to compile his collection of solutions to Martini's enigmatic canons.

It is worth noting that Martini almost certainly did not have the same ideas as Cherubini regarding the use of his list of expressions to resolve his own canons. The canons of the *Storia della musica* make use of only thirteen of the fifty-six expressions in Martini's list: mottoes 1, 2, 10, 21, 22, 25, 27, 30, 41, 42, 43, 48, and 51. These expressions appear in sixteen of the seventy-two canons solved by Cherubini: canons 1, 6, 7, 8, 11, 13, 17, 18, 23, 30, 34, 46, 49, 50[4], 53, and 54. This is because, as Cherubini so clearly indicates, several canons in the *Storia della musica* are not enigmatic, but are merely closed: their solution does not depend on enigmatic expressions, but only on the expressions assembled in the second part of Cherubini's table (the part that does not exist in Martini's list of *Motti o Enigmi*). In addition, instead of Latin expressions, Canon No. 47 has hints in Greek (which are absent from the table of Latin phrases). Besides these Greek tags, there are three Latin expressions which are used in the canons, but which do not occur in Martini's list: *Nec mihi, nec tibi, sed dividatur* (canon No. 28)[5], *Me pente, me tesseris phones* (canon No. 29), and *Qui deprimit [se, altissimo fit altior]* (canon No. 40).

Cherubini's work, and the centuries of material behind it — Martini's seven theoretical sources, Martini himself, and then Ginguené and Fétis — bear clear witness to the evolution of the term 'canon'. There is a clear shift from 'canon' as a rule in the form of a literary expression,

---

[3]. See the letter by Henry Expert in this volume, pp. 315ff.

[4]. Canon 50 makes use of two mottoes: *Cantus duarum facierum* and *Omne trinum perfectum*.

[5]. Obrecht, *Nec mihi nec tibi [sit], sed dividatur*, IJO 32. Let it me neither mine nor thine, but divide it (I Kings 3.26).

to 'canon' as a rule expressed in purely musical terms (the «proposta»), and finally to 'canon' as a piece of music. This shift is illustrated in Bontempi's explanation of what he calls a «cantilena artificiosa», the appearance of the term «canone chiuso» in Martini[6], and finally Fétis's amalgam of 'closed canon' and 'enigmatic canon'.

---

[6]. The term 'canoni chiusi' appears for the first time probably in 1673 in BONONCINI 1673, P. 2, p. 101. See COLLINS 1992, p. 136.

Comparative Tables

Table 1

Luigi Cherubini's
Table des mots latins, que les anciens compositeurs plaçaient souvent en tête des canons, avec l'explication du sens énigmatique qu'ils renferment, afin d'obtenir plus aisément la véritable solution d'un canon fermé

Table des mots latins,

que les anciens compositeurs plaçaient souvent en tête des canons,

avec l'explication du sens énigmatique qu'ils renferment,

afin d'obtenir plus aisément la véritable solution d'un canon fermé

		Explications	Explanations[1]	Canons[2]
1.	*Clama ne cesses*	Chacun de ces huit mots, ou énigmes, indique que la partie qui repond, chante toutes les notes du Canon, en suprimant tous les silences de l'Antécédent. (3*)	Each of these eight words, or enigmas, indicates that the answering voice sings all the notes of the canon while omitting all of the rests found in the antecedent. (4*)	18, 19
2.	*Otia dant vitia*			46
3.	*Dii faciant sine me non moriar ego*			
4.	*Omnia si perdas famam servare memento, qua semel emissa: postea nullus eris*			
5.	*Sperare et praestolari multos facit morari*			
6.	*Otia securis insidiosa nocent*			
7.	*Tarda solet magnis rebus in esse fides*			
8.	*Fuge morales* [sic]			
9.	*Misericordias et veritas obviaverunt sibi*	Les mots qui se succèdent depuis le n° 9, jusqu'au n° 20, signifient que du Conséquent (5***) il doit se former deux autres Parties, l'une qui commence par la première note de l'Antécédent en suivant jusqu'à la dernière, et l'autre commençant par la dernière note de l'Antécédent revient en retrogradant à la première.	Phrases 9-20 indicate that two other parts are formed from the consequent (6**): one that begins from the first note of the antecedent and continues until the last, and another that begins with the last note of the antecedent and proceeds by retrograde back to the first.	
10.	*Justitia et pax se osculatae sunt*			34
11.	*Nescit vos missa reverti*			
12.	*Semper contrarius esto*			
13.	*Signa te signa temere me tangis et angis, Romae tibi subito motibus ibit amor*			
14.	*Frangenti fidem fides frangatur eidem*			
15.	*Roma caput mundi si veteris, omnia vincit*			
16.	*Mitto tibi metulas, erige si dubitas*			
17.	*Cancrizat, vel canis more haebreorum*			
18.	*Retrograditur*			
19.	*Vadam et veniam ad vos*			
20.	*Principium, et finis*			
21.	*Symphoniziabis* [sic]	Le Conséquent repond à l'Unisson.	The consequent answers at the unison.	8
22.	*Omne trinum perfectum*	Que de l'Antécédent on forme deux Conséquents, dont il résulte un Canon à 3 Parties, le quel Canon, le plus souvent est à l'<u>Unisson</u> ou à l'<u>Octave</u>.	Two consequents are formed from the antecedent, producing a three-part canon, most often at the <u>unison</u> or <u>octave</u>.	30, 50
23.	*Trinitas et unitas*			
24.	*Trinitate in unitate veneremur*			
25.	*Sit trium series una. Tres in unum*			1, 11, 23
26.	*Vidi tres viri qui erant laesi homonem*			

27.	*Manet alta mente repostum*	*L'Antécédent peut avoir deux, trois Conséquents, et plus qui lui répondent.*	The antecedent may have two, three, or even more consequents.	6
28.	*Deponte non cadit, qui cum sapientia vadit*			
29.	*Tantum hoc repete, quantum cum aliis sociare videbis*	*Une petite phrase de chant dans une des Parties du Canon, doit recommencer autant de fois qu'il en faut pour remplir la durée du Canon dans les autres Parties.*	A short phrase in one of the voices of the canon must repeat as many times as required to match the duration of the canon in the other voices.	
30.	*Non qui inceperit, sed qui perseveraverit*			13
31.	*Itque, redítque frequens*			
32.	*Crescit* in Duplo, Triplo, &c.	*Le Conséquent doit doubler, ou tripler la valeur des figures notées dans l'Antécédent, ou la diminuer de la moitié, ou de deux tiers.*	The consequent must multiply (cresc-) or divide (decresc-) the duration of the rhythmic values in the antecedent by two or three.	
33.	*Decrescit*			
34.	*Dignora sunt priora*	*Le Conséquent doit repondre de manière à suivre par ordre la valeur des figures à commencer par la plus grande et progressivement passer graduellement de celle-ci jusqu'à la plus petite, c'est-à-dire, de la <u>Maxime</u> passer à la <u>Longue</u>, puis à la <u>Breve</u>, ensuite à la <u>Semibreve</u> ou <u>Ronde</u>, après à la <u>Minime</u> ou <u>Blanche</u>, et de celle-ci à la <u>Semiminime</u> ou <u>Noire</u> &c.*	The consequent must answer in such a way that it follows the order of the rhythmic values in the antecedent by starting with the longest value and progressively and gradually moving towards the shortest. This means the <u>maxim</u> is followed by the <u>long</u>, then the <u>breve</u>, <u>semibreve</u> or <u>whole note</u>, <u>minim</u> or <u>half note</u>, <u>crotchet</u> or <u>quarter note</u>, etc.	
35.	*Descende gradatim*	*Il peut y avoir dans une partie un passage de nature à être répété autant de fois qu'il faut pour remplir la durée du chant principal, et qu'en le répétant il soit haussé, ou baissé d'un Ton.*	There may be in one part a passage that is repeated as many times as is necessary to match the duration of the main voice. These repetitions should be raised or lowered by a whole step.	
36.	*Ascende gradatim*			
37.	*Et sic de singulis*	*Si la première note de l'Antécédent est marquée avec un point, le Conséquent doit pointer toutes les autres notes.*	If the first note of the antecedent is dotted, all notes must be dotted in the consequent.	
38.	*Nigra sum sed formosa*	*Le Conséquent doit chanter les notes Noires, comme si elles étaient des Blanches.*	All quarter notes in the consequent must appear as half notes.	
39.	*Coecus non judicat de colore*			

Table 1

40.	*Qui se exaltat humiliabitur*	*La reponse doit être l'opposé de l'Antécédent, c'est-à-dire que si celui-ci monte, le Conséquent doit descendre, et vice-versa.*	The response must be the opposite of the antecedent, meaning that if the antecedent ascends, the consequent must descend and vice versa.	
41.	*Qui se humiliat exaltabitur*			7
42.	*Plutonico subiit regna*			54
43.	*Contraria contrariis curantur*			49, 53
44.	*Qui non est mecum, contra me est*			
45.	*Duo adversi adverse in unum*			
46.	*De minimis non curat Praetor*	*Le Conséquent ne doit chanter ni les Blanches, ni les Noires, quoiqu'elles soient notées dans l'Antécédent.*	The consequent must include neither the half notes nor the quarter notes, even if they are notated in the antecedent.	
47.	*Me opportet minui, illum autem crescere*	*L'Antécédent diminue de moitié la valeur des notes, que le Conséquent a quadruplées.*	The antecedent halves the duration of the notes that the consequent quadrupled.	
48.	*Qui venit post me, ante me factus est*	*Le Conséquent a été composé, avant l'Antécédent.*	The consequent was composed prior to the antecedent.	17
49.	*Exurge in adjutorium mihi*	*La reponse est à l'Unisson.*	The response is at the unison.	
50.	*Respice in me: Ostende mihi faciem tuam*	*Le Conséquent execute les mêmes notes de l'Antécédent, mais dans le sens inverse comme si l'un et l'autre se regardaient.*	The consequent has the same notes of the antecedent, but in reverse order, as if each was looking at the other.	
51.	*Cantus duarum facierum*	*Le Conséquent peut chanter avec ou sans les silences marqués dans l'Antécédent, à l'exception du soupir si l'Antécédent l'a dans sa partie, afin de completer la mesure.*	The consequent may appear with or without the indicated rests found in the antecedent in order to complete the measure, except for quarter rests if they appear in the antecedent.	50
52.	*Tolle moras placido maneant suspiria cantu*			
53.	*Dum lucem habetis credite in lucem*	*Le Conséquent ne dit aucune note Noire de l'Antécédent, mais seulement celles qui sont Blanches.*	The consequent omits any quarter notes in the antecedent, reproducing only half notes.	
54.	*Qui sequitur me non ambulat in tenebris*			19
55.	*Post unum Tempus*	*Le Conséquent doit repondre après la valeur d'un temps, c'est-à-dire une mesure de ¢ ou de C.*	The consequent answers one beat later, i.e. one measure of cut time or common time.	3, 16
56.	*Ad Tonum infra*	*Le Conséquent doit repondre un Ton plus bas.*	The consequent replies a whole step lower.	5
57.	*Ad Tonum supra*	*Le Conséquent doit repondre un Ton plus haut.*	The consequent replies a whole step higher.	5, 41, 64
58.	*Ad Semi-Ditonum*	*Reponse à la Tierce mineure.*	Response at the minor third.	8

59.	*Ad Unissonum*	*À l'Unisson.*	At the unison.	9, 12, 20, 21, 27, 31, 43, 50, 53, 56, 57, 59, 66, 68, 69, 70
	Ad Diatessaron	*À la Quarte Supérieure.*	At the fourth higher.	7, 9, 13, 59
	Ad Diapason	*À l'Octave id.*	At the octave higher.	9, 27, 35, 45, 60, 61
	Ad Ditonum	*À la Tierce Majeure id.*	At the major third higher.	
	Ad Duodecimam	*À la Douzième id.*	At the twelfth higher.	18, 21
	Ad Diapente	*À la Quinte id.*	At the fifth higher.	21, 35, 41, 49, 52, 53
	Ad Diapason-Diatessaron	*À l'Octave de la Quarte id.*	An octave higher than the fourth above.	9
	Ad Diapason-Ditonum	*À l'Octave de la Tierce id.*	An octave higher than the third above.	15
	Ad Eptacordum	*À la Septième id.*	At the seventh higher.	27
	Ad Diapason-Diapente	*À l'Octave de la Quinte id.*	An octave higher than the fifth above.	35
		Lorsque les dénominations de ces intervalles sont précédés par Sub, cela veut dire que l'Intervalle est Inferieur ou au-dessous.	When the interval is preceded by 'sub', this means the interval is below.	14, 19, 24, 36, 43, 45, 50, 58, 60, 62, 70: Sub-Diapason 13, 14, 17, 22, 50, 52, 62: Sub-Diatessaron 36, 67, 72: Sub-Diapente 14, 62: Sub-Diapason-Diatessaron 36: Sub-Diapason-Diapente 27: Sub-Eptacordum
60.	*Ad Hypo-Diapason*	*À l'Octave grave ou inférieure.*	An octave lower.	20, 46
61.	*Ad Hyper-Diapason*	*À l'Octave aigue ou supérieure.*	An octave higher.	20[7], 46
	[There is nothing in the table related to number 62.]			
63.	*Crescit eundo*	*Chaque fois que le Canon recommence, il hausse d'un Ton.*	Each time the canon repeats it comes back in a whole step higher.	21
64.	*Decrescit eundo*	*À chaque reprise, il baisse d'autant.*	At each repeat it comes in a whole step lower.	26
65.	*Ad Epi-Diapason*	*À l'Octave aigue, ou Supérieure.*	An octave higher.	22

Table 1

66.	*Ad Epi-Diapente*	*À la Quinte aigue, ou supérieure.*	A fifth higher.	22
67.	*Ad Hypo-Diapente*	*À la Quinte inférieure.*	A fifth lower.	26
68.	*Ad Hyper-Diatessaron*	*À la Quarte supérieure.*	A fourth higher.	26
69.	*Ad Homophonum*	*À l'Unisson.*	At the unison.	25
70.	*Ad Equisonum*	*À l'Octave ou Double Octave à l'aigue, ou au grave.*	One or two octaves higher or lower.	25
71.	*Ad Diapente remissum*	*À la Quinte inférieure.*	A fifth lower.	28
72.	*Ad Diapente espensum [sic]*	*À la Quinte supérieure.*	A fifth higher.	28
73.	*Ad Nonam*	*À la Neuvième supérieure.*	A ninth higher.	28
74.	*Ter terni canite vocibus*	*De l'Antécédent on forme huit Conséquents, dont il résulte un Canon à 9 voix, le quel Canon, le plus souvent est à l'Unisson.*	Eight consequents are formed from the antecedent, producing a nine-part canon. This type of canon is most often at the unison.	32
75.	*Congenita haec tria sunt*	*Même explication, que celle donnée depuis le n° 22, jusqu'et compris le n° 26.*	Same explanation as given for Nos. 22-26 inclusive.	33
76.	*Diapente Diapason* *Diapason Diapente*	*Intervalle de Douzième.*	Interval of a twelfth.	54
77.	*Ter voce ciemus*	*Tous ces mots ont la même signification, et l'explication donnée depuis le n° 22, jusqu'au n° 26 de cette Table, doit servir d'explication à ceux-ci.*	All of these words have the same meaning. See Nos. 22-26 in this table.	38
78.	*Voce ter insonuit*			38
79.	*Ad Hypo-Diapason-Diapente*	*Intervalle de Douzième inférieure.*	Interval of a twelfth lower.	39
80.	*Ad Eptachordum infra*	*Septième inférieure.*	A seventh lower.	41
81.	*Ibit, redibit*	*Veut dire, que la partie à la quelle appartiennent ces mots, doit éxécuter le chant depuis le commencement jusqu'à la fin, et retourner de celle-ci au commencement en chantant la mélodie à reculon.*	This means that the part these words belong to must play out from beginning to end and then back to the beginning in retrograde motion.	42
82.	*Ad Tonum, infinit, et finit*	*Le Conséquent doit répondre à un Ton au-dessus; et les autres mots signifient que le Canon est sans fin, et qu'il peut en avoir une.*	The consequent must respond a whole step higher; the other words mean that the canon has no end, but that it could have one.	42
83.	*Six [sic] Vocum*	*Le Canon est à six voix.*	The canon has six voices.	49
84.	Ad Diapason, et Unissonum Vicissim	*À l'Octave supérieure, et à l'Unisson alternativement.*	Alternating between an octave higher and unison.	51

85.	*Tot tempora, tot sunt voces*	*Le Canon est composé d'autant de <u>Parties</u> ou <u>Voix</u> qu'il renferme de <u>Temps</u> ou de <u>Mesures</u>.*	The canon is composed of as many <u>parts</u> or <u>voices</u> as the number of beats or <u>measures</u>.	51
86.	*Ad Diapason intensum*	*À l'Octave inférieure.*	An octave lower.	55
87.	*Ad Diapason espensum*	*À l'Octave supérieure.*	An octave higher.	55
88.	*Ad Sub-Sesquiditonum*	*À la Tierce mineure au-dessous.*	A minor third lower.	59
89.	*Ad Septimam infra*	*À la Septième inférieure.*	A seventh lower.	65
90.	*Ad Decimam*	*À la Dixième supérieure.*	A tenth higher.	67
91.	*Ad Tertiam infra*	*Tierce inférieure.*	A third lower.	68

[1]. This column with English translations does not appear in Cherubini's original.

[2]. This column does not appear in Cherubini's original either; it was added by the author.

[3]. (*) On appelle Antécédent la partie qui propose le Canon.

[4]. (*) The 'antecedent' is the first statement of the canon.

[5]. (**) Le Conséquent est la réponse ou la résolution de l'Antécédent. Il peut y avoir dans un Canon plusieurs Conséquents, et leur quantité établit celle des Parties.

[6]. (**) The 'consequent' is the antecedent's response or solution. In a canon there may be multiple consequents, and their number determines the number of voices.

[7]. Hyper-Diatessaron in Martini's original.

Table 2

Cherubini's
Table des mots latins

vs.

Martini's Lists of
Motti o Enigmi and
Vocaboli Italiani, Latini e Greci

Cherubini's *Table de mots latis* vs.
Martini's Lists of *Motti o Enigmi* and *Vocaboli Italiani, Latini e Greci*

Canons[1]	Cherubini's Table		Martini's *Esemplare*[2]	
18	1. Clama ne cesses	Chacun de ces huit mots, ou énigmes, indique que la partie qui repond, chante toutes les notes du Canon en suprimant [sic] tous les silences de l'Antécédent.	1. Clama ne cesses	Ciascun di questi otto Motti, o Enigmi indica, che il Conseguente, o la Parte, che risponde, tralascia le Pause dell'Antecedente, e segue a cantare le sole Note.
46	2. Otia dant vitia		2. Ocia dant vitia	
	3. Dii faciant sine me non moriar ego		3. Dii faciant sine me non moriar ego	
	4. Omnia si perdas famam servare memento, qua semel emissa: postea nullus eris		4. Omnia si perdas famam servare memento, Qua semel amissa, postea nullus eris	
	5. Sperare et praestolari multos facit morari		5. Sperare & praestolari [sic] multos facit morari	
	6. Otia securis insidiosa nocent		6. Ocia securis insidiosa nocent	
	7. Tarda solet magnis rebus in esse fides		7. Tarda solet magnis rebus inesse fides	
	8. Fuge morales [sic]		8. Fuge morulas	
	9. Misericordias et veritas obviaverunt sibi	Les mots qui se succèdent depuis le n° 9, jusqu'au n° 20, signifient que du Conséquent (3**) il doit se former deux autres Parties, l'une qui commence par la première note de l'Antécédent en suivant jusqu'à la dernière, et l'autre commençant par la dernière note de l'Antécédent revient en retrogradant à la Première.	9. Misericordias & veritas obviaverunt sibi	Questi altri Motti, che vengono in appresso fino al Num. 20 significano, che dal Conseguente ne dobbiamo ricavare due altre Parti, che rispondono, l'una che comincia dalla prima Nota dell'Antecedente, e procede ordinariamente fino al fine; l'altra comincia dall'ultima Nota dell'Antecedente, e proseguisce all'indietro fino alla prima Nota.
34	10. Justitia et pax se osculatae sunt		10. Justicia & pax se osculatae sunt	
	11. Nescit vos missa reverti		11. Nescit vos missa reverti	
	12. Semper contrarius esto		12. Semper contrarius esto	
	13. Signa te signa temere me tangis et angis, Romae tibi subito motibus ibit amor		13. Signa te signa temere me tangis & angis, Romae tibi subito motibus ibit amor	
	14. Frangenti fidem fides frangatur eidem		14. Frangenti fidem fides frangatur eidem	
	15. Roma caput mundi si veteris, omnia vincit		15. Roma caput mundi, si veteris, omnia vincit	
	16. Mitto tibi metulas, erige si dubitas		16. Mitto tibi metulas, erige si dubitas	
	17. Cancrizat, vel canis more Haebreorum		17. Cancrizat, vel canis more Haebreorum	
	18. Retrograditur		18. Retrograditur	
	19. Vadam et veniam ad vos		19. Vadam & veniam ad vos	
	20. Principium, et finis		20. Principium, & finis	
8	21. Symphoniziabis [sic]	Le Conséquent repond à l'Unisson.	21. Symphonizabis	Il Conseguente risponde all'Unissono.

30, 50	22. Omne trinum perfectum	Que de l'Antécédent on forme deux Conséquents, dont il résulte un Canon à 3 Parties, le quel Canon, le plus souvent est à l'Unisson ou à l'Octave.	22. Omne trinum perfectum	Che dall'Antecedente si ricavino due Conseguenti, o due Parti, che rispondino, affinchè si formi il Canone a 3. Voci, il quale per lo più vuol essere all'Unissono, o all'Ottava.
	23. Trinitas et unitas		23. Trinitas & unitas	
	24. Trinitate in unitate veneremur		24. Trinitatem in unitate veneremur	
1, 11, 23	25. Sit trium series una. Tres in unum		25. Sit trium seriès una	
	26. Vidi tres viri qui erant laesi homonem		26. Vidi tres viri qui erant laesi homonem	
6	27. Manet alta mente repostum	L'Antécédent peut avoir deux, trois Conséquents, et plus qui lui repondent.	27. Manet alta mente repostum	Possano rispondere all'Antecedente due, tre, e più Voci.
	28. Deponte [sic] non cadit, qui cum sapientia vadit		28. De ponte non cadit, qui cum sapientia vadit	
	29. Tantum hoc repete, quantum cum aliis sociare videbis	Une petite phrase de chant dans une des Parties du Canon, doit recommencer autant de fois qu'il en faut pour remplir la durée du Canon dans les autres Parties.	29. Tautum [sic] hoc repete, quantum cum aliis sociare videbis	Una piccola Cantilena, che ritrovasi in una Parte deve repplicarsi fin'a tanto che siano terminate le altre Parti della Composizione.
13	30. Non qui inceperit, sed qui perseveraverit		30. Non qui inceperit, sed qui perseveraverit	
	31. Itque, reditque frequens		31. Itque, reditque frequens	
	32. Crescit in Duplo, Triplo, &c.	Le Conséquent doit doubler, ou tripler la valeur des figures notées dans l'Antécédent, ou la diminuer de la moitié, ou de deux tiers.	32. Crescit in Duplo, Triplo, &c.	Il Conseguente deve radoppiare, o triplicare, &c. il valore delle Figure; o diminuirlo la metà, o due terzi.
	33. Decrescit in Duplo, Triplo, &c.		33. Decrescit in Duplo, Triplo, &c.	
	34. Dignora sunt priora	Le Conséquent doit repondre de manière à suivre par ordre la valeur des figures à commencer par la plus grande et progressivement passer graduellement de celle-ci jusqu'à la plus petite, c'est-à-dire, de la Maxime passer à la Longue, puis à la Breve, ensuite à la Semibreve ou Ronde, après à la Minime ou Blanche, et de celle-ci à la Semiminime ou Noire &c.	34. Dignora sunt priora	Si devono cantar dal Conseguente le Figure per ordine del loro maggior valore, cioè prima le Massime, indi le Longhe, poscia le Brevi, le Semibrevi, le Minime, le Semiminime, &c.

Table 2

	35. Descende gradatim	Il peut y avoir dans une partie un passage de nature à être repeté autant de fois qu'il faut pour remplir la durée du chant principal, et qu'en le repétant il soit haussé, ou baissé d'un Ton.	35. Descende gradatim	Se una Parte forma una piccola Cantilena, questa deve repplicarsi fin tanto che sia teminata la Composizione; e nel repplicarsi deve alzarsi, o abbassarsi un Tuono.
	36. Ascende gradatim		36. Ascende gradatim	
	37. Et sic de singulis	Si la première note de l'Antécédent est marquée avec un point, le Conséquent doit pointer toutes les autres notes.	37. Et sic de singulis	Se alla prima Nota dell'Antecedente trovasi segnato il Punto, debbonsi cantare dal Conseguente tutte le altre Note col Punto.
	38. Nigra sum sed formosa	Le Conséquent doit chanter les notes, Noires comme si elles étaient des Blanches.	38. Nigra sum sed formosa	Il Conseguente deve cantare le Note nere, come se fossero bianche.
	39. Coecus [sic] non judicat de colore		39. Caecus non iudicat de colore	
	40. Qui se exaltat humiliabitur	La reponse doit être l'opposé de l'Antécédent, c'est-à-dire que si celui-ci monte, le Conséquent doit descendre, et vice-versa.	40. Qui se exaltat humiliabitur	La Risposta deve cantarsi al contrario in maniera tale, che se l'Antecedente ascende, il Conseguente discenda, e se l'Antecedente discende, il Conseguente ascende.
7	41. Qui se humiliat exaltabitur		41. Qui se humiliat exaltabitur	
54	42. Plutonico [sic] subiit regna		42. Plutonica subiit regna	
49, 53	43. Contraria contrariis curantur		43. Contraria contrariis curantur	
	44. Qui non est mecum, contra me est		44. Qui non est mecum, contra me est	
	45. Duo adversi adverse in unum		45. Duo adversi adverse in unum	
	46. De minimis non curat Praetor	Le Conséquent ne doit chanter ni les <u>Blanches</u>, ni les <u>Noires</u>, quoique elles soient notées dans l'Antécédent.	46. De Minimis non curat Praetor	Non si cantano dal Conseguente, benchè scritte nell'Antecedente, nè le Minime, nè le Semiminime.
	47. Me opportet minui, illum autem crescere	L'Antécédent diminue de moitié la valeur des notes, que le Conséquent a quadruplées.	47. Me opportet minui, illum autem crescere	L'Antecedente diminuisce per metà il valor delle Figure, e il Conseguente lo accresce in quadruplo.
17	48. Qui venit post me, ante me factus est	Le Conséquent a été composé, avant l'Antécédent.	48. Qui venit post me, ante me factus est	Il Conseguente è stato composto prima dell'Antecedente.

	49. Exurge in adjutorium mihi	La reponse est à l'Unisson.	49. Exurge in adjutorium mihi	Il Conseguente risponde all'Unissono.
			50. Vous jejuneres le quattr temps	Il Conseguente deve rispondere dopo il valore di quattro Tempi, cioè di quattro Brevi.
	50. Respice in me: Ostende mihi faciem tuam	Le Conséquent execute les mêmes notes de l'Antécédent, mais dans le sens inverse comme si l'un et l'autre se regardaient.	51. Respice in me: Ostende mihi faciem tuam	Che il Conseguente canta l'istesse Note dell'Antecedente, ma al contrario voltando la faccia l'uno verso dell'altro.
50	51. Cantus duarum facierum	Le Conséquent peut chanter avec ou sans les silences marqués dans l'Antécédent, à l'ecception du soupir si l'Antécédent l'a dans sa partie, afin de completer la mesure.	52. Cantus duarum facierum	Si può cantare il Conseguente con le Pause, e senza le Pause, ritenendo però sempre il sospiro, o sia quarto di Battuta, se trovasi scritto nell'Antecedente, affinchè resti compiuta la Battuta.
	52. Tolle moras placido maneant suspiria cantu		53. Tolle moras placido maneant suspiria cantu	
	53. Dum lucem habetis credite in lucem	Le Conséquent ne dit aucune note Noire de l'Antécédent, mais seulement celles qui sont Blanches.	54. Dum lucem habetis credite in lucem	Il Conseguente non canta alcuna Nota nera, ma solamente le bianche.
	54. Qui sequitur me non ambulat in tenebris		55. Qui sequitur me non ambulat, in tenebris	
			56. Intendami chi può, che m'intend'io	L'annesso Esempio servirà di spiegazione a quest'ultimo Enigma.
3, 16	55. Post unum Tempus	Le Conséquent doit Repondre après la valeur d'un Temps, c'est-à-dire une mesure de ₵ ou de **C**.	p. xxiv Post unum Tempus	Il Conseguente deve rispondere dopo la Pausa di uno Tempo.
5	56. Ad Tonum infra	Le Conséquent doit repondre un <u>Ton</u> plus bas.	p. xxiii Ad Tonum	Alla Seconda maggiore.
5, 41, 64	57. Ad Tonum supra	Le Conséquent doit repondre un <u>Ton</u> plus haut.	p. xxiii Ad Tonum [Supra]	Alla Seconda maggiore [sopra].
8	58. Ad Semi-Ditonum	Réponse à la Tierce-mineure.	p. xxiii Ad Semiditonum	Alla Seconda minore[4].
9	59. Ad Unissonum	À l'Unisson.	p. xxiii Ad Unissonum	All'Unissono.
7, 9, 13	Ad Diatessaron	À la Quarte supérieure.	p. xxiii Ad Diatessaron	Alla Quarta.

Table 2

9, 15, 27, 35, 45, 60, 61	Ad Diapason	À l'Octave id.	p. xxiii Ad Diapason	All'Ottava.
15	Ad Ditonum	À la Tierce Majeure id.	p. xxiii Ad Ditonum	Alla Terza maggiore.
21	Ad Duodecimam	À la Douzième id.	p. xxiii Ad Duodecimam	Alla Duodecima.
21, 35, 41, 49, 52, 53	Ad Diapente	À la Quinte id.	p. xxiii Ad Diapente	Alla Quinta.
9	Ad Diapason-Diatessaron	À l'Octave de la Quarte id.	p. xxiii Ad Diapason-Diatessaron	All'Undecima.
	Ad Diapason-Ditonum	À l'Octave de la Tierce id.	p. xxiii Ad Diapason cum Ditono, vel Triemitonio	Alla Decima min., o mag.
27	Ad Eptacordum	À la Septième id.	p. xxiii Ad Heptachordum min., Ad Heptachordum maj.	Alla Settima minore. Alla Settima maggiore.
35	Ad Diapason-Diapente	À l'Octave de la Quinte id.	p. xxiii Ad Diapason-Diapente	Alla Duodecima.
		Lorsque les dénominations de ces Intervalles sont précédés par Sub, cela veut dire que l'Intervalle est Inférieur ou au-dessous.		
20, 46	60. Ad Hypo-Diapason	À l'Octave grave ou Inférieure.	p. xxiv Hypo-Diapason	All'Ottava sotto.
20, 46	61. Ad Hyper-Diapason	À l'Octave aigue ou supérieure.	p. xxiv Hyper[-Diapason]	[All'Ottava] sopra.
	[There is nothing in the table related to number 62.]			
21	63. Crescit eundo	Chaque fois que le Canon recommence, il hausse d'un Ton.		
26	64. Decrescit eundo	À chaque reprise, il baisse d'autant.		
22	65. Ad Epi-Diapason	À l'Octave aigue, ou supérieure.	p. xxiv Epi-Diapason	All'Ottava sopra.
22	66. Ad Epi-Diapente	À la Quinte aigue, ou supérieure.	p. xxiv Epi-Diapente	Alla Quinta sopra.
26	67. Ad Hypo-Diapente	À la Quinte Inférieure.	p. xxiv Hypo[-Diapente]	Alla Quinta [sotto].
26	68. Ad Hyper-Diatessaron	À la Quarte supérieure.	p. xxiv Hyper[-Diatessaron]	Alla [Quarta] sopra.
25	69. Ad Homophonum [sic]	À l'Unisson.	p. xxiii Homophonur	All'Unissono.
25	70. Ad Equisonum	À l'Octave ou double Octave à l'aigue, ou au grave.		

28	71. Ad Diapente remissum	À la Quinte Inférieure.	Diapason remissum MARTINI 1775, p. 265, citing P. Costanzo Porta, Opera Liber 52, Motectorum 5. 6. 7. & 8. Vocum, 1580.	
28	72. Ad Diapente expensum [*sic*]	À la Quinte supérieure.		
28	73. Ad Nonam	À la Neuvième supérieure.	p. xxiii Ad Nonam minorem, vel majorem	Alla Nona minore, o mag.
32	74. Ter terni canite vocibus[5]	De l'Antécédent on forme huit Conséquents, dont il résulte un Canon à 9 voix, le quel Canon, le plus souvent est à l'Unisson.		
33	75. Congenita haec tria sunt	Même explication, que celle donnée depuis le n° 22, jusqu'et compris le n° 26.		
	76. Diapente Diapason	Intervalle de Douzième.		
54	76. Diapason Diapente		p. xxiii Ad Diapason-Diapente	Alla Duodecima.
38	77. Ter voce ciemus[6]	Tous ces Mots ont la même signification, et l'explication donnée depuis le n° 22, jusqu'au n° 26 de cette Table, doit servir d'explication à ceux-ci.		
38	78. Voce ter insonuit[7]			
39	79. Ad Hypo-Diapason-Diapente	Intervalle de Douzième Inférieure.	p. xxiv Hypo[-Diapason-Diapente]	Alla [Duodecima] sotto.
41	80. Ad Eptachordum infra	Septième Inférieure.	p. xxiii Ad Heptachordum min. Ad Heptachordum maj.	Alla Settima minore. Alla Settima maggiore.
42	81. Ibit, redibit	Veut dire, que la partie à la quelle appartiennent ces mots, doit executer le chant depuis le commencement jusqu'à la fin, et retourner de celle-ci au commencement en chantant la mélodie à reculon.		

Table 2

42	82. Ad Tonum, infinit, et finit	Le Conséquent doit répondre à un Ton au-dessus; et les autres mots signifient que le Canon est sans fin, et qu'il peut en avoir une.	p. xxi Finito, Infinito	[Canone] Finito è quello, che termina con Cadenza nell'istesso modo, che terminano tutte le Composizioni [...]. [Canone] Infinito, che chiamasi anche Circolare, è quello, il quale giunto al fine ritorna da capo fin'a tanto, che piace ai Cantori.
49	83. Six [sic] Vocum	Le Canon est à six voix.		
51	84. Ad Diapason, et Unissonum Vicissim	À l'Octave supérieure, et à l'Unisson alternativement.		
51	85. Tot tempora, tot sunt voces	Le Canon est composé d'autant de <u>Parties</u> ou <u>Voix</u> qu'il renferme de <u>Temps</u> ou de <u>Mesures</u>.		
55	86. Ad Diapason intensum	À l'Octave Inférieure.	Diapason intensum MARTINI 1775, pp. 265, 270. Example by P. Costanzo Porta, Opera Liber 52, Motectorum 5. 6. 7. & 8. Vocum, 1580.	
55	87. Ad Diapason espensum [sic]	À l'Octave supérieure.		
59	88. Ad Sub-Sesquiditonum	À la Tierce mineure au-dessous.		
65	89. Ad Septimam infra	À la Septième Inférieure.	p. xxiii Ad Septimam minorem Ad Septimam majorem	Alla Settima minore. Alla Settima maggiore.
67	90. Ad Decimam	À la Dixième supérieure.	p. xxiii Ad Decimam minor., vel majorem	Alla Decima min., o mag.
	91. Ad Tertiam infra	Tierce Inférieure.	p. xxiii Ad Tertiam minorem Ad Tertiam majorem	Alla Terza minore. Alla Terza maggiore.

[1]. Numbers correspond to Cherubini's collection.

[2]. MARTINI 1775, pp. xxii-xxvi. The numbers of the first part, Martini's No. 1-56, correspond to the numbering of the list of *Motti, o Enigmi*, on pp. xxv-xxvi. Martini's expressions of the second part of this table, matching with Cherubini's No. 55 onwards, appear on pp. xxii-xxiv of MARTINI 1775. These expressions are not part of Martini's list of *Motti, o Enigmi*. The most of them are instead part of his list of *Vocaboli Italiani, Latini e Greci*.

[3]. (**) Le Conséquent est la réponse ou la résolution de l'Antécédent. Il peut y avoir dans un Canon plusieurs Conséquents, et leur quantité établit celle des Parties.

[4]. This is a Padre Martini's mistake. Cherubini is correct. See p. 41, fn. 135.

[5]. This motto appears in Mozart KV 89ᵃ II (73r), 2, probably composed in Bologna in 1770.

[6]. This motto appears in Mozart KV 89ᵃ II (73r), 4, probably composed in Bologna in 1770.

[7]. This motto appears in Mozart KV 89ᵃ II (73r), 4, probably composed in Bologna in 1770.

Table 3

Padre Martini's Sources
for his
Motti o Enigmi

The table below relates all the mottoes in Martini's list of *Motti o Enigmi* (*Esemplare*, pp. xxv-xxvi) to their theoretical sources. The theoretical sources cited here refer exclusively to the treatises mentioned by Martini in footnote no. 3 on page xxv. When a motto has not been found in one of the theoretical sources given by Martini, and a practical source has been identified, this practical source is then cited. For example, motto no. 20 was not found in one of the treatises mentioned by Martini, but it was found in one of his practical sources, Giovanni Maria Nanino. Sometimes, as in the case of motto no. 23, a Martini's practical source is known in addition to the theoretical source; this practical source is then mentioned.

Most of the mottoes in Martini's list can be found in many other theoretical and practical works not mentioned in Martini's footnote[1]. These other sources are not given here, with one exception: motto no. 29. This motto has not been found in any of Martini's theoretical sources, but is cited by Zacconi.

Martini's explanations, as it appears on pages xxv-xxvi of his *Esemplare*, are given in the original Italian, accompanied by an English translation. Often, the same explanation applies to several mottoes. The first explanation relates to mottoes 1-8, for example. Each motto is then given separately, first in the original Latin, French or Italian, then in an English translation.

When the motto has been used in a canon in Cherubini's collection, the number of the canon is given. For example, motto no. 1 is used in canon no. 18.

Next come the sources. The explanatory texts for the mottoes as they appear in each of Martini's sources are given on the left in the original language and on the right in an English translation. When the source mentions a work or composer which used the motto, that work or composer is given. For example, Finck mentions an example by Josquin for motto no. 1. When the work in which the motto appears is known, the work is then cited, as in this example of Josquin quoted by Finck: the motto appears in the Agnus III of the *Missa l'Homme armé*. The same motto no. 1 is also cited by Cerone in an example of a work by Giovanni Maria Nanino. However, Cerone makes no specific mention of the work by Nanino in which the motto appears. Nanino's work is therefore not cited in the list below.

When there is a difference in the version of the motto as it appears in Martini and in one of his sources, the version that differs from Martini's is given just before the related source. For example, motto no. 17, which in Martini is «Cancrizat, vel canis more Haebreorum», in Finck appears only as «Cancrizat».

One expression in Martini's list was not found in the sources Martini himself indicated: *Fuge morulas* (M.8). Another expression that could not be found among the theoretical sources cited by Martini, *Vadam et veniam ad vos*, was found instead in a work by one of Martini's practical sources: 'O Rex gloriae Quatuor vocibus', Agnus Dei I, from the *Liber Primus Missarum* by Alonso [Alphonsi] Lobo de Borja, published in Madrid in 1602. *Tantum hoc repete, quantum cum aliis sociare videbis* (M.29), also could not be found among Martini's theoretical sources, but is cited by Ludovico Zacconi in his *Prattica di musica* (1596), Libro secondo, Cap. LII, p. 129. The example appears in the Motetto *Deus qui nos Patrem, & Matrem honorare praecepisti* by Clemens non Papa.

---

[1]. For a more complete list of sources for each motto, see Bonnie Blackburn's *Catalogue of enigmatic canonic inscriptions*, in SCHILTZ 2015, pp. 367-477.

Motti 1-8

Ciascun di questi otto Motti, o Enigmi indica, che il Conseguente, o la Parte, che risponde, tralascia le Pause dell'Antecedente, e segue a cantare le sole Note.

Each of these eight mottoes, or enigmas, indicates that the consequent, or the answering part, omits the rests of the antecedent, and sings only the notes.

1. Clama ne cesses
Don't cease crying out

Martini, **Canon No. 18**
AARON (*Libri tres*, 1516), f. 26

Missa est Iosquini, in qua quidem in parte illa, quae est Agnus dei, Canon talis est: Clama, ne cesses, *ubi uult in parte illa, quae in cantu est pausata pausis trium temporum singulis, ut pausae illae numerabiles non sint, sed ut solam moneant longarum quantitatem perfectarum, quae singulae quidem sex semibreues complectantur. Ex quo etiam breuium sequitur alteratio, quemadmodum supra in capite Modi minoris diximus.*	There is a mass by Josquin's in which in the Agnus the canon is *Clama, ne cesses* where he wishes, in the part in which there is a silence of three rests of one tempus each, that these rests should not be counted, but merely remind the quantity of the perfect longs, which each contain six semibreves. From which there also follows the alteration of the breves, as we said above in the chapter on minor mode.

GLAREAN (*Dodecachordon*, 1547), p. 206

Item, clama ne cesses, pro, omitte pausas.	Idem, 'Don't stop crying out' for 'omit rests'.

FINCK (*Practica musica*, 1556, book 3), Bb 4v / Cc 3v
Josquin, *Missa l'Homme armé super voces musicales*, Agnus III

Hic obseruabis: cantum, qui aliquem istorum canonum habet, cantari debere omissis pausis, etiamsi pausae adscriptae fuerint.	Here you will observe that a chant that has any of these canons must be sung omitting the rests, even if rests would have been written.

CERONE (*Melopeo*, 1613, book 22), *Enigma com outra differente Cruz*, Num. XXXXIII, ff. 1130-1131
Giovanni Maria Nanino

Y porque en ella no ay cosa dificultosa ni secreta, passaremos adelande, sin perder tempo en hazer su particular declaracion, solo ponremos el principio de la Resolucion.	And because there is nothing difficult or secret in it, we will continue without wasting time in making a particular declaracion, and only give the beginning of the resolution.

BONTEMPI (*Historia*, 1695), p. 232

Clama ne cesses, *che non si contano mai le Pause, ancorche vi sieno scritte.*	*Clama ne cesses* [indicates] that the Pauses are never counted, even if they are written.

2. Ocia dant vitia
Idleness begets vice

Martini, **Canon No. 46**
FINCK (*Practica musica*, 1556, book 3), Bb 4v

Hic obseruabis: cantum, qui aliquem istorum canonum habet, cantari debere omissis pausis, etiamsi pausae adscriptae fuerint.	Here you will observe that a chant that has any of these canons must be sung omitting the rests, even if rests would have been written.

Luciane Beduschi

3. Dii faciant sine me non moriar ego
May the gods bring it about that 'I' does not die without me

Finck (*Practica musica*, 1556, book 3), Bb 4v
Hic obseruabis: cantum, qui aliquem istorum canonum habet, cantari debere omissis pausis, etiamsi pausae adscriptae fuerint.
Here you will observe that a chant that has any of these canons must be sung omitting the rests, even if rests would have been written.

4. Omnia si perdas famam servare memento, Qua semel amissa, postea nullus eris
If you lose everything, remember to keep your good name; once you have lost that, you will after that be no one

Finck (*Practica musica*, 1556, book 3), Bb 4v
Hic obseruabis: cantum, qui aliquem istorum canonum habet, cantari debere omissis pausis, etiamsi pausae adscriptae fuerint.
Here you will observe that a chant that has any of these canons must be sung omitting the rests, even if rests would have been written.

5. Sperare & prestolari multos facit morari
Hoping and wanting makes many become fool

Finck (*Practica musica*, 1556, book 3), Bb 4v
Hic obseruabis: cantum, qui aliquem istorum canonum habet, cantari debere omissis pausis, etiamsi pausae adscriptae fuerint.
Here you will observe that a chant that has any of these canons must be sung omitting the rests, even if rests would have been written.

6. Ocia securis insidiosa nocent
Treacherous ease hurts the careless

Finck (*Practica musica*, 1556, book 3), Bb 4v
Hic obseruabis: cantum, qui aliquem istorum canonum habet, cantari debere omissis pausis, etiamsi pausae adscriptae fuerint.
Here you will observe that a chant that has any of these canons must be sung omitting the rests, even if rests would have been written.

7. Tarda solet magnis rebus inesse fides
Great things are usually slow to be believed

Finck (*Practica musica*, 1556, book 3), Bb 4v
Hic obseruabis: cantum, qui aliquem istorum canonum habet, cantari debere omissis pausis, etiamsi pausae adscriptae fuerint.
Here you will observe that a chant that has any of these canons must be sung omitting the rests, even if rests would have been written.

8. Fuge morulas
Flee delays

Sources not identified.

Table 3

Motti 9-20

Questi altri Motti, che vengono in appresso fino al Num. 20 significano, che dal Conseguente ne dobbiamo ricavare due altre Parti, che rispondeno, l'una che comincia dalla prima Nota dell'Antecedente, e procede ordinariamente fino al fine; l'altra comincia dall'ultima Nota dell'Antecedente, e proseguisce all'indietro fino alla prima Nota.

These other mottoes which follow up to no. 20, mean that from the consequent we must form two other parts that answer: one that begins from the first note of the antecedent and proceeds normally to the end, and another that begins from the last note of the antecedent and proceeds backwards to the first note.

9. Misericordias & veritas obviaverunt sibi
Mercy and truth have met each other

FINCK (*Practica musica*, 1556, book 3), Bb 4v / Dd 3r
Senfl, *Crux fidelis*, 3.P. (B and T)

Hos Canones addunt, quando uolunt significare ex una uoce duas cantandas esse, quarum altera, incipiendo ab initiali nota, iusto ordine usque ad finem progreditur: altera uero a finali incipiens, procedit contrario modo, donec ad initialem perueniat.	They add these canons when they want to indicate that two voices are to be sung from one, of which the one, beginning at the initial note, progresses in the normal order to the end, while the other, beginning at the final, proceeds by contrary motion until it arrives at the initial.

CERONE (*Melopeo*, 1613, book 22), *Enigma com outra differente Cruz*, Num. XXXXIII, ff. 1130-1131
Giovanni Maria Nanino

Y porque en ella no ay cosa dificultosa ni secreta, passaremos adelande, sin perder tempo en hazer su particular declaracion, solo ponremos el principio de la Resolucion.	And because there is nothing difficult or secret in it, we will continue without wasting time in making a particular declaracion, and only give the beginning of the resolution.

10. Justicia & pax se osculatae sunt
Justice and peace have kissed each other

Martini, **Canon No. 34**
FINCK (*Practica musica*, 1556, book 3), Bb 4v / Dd 3r
Senfl, *Crux fidelis*, D and A

Hos Canones addunt, quando uolunt significare ex una uoce duas cantandas esse, quarum altera, incipiendo ab initiali nota, iusto ordine usque ad finem progreditur: altera uero a finali incipiens, procedit contrario modo, donec ad initialem perueniat.	They add these canons when they want to indicate that two voices are to be sung from one, of which the one, beginning at the initial note, progresses in the normal order to the end, while the other, beginning at the final, proceeds by contrary motion until it arrives at the initial.

CERONE (*Melopeo*, 1613, book 22), *Enigma com outra differente Cruz*, Num. XXXXIII, ff. 1130-1131
Giovanni Maria Nanino

Y porque en ella no ay cosa dificultosa ni secreta, passaremos adelande, sin perder tempo en hazer su particular declaracion, solo ponremos el principio de la Resolucion.	And because there is nothing difficult or secret in it, we will continue without wasting time in making a particular declaracion, and only give the beginning of the resolution.

Luciane Beduschi

11. Nescit vos missa reverti
The voice once uttered not know how to return

Finck (*Practica musica*, 1556, book 3), Bb 4v

Hos Canones addunt, quando uolunt significare ex una uoce duas cantandas esse, quarum altera, incipiendo ab initiali nota, iusto ordine usque ad finem progreditur: altera uero a finali incipiens, procedit contrario modo, donec ad initialem perueniat.	They add these canons when they want to indicate that two voices are to be sung from one, of which the one, beginning at the initial note, progresses in the normal order to the end, while the other, beginning at the final, proceeds by contrary motion until it arrives at the initial.

12. Semper contrarius esto
Always be contrary

Finck (*Practica musica*, 1556, book 3), Bb 4v

Hos Canones addunt, quando uolunt significare ex una uoce duas cantandas esse, quarum altera, incipiendo ab initiali nota, iusto ordine usque ad finem progreditur: altera uero a finali incipiens, procedit contrario modo, donec ad initialem perueniat.	They add these canons when they want to indicate that two voices are to be sung from one, of which the one, beginning at the initial note, progresses in the normal order to the end, while the other, beginning at the final, proceeds by contrary motion until it arrives at the initial.

13. Signa te signa temere me tangis & angis, Romae tibi subito motibus ibit amor
Cross, cross yourself, you are rash to touch and vex me,
For by my labours Rome shall suddenly come to you, the object of your wishes

Finck (*Practica musica*, 1556, book 3), Bb 4v

Hos Canones addunt, quando uolunt significare ex una uoce duas cantandas esse, quarum altera, incipiendo ab initiali nota, iusto ordine usque ad finem progreditur: altera uero a finali incipiens, procedit contrario modo, donec ad initialem perueniat.	They add these canons when they want to indicate that two voices are to be sung from one, of which the one, beginning at the initial note, progresses in the normal order to the end, while the other, beginning at the final, proceeds by contrary motion until it arrives at the initial.

14. Frangenti fidem fides frangatur eidem
To him who breaks faith, let faith be broken

Finck (*Practica musica*, 1556, book 3), Bb 4v

Hos Canones addunt, quando uolunt significare ex una uoce duas cantandas esse, quarum altera, incipiendo ab initiali nota, iusto ordine usque ad finem progreditur: altera uero a finali incipiens, procedit contrario modo, donec ad initialem perueniat.	They add these canons when they want to indicate that two voices are to be sung from one, of which the one, beginning at the initial note, progresses in the normal order to the end, while the other, beginning at the final, proceeds by contrary motion until it arrives at the initial.

15. Roma caput mundi, si verteris, omnia vincit
Roma the head of the world; if you turn it, conquers all

Finck (*Practica musica*, 1556, book 3), Bb 4v

Table 3

Hos Canones addunt, quando uolunt significare ex una uoce duas cantandas esse, quarum altera, incipiendo ab initiali nota, iusto ordine usque ad finem progreditur: altera uero a finali incipiens, procedit contrario modo, donec ad initialem perueniat.	They add these canons when they want to indicate that two voices are to be sung from one, of which the one, beginning at the initial note, progresses in the normal order to the end, while the other, beginning at the final, proceeds by contrary motion until it arrives at the initial.

16. Mitto tibi metulas, erige si dubitas
I send you metulas, stand them up if you are in doubt

FINCK (*Practica musica*, 1556, book 3), Cc 1r

Indicatur, cantum simpliciter ab ultima nota incipiendo retro cantari debere.	Indicates that the chant, starting from the last note, simply must be sung backwards.

17. Cancrizat, vel canis more Haebreorum
He goes like a crab, or dog after the manner of the Hebrews

Cancrizat
FINCK (*Practica musica*, 1556, book 3), Cc 1r / Ee r

Indicatur, cantum simpliciter ab ultima nota incipiendo retro cantari debere.	Indicates that the chant, starting from the last note, simply must be sung backwards.

BONTEMPI (*Historia*, 1695), p. 232
Josquin, *Missa l'Homme armé super voces musicales*, Qui tollis; Et incarnatus

Cancrizat, *che si devono cominciare a cantar nel fine.*	*Cancrizat* [indicates] that one should start singing from the end.

18. Retrograditur
It goes backwards

FINCK (*Practica musica*, 1556, book 3), Cc 1r

Indicatur, cantum simpliciter ab ultima nota incipiendo retro cantari debere.	Indicates that the chant, starting from the last note, simply must be sung backwards.

19. Vadam & veniam ad vos
I will go and come to you

Vado. oineV
CERONE (*Melopeo*, 1613, book 22), *Enigma de la Cruz*, Num. XX, f. 1095

Aqui no ay tanta necessidad de declaracion, come de Resolucion: pues harto claro se conoce, que el Baxo y el Tenor començam differentemente, desde el pie de la Cruz, y ayuntanse en el arbol: cantando las notas cada uno por su verso; que viene aser; el uno contrario al otro [...]. Mas el contralto canta su parte sobre del braço de la Cruz, andando una vez, y otra volviendo: que por esto de una parte tiene escrito, Vado; que muestra camino derecho; y de otra, oineV: con que nos avisa que canta al contrario.	Here there is not so much a need for an explanation as for a solution: for it is quite clear that the bass and the tenor begin differently, from the foot of the cross, and join each other at the tree, singing the notes each from his side, that is, the one contrary to the other [...]. And the contralto sings its part on the arm of the cross, once going, then returning: this is why on one side it has the inscription Vado, showing the way to the right, and on the other oineV which tells us that it sings in the reverse.

ALONSO [Alphonsi] LOBO de Borja, 'O Rex gloriae Quatuor vocibus', *Liber Primus Missarum*, Agnus Dei I, Madrid, 1602

Luciane Beduschi

20. Principium, & finis
The beginning and the end

Giovanni Maria NANINO, [No. 143] 'Canon principium et finis', *Contrapunti sopra un Canto Fermo* (I-Bc T 225 / I-Bc C 36). *Joannis Mariae Nanini in Cappella Pontificia musici motecta, ut vulgo appellantur varie et nova inventione elaborata, quae ternis et quinis vocibus concinuntur*, Venice, Angelo Gardano, 1586.

Motto 21

Il Conseguente risponde all'Unissono.
The consequent answers at the unison.

---

21. Symphonizabis
You will sound together

Martini, **Canon No. 8**
ROSSI (*Organo*, 1618), p. 13
Palestrina, *Magnificat sexti toni a 4*, 'Sicut erat' (Vatican CG XII, 2, fols. 214ᵛ-220ʳ)

Il Palestrina nella Messa, Brevis, dice, Symphonizabis, *che vuol dire cantar l'istesse note, con l'istessa voce.*	Palestrina in the Missa Brevis says *Symphonizabis*, which means to sing the same notes, with the same voice.

Motti 22-26

Che dall'Antecedente si ricavino due Conseguenti, o due Parti, che rispondino, affinchè si formi il Canone a 3 Voci, il quale per lo più vuol essere all'Unissono, o all'Ottava.

From the antecedent are derived two consequents, or two parts that respond, producing a three-part canon, most often at the unison or octave.

22. Omne trinum perfectum
Every triad is perfect

Martini, **Canons No. 30, 50**
FINCK (*Practica musica*, 1556, book 3), Cc 1r / Ff 3v
Senfl

Hi canones usurpantur ad significandum, tres uoces ex una cantandas esse.	These canons are used to signify that three voices must be sung from one.

GLAREAN (*Dodecachordon*, 1547), p. 444
Lutuichi Senflij Tigurini Hypoaeolius, Canon. Omne trinum perfectum

Table 3

In huiuscemodi sanè Symphonijs, ut libere dicam quae sentio, magis est ingenij ostentatio quàm auditum reficiens adeo iucunditas, quale & hoc cuius nostri Lutuichi Senflij Tigurini, docti nostra ætate Symphonetæ. Cui ipse Cantorum more Canonem præfixit. Omne trinum perfectum. *Caeterum pro inceptione poterat & hic præfigi Canon ex Odysseæ. V.* [Greek text]. *Quod in Æneide Virgilius ita uertit: O terque quaterque beati. Sed Ænigma non admodum difficile eruditus lector facile discuti et cônsiderata diapente Diatessaron ac diapason consonantiarum ratione, ad eum modum quo Macrobius, quod diximus, Virgilianum discussit.*

In compositions of this kind, to say frankly what I believe, there is more display of skill than there is enjoyment which truly refreshes the hearing; of such a kind is the following example of our countryman, Ludwig Senfl of Zurich, a learned composer of our time. According to the custom of singers he has prefixed to it the inscription *Omne trinum prefectum*. Moreover, at the beginning, this inscription from book 5 of the Odyssey could also have been prefixed: [Greek text], which Virgil translates in the Aeneid in this way: O three and four times blessed. But an educated reader will easily solve this not very difficult riddle by considering the relationship of the fifth, fourth, and octave consonances, according to the way in which Macrobius solved the Vergilian inscription which we quoted.

23. Trinitas & unitas
Trinity and Unity

FINCK (*Practica musica*, 1556, book 3), Cc 1r / Ff 3v
Josquin, *Missa l'Homme armé super voces musicales*, Agnus II

Hi canones usurpantur ad significandum, tres uoces ex una cantandas esse. These canons are used to signify that three voices must be sung from one.

Manuel CARDOSO, *Missa Tradent enim vos*, Agnus

24. Trinitatem in unitate veneremur
That we worship the Trinity in Unity

FINCK (*Practica musica*, 1556, book 3), Cc 1r / Ff 4v
Anon., textless

Hi canones usurpantur ad significandum, tres uoces ex una cantandas esse. These canons are used to signify that three voices must be sung from one.

25. Sit trium series una
Let there be one sequence of three

Martini, **Canons No. 1, 11, 23**
FINCK (*Practica musica*, 1556, book 3), Cc 1r / Ff 4r
Anon., textless

Hi canones usurpantur ad significandum, tres uoces ex una cantandas esse. These canons are used to signify that three voices must be sung from one.

Tres in unum[1]
CERONE (*Melopeo*, 1613, book 22), *Enigma con tres Tiempos*, Num. 1, f. 1075
Josquin, *Missa L'Homme armé*, Agnus Dei

Luciane Beduschi

Iusquin hizo un Tercio en el Agnus Dei segundo, de la Missa Lomme arme super voces musicales *à 4 vozes, formado con tres differentes Tiempos, pero muy seco en el letrero, pues no dize mas de assi: Tres in unum. En este Canon todas três partes comiençam juntamente, pero com diferentes valores, y en diversas vozes [...].*

Josquin composed a Tercio for the second Agnus Dei of the *Missa L'homme armé super voces musicales* for 4 voices, with three different metres, but very dry in its text, because it does not say more than Tres in unum. In this canon all three parts begin together, but with different values, and in different voices [...]

26. Vidi tres viri qui erant laesi homonem
I saw — three men who had been injured — a wight

FINCK (*Practica musica*, 1556, book 3), Cc 1r
Hi canones usurpantur ad significandum, tres uoces ex una cantandas esse.

These canons are used to signify that three voices must be sung from one.

Motti 27-28

Possano rispondere all'Antecedente due, tre, e più Voci.
Two, three or more voices may respond to the antecedent.

27. Manet alta mente repostum
There remain stored in the depths of her mind

Martini, **Canon No. 6**
FINCK (*Practica musica*, 1556, book 3), Cc 1r-v / Ggr
Senfl, textless, in Stomius, *Prima ad Musicen instruction*
Significatur artificiose cantilenam factam esse, ita ut ex una uoce duae uel tres aliae, aut etiam plures cantari possint.

Signifies that a cantilena is artistically made so that two or three voices, or even more, can be sung from one voice.

28. De ponte non cadit, qui cum sapientia vadit
He will not fall from the bridge who goes wisely

FINCK (*Practica musica*, 1556, book 3), Cc 1v
Significatur artificiose cantilenam factam esse, ita ut ex una uoce duae uel tres aliae, aut etiam plures cantari possint.

Signifies that a cantilena is artistically made so that two or three voices, or even more, can be sung from one voice.

Motti 29-31

Una piccola Cantilena, che ritrovasi in una Parte deve repplicarsi fin'a tanto che siano terminate le altre Parti della Composizione.
A small cantilena, found in one part, must repplicate itself until the other parts of the composition are finished.

29. Tantum hoc repete, quantum cum aliis sociare videbis
Repeat this as often as you will see it associated with the others

ZACCONI (*Prattica*, 1592), Libro secondo, Cap. LII, 'Se con un segno solo, si può far repetere una cosa piu volte', p. 129
Clemens non Papa, Motetto *Deus qui nos Patrem, & Matrem honorare praecepisti*

Table 3

Con parole sotto che dicano: Pater meus & mater mea dereliquerunt me, Dominus autem assumpsit me; *dove che il si convien repplicar cinque volte; non tanto perche l'altre parte prima non finiscano quanto perche egli stesso conoscendo che gl'indissi non possano dimostrar altro che una semplice repetitione, col porti di sopra queste parole:* Tantum hoc repete, quantum cum alijs sociare videbis, *n'insegna & dimostra come simil sorte di cantilene s'habbiano da formare.*

With words beneath, that say *Pater meus & mater mea dereliquerunt me, Dominus autem assumpsit me*, where it is suitable to repeat five times, not so much because the other parts do not finish first than knowing that the hints cannot demonstrate anything else than a simple repetition, by carrying above these words: *Tantum hoc repete, quantum cum alijs sociare videbis*, which teaches and demonstrates how similar kinds of cantilenes have to be formed.

30. Non qui inceperit, sed qui perseveraverit
Not he who shall have begun, but he who shall have persevered

Martini, **Canon No. 13**
FINCK (*Practica musica*, 1556, book 3), Cc 1r / Mm 2r
Andreas de Silva, *Nigra sum*

Significat, cantilenam, absoluta serie notarum, iterum atque iterum ab initio repetendam, donec reliquae uoces etiam cessent.

Signifies that the whole series of notes of a cantilena must be repeated from the beginning again and again until the other voices stop.

31. Itque, reditque frequens
He goes there and back frequently

FINCK (*Practica musica*, 1556, book 3), Cc 1r
Significat, cantilenam, absoluta serie notarum, iterum atque iterum ab initio repetendam, donec reliquae uoces etiam cessent.

Signifies that the whole series of notes of a cantilena must be repeated from the beginning again and again until the other voices stop.

Motti 32-33
Il Conseguente deve radoppiare, o tripliare, &c. il valore delle Figure; o diminuirlo la metà, o due terzi.
The consequent must double or triple, etc., the value of the notes, or decrease it by half or two-thirds.

32. Crescit in Duplo, Triplo, &c.
Increase the double, triple, etc.

FINCK (*Practica musica*, 1556, book 3), Cc 1v / Ggv
Isti Canones admodum uulgares sunt, ijsque pro arbitrio symphonistae utuntur.

These canons are utterly common, they are used at the discretion of the symphonistae.

Crescat in duplum
BONTEMPI (*Historia*, 1695), p. 232
E dinotano Crescat in duplum, *che le Note e le Pause crescono il doppio.*

And *Crescat in duplum* indicates that the notes and rests double.

Luciane Beduschi

33. Decrescit in Duplo, Triplo, &c.
Decrease the double, triple, etc.

FINCK (*Practica musica*, 1556, book 3), Cc 1v

Isti Canones admodum uulgares sunt, ijsque pro arbitrio symphonistae utuntur.	These canons are utterly common, they are used at the discretion of the symphonistae.

Motto 34

Si devono cantar dal Conseguente le Figure per ordine del loro maggior valore, cioè prima le Massime, indi le Longhe, poscia le Brevi, le Semibrevi, le Minime, le Semiminime, &c.

In the consequent, the notes should be sung in the order of their longest values, that is, first the maxims, then the longs, then the breves, the semibreves, the minims, the semiminims, etc.

34. Dignora sunt priora
The more worthy have precedence

FINCK (*Practica musica*, 1556, book 3), Cc 1v / Gg 4r

Id est, notae quae maiorem habent ualorem, primum cantandae sunt, deinde illae quae minus ualent: ut longa breuem superat ualore, breuis semibreuem, semibreuis minimam, et caetera simili modo de pausis iudicandum est.	This is, that the notes of longer value must be sung first, then the ones with shorter value; so that a long note precedes a breve, a breve a semibreve, a semibreve a minim, and the rests must be judged in the same way.

Sunt digniora priora
BONTEMPI (*Historia*, 1695), p. 232

Sunt digniora priora, *che si cantano prima le Massime, poi le Lunghe, e poi le Brevi, & in simil guisa le altre Note secondo i gradi loro collocate fra molte altre che vi sono scritte.*	*Sunt digniora priora* [indicates] that the maxims are sung first, then the longs, then the breves, and in the same way the other notes following the ranks allocated to them among many others that are written.

Motti 35-36

Se una Parte forma una piccola Cantilena, questa deve repplicarsi fin tanto che sia teminata la Composizione; e nel repplicarsi deve alzarsi, o abbassarsi un Tuono.

If a part forms a small cantilena, it must repeat itself until the end of the composition. When it repeats itself it must raise or lower a tone.

35. Descende gradatim
Descend stepwise

FINCK (*Practica musica*, 1556, book 3), Cc 1v / Hh 2v
La Rue, *Missa Cum iocunditate*, Sanctus

Quando aliqua clausula, in cantilena quae plurium uocum est, in una tantum uoce saepius ponitur, tunc ea singulis uicibus per secundam deprimenda est.	When some phrase [clausula], in a cantilena of several voices, appears more often in one single voice, then this must be lowered by a second in each single repetition.

BONTEMPI (*Historia*, 1695), p. 232

Table 3

Descende gradatim, *che ogni volta che si arriva al Ritornello, segno espresso con due linee perpendicolari e paralelle con quattro punti segnati due in ciaschedun lato, si ricomincia, ma sempre un Tuono piu grave.*

Descende gradatim [indicates that] every time you arrive at the Ritornello, a sign expressed with two perpendicular and parallel lines with four dots marked two on each side, you start again, but always a tone lower.

36. Ascende gradatim
Ascend stepwise

Ascendo ad Patrem meum
Cerone (*Melopeo*, 1613, book 22), *Enigma, que en la Repeticion sube un punto*, Num. VIII, f. 1081
Giovanni Maria Nanino

Mas el mysterio de aquel letrero, Ascendo ad Patrem meum, *es que en llegando à la Repeticion, se ha de subir el Canto un punto mas en alto: esto es, que comiença de nuevo la Fuga,* Re fa sol la, &c. *pero cantase una boz mas subido de lo se cantò la primera vez* [...].

In addition, the mystery of that text, *Ascendo ad Patrem meum*, is that arriving at the repetition, the cantus must go up one degree: that is that the fugue starts again, *Re fa sol la &c.*, but it is sung one voice higher than where it was sung the first time [...].

Motto 37
Se alla prima Nota dell'Antecedente trovasi segnato il Punto, debbonsi cantare dal Conseguente tutte le altre Note col Punto.
If the first note of the antecedent is dotted, all notes must be dotted in the consequent.

37. Et sic de singulis
And thus for each one

Finck (*Practica musica*, 1556, book 3), Cc 1v / Hh 4v
Josquin, *L'Homme armé*

Id est, quod initiali notae accidit, reliquis identidem accidat: exempli gratia, si primae notae punctum additum fuerit, tunc singulis sequentibus, cuiuscunque Formos sint, puncta addenda esse censeas.

That is, that what happens to the first note also happens to the others. For instance, if a dot is added to the first note, then consider that a dot must be added to each of the following, of what species they may be.

Motti 38-39
Il Conseguente deve cantare le Note nere, come se fossero bianche.
All quarter notes in the consequent must be sung as half notes.

38. Nigra sum sed Formosa
I am black but beautiful

Finck (*Practica musica*, 1556, book 3), Cc 1r
Plaerunque significat, notas coloratas seu nigras, pro albis canendas esse.

Signifies most of the time that colored or black notes must be sung as whites.

Bontempi (*Historia*, 1695), p. 232
Nigra sum sed formosa, *che essendovi le Note nere si cantano per bianche.*

Nigra sum sed formosa [indicates] that black notes are sung as whites.

Luciane Beduschi

39. Caecus non iudicat de colore
A blind man does not judge by color

Angleria [Cima], (*Regola del contraponto*, 1622), p. 121

Motti 40-45

La Risposta deve cantarsi al contrario in maniera tale, che se l'Antecedente ascende, il Conseguente discenda, e se l'Antecedente discende, il Conseguente ascende.

The answer must be sung backwards in such a way that, if the antecedent ascends, the consequent descends, and if the antecedent descends, the consequent ascends.

---

40. Qui se exaltat humiliabitur
He who exalts himself shall be humbled

Finck (*Practica musica*, 1556, book 3), Cc 2v
Hoc est, quantum ascendit nota, tantum descendere illam imagineris, et contra.

That is, how much a note ascends, as much you will imagine it to descend, and the reverse.

Cerone (*Melopeo*, 1613, book 22), *Enigma de los três caminhos*, Num. xxi, f. 1098
Adonde el prim. Tiple (pues no tiene pausa) comiença primero; el qual, tomando-se à la parte alta, sube y baxa: que por esto tiene su lettra, que dize Qui se exaltat, humiliabitur.

Where the first treble (because it has no pause) starts first; which, taking the upper part, goes up and down: that is why it has the expression that says *Qui se exaltat, humiliabitur*.

41. Qui se humiliate exaltabitur
He who humbles himself shall be exalted

Martini, **Canon No. 7**
Finck (*Practica musica*, 1556, book 3), Cc 2v / Nn 1v
Anon., *Languir me fais*
Quamuis hunc canonem in Gallica cantilena, Languir me fais, *paulo aliter deprehendo, in qua inuestigaui, quod non solum descendentes notae uoce sublata cani debent, sed ipsa quoque cantio etsi tantum quatuor uocum apparet, ex illarumque numero est, quibus supra scriptus est canon,* Qui se humiliat exaltabitur: *Tamen ex quatuor positis insuper quinta artificiose promanat, hoc modo: quatuor uoces ordiuntur cantum, singulae quidem eo sono, quem clauis signata postulat. quinta uero uox pausat duos uulgares tactus, et quinto interuallo infra illam uocem, ex qua deriuatur, orditur. Exempli gratia: praecedens uox orditur in Ffaut: altera uero quae duas pausas habet in bfa♮mi, quinta infra illam canitur, deinde etiam quoties occurrit pausa, sequens non eundem retinet sonum, sed post obseruatam pausam illam, attollitur in sono semper per secundam, idque obseruat ad finem usque.*

Although I find this canon in a slightly different form in the French chanson *Languir me fais*, in which I have established that not only should the descending notes be sung at high pitch, but the chanson itself, although it appears to be for only four voices, and is one of those over which is written the canon *Qui se humiliate exaltabitur*. Yet out of the four written voices a fifth emerges as well by artifice, as follows: the four voices begin the song, each at that pitch which the signed clef requires; the fifth voice rests for two ordinary tactus, and begins at the interval of a fifth below that voice from which it is derived. For example: the preceding voice begins on Ffaut: the other that has two rests is sung on b-fa-bquadrum-mi, a fifth below it; then too whenever a rest occurs, the following voice does not keep up the same sound, but after observing the rest is always raised in sound by a second, and observes the rule right to the end.

Table 3

Cerone (*Melopeo*, 1613, book 22), *Enigma de los três caminhos*, Num. xxi, f. 1098

Luego despues de quatro Compasses, entra el segundo Tiple, el qual abaxa y sube; y para los advertir desto, tiene el letreiro: Qui se humiliat, exaltabitur.	Then, after four bars, the second treble enters, which goes down and up; and to warn about this, there is the sign *Qui se humiliat, exaltabitur.*

42. Plutonica subiit regna
He went down into the realm of Pluto

Martini, **Canon No. 54**

Finck (*Practica musica*, 1556, book 3), Cc 2v

Hoc est, quantum ascendit nota, tantum descendere illam imagineris, et econtra.	That is, how much a note ascends, as much you will imagine it to descend, and the reverse.

43. Contraria contrariis curantur
Everything is cured by its contrary

Martini, **Canon No. 49, 53**

Finck (*Practica musica*, 1556, book 3), Cc 2v / Mm 3v

Hoc est, quantum ascendit nota, tantum descendere illam imagineris, et econtra.	That is, how much a note ascends, as much you will imagine it to descend, and the reverse.

44. Qui non est mecum, contra me est
He who is not with me is against me

Cerone (*Melopeo*, 1613, book 22), Enigma adonde dos partes proceden al contrario de las dos principales, Num. vi, f. 1080
Giovanni Maria Nanino

[...] *Mas los otros dos (que es el primero y el tercero)* [...] *proceden al contrario: la qual operacion se avisa con dezir:* Qui non est mecum contra me est.	[...] But the other two [voices] (which is the first and the third) [...] proceed in contrary [motion]: this operation is notified stating *Qui non est mecum contra me est.*

Rossi (*Organo*, 1618), 13, 18
Don Tomasso Sanguineto Genovese canonico di sturla

Don Tomasso Sanguineto Genovese canonico di sturla, famoso à suoi tempi in questa scienza, fà questo roverscio, dicendo à questo modo: Qui non est mecum contra me est.	Don Tomasso Sanguineto, a Genovese canon of Sturla, famous in his day for this knowledge, made this contrary, saying in this way *Qui non est mecum contra me est.*

45. Duo adversi adverse in unum
The two adversaries come to one oppositely

Glarean (*Dodecachordon*, 1547), pp. 464-465
Mouton, Salve mater salvatoris

Luciane Beduschi

In priore hac cantione ita Basin instituit, ut nihilo secius ex ea uoce Altum canas ex aduerso constitutus, ijsdem etiam notulis, se ad te uersis. Ita duo suam uterque uocem incinent ex una. Idque in Diapason & duorum temporum spacio sese consequentes, ita ut Basis in D. magno incipiat, Altus post duo tempora in d paruo. Preterea ut Altus ita descendat, quemadmodum Basis ascendit: Cantio Dodrii Phrasin sapit, quod in Tenore potissimum cernitur, qui pulchre Dorius est. Sed Resolutionem eius nihilominus adposuimus, quod illi uocant. Ad longum.	In this first song he arranged the Bass so that you may sing the Alto no less from the same voice taken in the opposite, with the same notes, but in your direction. Thus, two may sing each his voice from one. And they follow themselves at the distance of an octave and of two *tempora*, so that the Bass begins on large D, the Alto after two *tempora* on little d. Moreover, that the Alto descends as the Bass ascends. The song resembles the phrasis of the Dorian, which is recognized particularly in the tenor, which is beautifully Dorian. But nonetheless we added the resolution which we call *Ad longum*.

Motto 46

Non si cantano dal Conseguente, benchè scritte nell'Antecedente, nè le Minime, nè le Semiminime.
The consequent must not sing half notes or quarter notes, even if they are written in the antecedent.

46. De Minimis non curat Praetor
The magistrate is not concerned with trifles

Pretore de minimis non curat
CERONE (*Melopeo*, 1613, book 22), *Enigma del espejo*, Num. XXXX (Tenore, e Alto), f. 1123

Mas de las dos partes, que aqui en este Canto estan encerradas, ninguna dellas cantan los puntos seguidos; porque el Tenor (que sirve de Baxo) va sacando, y cantando solamente las notas y pausas de Breve y Semibreve, dexando à parte todas las demas, que son de menor valia; como es la Minima, &c. y para avisarmos desto, dize el mote De minimis non curat Praetor.	And of the two parts that are contained in this song, none sings the notes in order; for the tenor (which serves as bass) is extracting and singing only the notes and pauses of breve and semibreve, leaving aside all the others of lesser value, as the minima, etc. To warn us of this, the moto says *De minimis non curat Praetor.*

De minimis non curat pretor
ROSSI (*Organo*, 1618), p. 13

Josquin, *Missa Malheur me bat*, Agnus I

L'istesso [Josquin] nella Messa mal'heur; dice: De minimis non curat prętor: *che vuol dire, che il giudice non fà stima delle cose leggiere, ò de' peccati piccioli: dando ad intendere che si devon cantare tutte le figure maggiori eccetto che le minime, & per consequenza le altre inferiori: & cosi si deve intendere delle Pause minime.*	The same [Josquin] in the Messa Mal'heur says *De minimis non curat prętor*, i.e. that the judge does not value trifling things, or petty sins. This means that all the major figures must be sung except the minims, and therefore anything smaller, and this is how we must understand the minim rests.

BONTEMPI (*Historia*, 1695), p. 232

De minimis non curat Prætor, *che non si cantano benche scritte, ne le Minime ne le Semiminime.*	*De minimis non curat Prætor* [indicates] that although written, neither minims nor semiminims are sung.

Motto 47

L'Antecedente diminuisce per metà il valor delle Figure, e il Conseguente lo accresce in quadruplo.
The antecedent halves the value of the notes, and the consequent quadruples it.

Table 3

47. Me opportet minui, illum autem crescere
I must decrease, but he must increase

Cerone (*Melopeo*, 1613, book 22), *Enigma que diminuye y aumenta el valor de las notas*, Num. xxviiii, f. 1108
Pietro Cerone?

En este Canon ay dos partes ambas secretas, aunque contrarias en el effecto, por quanto una parte diminuye el valor de las notas, y la otra lo aumenta: de modo que ninguna dellas canta con el valor, que muestra la senal indicial del tiempo q es este ¢; *el qual dize que la Breve vale dos Compases, la Semibreve uno, la Minima medio, y la Seminima la quarta parte. Que por causa del letrero,* Me oportet minui, *altera este valor el que canta la parte principal, y diminuye su natural cantidad; cantando la Breve en consideracion de Semibreve, la Semibreve de Minima, la Minima de Semiminima, y la Semiminima de Corchea; come si el Canto cantara* per dimidium, *y tubiera estotra senal* ¢. *Mas la parte Consiguiente obra todo al cōtrario, pues aumenta el valor à las notas à causa de la letra que dize* ...illum autem crescere: *y es que canta la Semibreve en consideracion de Breve, la Minima de Semibreve, y la Semiminima de Minima.*

In this canon there are two parts, both secret, although of opposite effect, because one part decreases the values of the notes and the other increases them, so that none of them sings with the values shown by the time signature which is ¢, which means that the breve counts two bars, the semibreve one, the minim half and the semiminim a fourth. Because of the inscription *Me oportet minui*, the one who sings the principal part alters this value and diminishes its natural quantity, singing the breve as a semibreve, the semibreve as a minim, the minim as a semiminim and the semiminim as a quaver, as if the cantus sang *per dimidium* and took this other time signature ¢. But the part that follows works totally in opposition, since it augments the value of the notes because of the text with says ...*illum autem crescere*, that is that it sings the semibreve as a breve, the minim as a semibreve and the semiminim as a minim.

Motto 48

Il Conseguente è stato composto prima dell'Antecedente.
The consequent was composed prior to the antecedent.

48. Qui venit post me, ante me factus est
He who comes after me was made before me

Martini, **Canon No. 17**
Cerone (*Melopeo*, 1613, book 22), *Enigma que diminuye y aumenta el valor de las notas*, Num. xxviiii, f. 1108
Pietro Cerone?

Ay despues esta tercera voz, que acompana la dos enigmaticas, harto clara y sin emberaço.

And then this third voice, which accompanies the two enigmatic ones, is very clear and without difficulty.

Motto 49

Il Conseguente risponde all'Unissono.
The consequent responds at the unison.

49. Exurge in adjutorium mihi
Rise up to help me

Rossi (*Organo*, 1618), p. 13
Pipelare, *Missa l'Homme armé*, Agnus III, B^2

Gio. Mouton in un'Agnus Dei nella parte del Basso, dice: exurge in adiutorium mihi: *chiama un'altro Basso che faccia l'istessa fuga il motto è chiaro.*

Gio. Mouton, in the bass part of an Agnus Dei, says: *exurge in adiutorium mihi*; call another bass to do the same fugue. The motto is clear.

Motto 50

Il Conseguente deve rispondere dopo il valore di quattro Tempi, cioè di quattro Brevi.

The consequent must answer after the value of four beats, i.e. four breves.

50. Vous jejuneres le quattr temps
You will fast in the four seasons

Rossi (*Organo*, 1618), p. 13
Josquin, *Missa de Beata Virgine*, Sanctus, Agnus I, Agnus III

Iusquino nella Messa della Madonna dice questo motto in lingua francesca, Vous jejuneres le quattr' temps, *cioè voi degiunerete le quattro tempora dell'anno, motto gratioso: che vuol dire che il cantore in quella cantilena ò fuga, uno aspetti quattro tempi che faranno otto tatti ò battute.*

Josquin in his Messa della Madonna uses this motto in French, *Vous jejuneres le quattr' temps*, that is, you will fast the four seasons of the year, an elegant motto, which means that in that cantilena or fugue the singer waits four tempi which will be eight tatti or battute.

Motto 51

Che il Conseguente canta l'istesse Note dell'Antecedente, ma al contrario voltando la faccia l'uno verso dell'altro.

The consequent sings the same notes as the antecedent, but on the contrary, the face of one turning towards the other.

51. Respice in me: Ostende mihi faciem tuam
Look into me: show me your face

Martini, **Canon No. 50**
CERONE (*Melopeo*, 1613, book 22), *Enigma, que para conocerle, se han de poner los Cantores enfrente*, Num. IX, f. 1082
Pietro Cerone

No ay duda, que este Canon assi mesmo na vaya cantando al cōtrario [...]. Y porque se conozca el effecto contrario que haze, y juntamente para mayor facilidad del segundo Cantante, tiene el letrero: Respice in me; Ostende mihi faciem tuam. *Con esto digo, viene à mostrar que los que cantan han de estar hueltos con las caras, mirando el uno hazia el otro, que tiene el libro en mano; pero de manera, que entrambos puedan ver el Canto.*

There is no doubt that this canon similarly goes singing in contrary motion. [...] To make known the effect of contrary motion, and also for the greater ease of the second singer, it has the text *Respice in me; Ostende mihi faciem tuam*. With this saying, it shows that those who sing must face each other, looking the one toward the other who holds the book in hand, but in such a way that both can see the chant.

Motti 52-53

Si può cantare il Conseguente con le Pause, e senza le Pause, ritenendo però sempre il sospiro, o sia quarto di Battuta, se trovasi scritto nell'Antecedente, affinchè resti compiuta la Battuta.

The consequent can be sung with or without the rests, but always with the quarter rests, i.e. the quarter of the measure, if written in the antecedent, so that the measure remains complete.

Table 3

52. Cantus duarum facierum
A song of two faces

Cantus duarum facierum
[Tolle moras placido maneant suspiria cantu]
Finck (*Practica musica*, 1556, book 3), Cc 1r / Ii 3v
Moulu, *Missa Alma redemptoris mater/A deux visages*, Kyrie

Id est, qui potest cum et sine pausis cantari, attamen ut suspiria tantum maneant quae tactus incolumitati inseruiunt, iuxta uersum: Tolle moras placido maneant suspiria cantu.	This is, that which can be sung with or without pauses, but so that the suspiria should remain that serve the integrity of the tactus according to the verse *Tolle moras placido maneant suspiria cantu* [Take the delays away, let your breath remain calmly in the song].

53. Tolle moras placido maneant suspiria cantu
Take the delays away, let your breath remain calmly in the song

See above, No. 52

Motti 54-55

Il Conseguente non canta alcuna Nota nera, ma solamente le bianche.	The consequent sings no black notes, only the white ones.

54. Dum lucem habetis credite in lucem
Whilst you have light, believe in light

Aaron (*Libri tres*, 1516), f. 26

Invenies etiam aliquando Cantilenam, in qua sint notae albae ac nigrae, & albae quidem notae tantummodo canendae erunt, in qua Canon erit huiusmodi, Dum lucem habetis credite in lucem. *Hic etiam non difficulter deprehendetur, compositorem uoluisse nigras xplode, & albas tantum cani.*	You will also sometimes find a Cantilena in which there are white and black notes, and indeed only the white notes are to be sung, in which there will be a canon of this kind, *Dum lucem habetis, credite in lucem*. Here too it will be apprehended without difficulty that the composer wished the black notes to be banished and only the white ones to be sung.

55. Qui sequitur me non ambulat, in tenebris
He who follows me shall not walk in darkness

Bontempi (*Historia*, 1695), p. 232

Qui sequitur me non ambulat in tenebris, *che la seconda Parte non canta alcuna Nota nera.*	*Qui sequitur me non ambulat in tenebris* [indicates] that the second part does not sing black notes.

Qui ambulat in tenebris nescit quo vadat / Qui sequitur me non ambulat, in tenebris
Cerone (Melopeo, 1613, book 22), *Enigma adonde una voz canta solamente las notas blancas*, Num. XXVII, f. 1105
Pietro Cerone, Mass

La declaracion deste Canon es, que la parte Consiguiente dexa las notas negras, y canta solamente las blancas.	The *declaracion* of this canon is that the consequent part omits the black notes and sings only the white ones.

Luciane Beduschi

Motto 56

L'annesso Esempio sevirà di spiegazione a quest'ultimo Enigma[3].
The attached example will serve as an explanation of this last enigma.

56. Intendami chi può, che m'intend'io
Understand me who can, for I understand myself

Angleria [Cima], (*Regola del contraponto*, 1622), p. 121

[1]. In Cherubini's table, the motto is *Sit trium series una. Tres in unum.*
[2]. Rossi attributes erroneously to Mouton.
[3]. See Martini 1775, pp. xxvi, xxvii.

Table 4

Martini's *Esemplare*
vs.
Finck's *Practica musica*

	Martini (*Esemplare*, pp. xxv-xxvi)	Finck (*Practica musica*, Liber Tertius)
M.1. *Clama ne cesses* (Bb 4v / Cc 3v) M.2. *Ocia dant vitia* (Bb 4v) M.3. *Dii faciant sine me non moriar ego* (Bb 4v) M.4. *Omnia si perdas famam servare memento, qua semel emissa: postea nullus eris* (Bb 4v) M.5. *Sperare et praestolari multos facit morari* (Bb 4v) M.6. *Ocia securis insidiosa nocent* (Bb 4v) M.7. *Tarda solet magnis rebus inesse fides* (Bb 4v)	Ciascun di questi otto Motti, o Enigmi indica, che il Conseguente, o la Parte, che risponde, tralascia le Pause dell'Antecedente, e segue a cantare le sole Note.	*Hic obseruabis: cantum, qui aliquem istorum canonum habet, cantari debere omissis pausis, etiamsi pausae adscriptae fuerint.* Here you will observe that a chant that has any of these canons must be sung omitting the rests, even if rests would have been written.
M.9. *Misericordias et veritas obviaverunt sibi* (Bb 4v / Dd 3r) M.10. *Justitia et pax se osculatae sunt* (Bb 4v / Dd 3r) M.11. *Nescit vox missa reverti* (Bb 4v) M.12. *Semper contrarius esto* (Bb 4v) M.13. *Signa te signa temere me tangis et angis, Romae tibi subito motibus ibit amor* (Bb 4v) M.14. *Frangenti fidem fides frangatur eidem* (Bb 4v) M.15. *Roma caput mundi si veteris, omnia vincit* (Bb 4v)	Questi altri Motti, che vengono in appresso fino al Num. 20 significano, che dal Conseguente ne dobbiamo ricavare due altre Parti, che rispondino, l'una che comincia dalla prima Nota dell'Antecedente, e procede ordinariamente fino al fine; l'altra comincia dall'ultima Nota dell'Antecedente, e proseguisce all'indietro fino alla prima Nota.	*Hos Canones addunt, quando uolunt significare ex una uoce duas cantandas esse, quarum altera, incipiendo ab initiali nota, iusto ordine usque ad finem progreditur: altera uero a finali incipiens, procedit contrario modo, donec ad initialem perueniat.* They add these canons when they want to indicate that two voices are to be sung from one, of which the one, beginning at the initial note, progresses in the normal order to the end, while the other, beginning at the final, proceeds by contrary motion until it arrives at the initial.
M.16. *Mitto tibi metulas, erige si dubitas* (Cc 1r) M.17. *Cancrizat* (Cc 1r / Ee r) M.18. *Retrograditur* (Cc 1r)		*Indicatur, cantum simpliciter ab ultima nota incipiendo retro cantari debere.* Indicates that the chant, starting from the last note, simply must be sung backwards.
M.22. *Omne trinum perfectum* (Cc 1r / Ff 3v) M.23. *Trinitas et unitas* (Cc 1r / Ff 3v) M.24. *Trinitate in unitate veneremur* (Cc 1r / Ff 4v) M.25. *Sit trium seriès una* (Cc 1r / Ff 4r) M.26. *Vidi tres viri qui erant laesi homonem* (Cc 1r)	Che dall'Antecedente si ricavino due Conseguenti, o due Parti, che rispondino, affinchè si formi il Canone a 3. Voci, il quale per lo più suol essere all'Unissono, o all'Ottava.	*Hi canones usurpantur ad significandum, tres uoces ex una cantandas esse.* These canons are used to signify that three voices must be sung from one.

M.27. *Manet alta mente repostum* (Cc 1r-v / Ggr) M.28. *De ponte non cadit, qui cum sapientia vadit* (Cc 1v)	*Possano rispondere all'Antecedente due, tre, e più Voci.*	*Significatur artificiose cantilenam factam esse, ita ut ex una uoce duae uel tres aliae, aut etiam plures cantari possint.* Signifies that a cantilena is artistically made so that two or three voices, or even more, can be sung from one voice.
M.30. *Non qui inceperit, sed qui perseveraverit* (Cc 1r / Mm 2r) M.31. *Itque, reditque frequens* (Cc 1r)	*Una piccola Cantilena, che ritrovasi in una Parte deve repplicarsi fin'a tanto che siano terminate le altre Parti della Composizione.*	*Significat, cantilenam, absoluta serie notarum, iterum atque iterum ab initio repetendam, donec reliquae uoces etiam cessent.* Signifies that the whole series of notes of a cantilena must be repeated from the beginning again and again until the other voices stop.
M.32. *Crescit in Duplo, Triplo, &c.* (Cc 1v / Ggv) M.33. *Decrescit* (Cc 1v)	*Il Conseguente deve radoppiare, o tripliare, &c. il valore delle Figure; o diminuirlo la metà, o due terzi.*	*Isti Canones admodum uulgares sunt, ijsque pro arbitrio symphonistae utuntur.* These canons are utterly common, they are used at the discretion of the symphonistae.
M.34. *Dignora sunt priora* (Cc 1v / Gg 4r)	*Si devono cantar dal Conseguente le Figure per ordine del loro maggior valore, cioè prima le Massime, indi le Longhe, poscia le Brevi, le Semibrevi, le Minime, le Semiminime, &c.*	*Id est, notae quae maiorem habent ualorem, primum cantandae sunt, deinde illae quae minus ualent: ut longa breuem superat ualore, breuis semibreuem, semibreuis minimam, et caetera simili modo de pausis iudicandum est.* This is, that the notes of longer value must be sung first, then the ones with shorter value; so that a long note precedes a breve, a breve a semibreve, a semibreve a minim, and the rests must be judged in the same way.
M.35. *Descende gradatim* (Cc 1v / Hh 2v)	*Se una Parte forma una piccola Cantilena, questa deve repplicarsi fin tanto che sia teminata la Composizione; e nel repplicarsi deve alzarsi, o abbassarsi un Tuono.*	*Quando aliqua clausula, in cantilena quae plurium uocum est, in una tantum uoce saepius ponitur, tunc ea singulis uicibus per secundam deprimenda est.* When some phrase (*clausula*), in a cantilena of several voices, appears more often in one single voice, then this must be lowered by a second in each single repetition.
M.37. *Et sic de singulis* (Cc 1v / Hh 4v)	*Se alla prima Nota dell'Antecedente trovasi segnato il Punto, debbonsi cantare dal Conseguente tutte le altre Note col Punto.*	*Id est, quod initiali notae accidit, reliquis identidem accidat: exempli gratia, si primae notae punctum additum fuerit, tunc singulis sequentibus, cuiuscunque speciei sint, puncta addenda esse censeas.* That is, that what happens to the first note also happens to the others. For instance, if a dot is added to the first note, then consider that a dot must be added to each of the following, of what species they may be.

Table 4

M.38. *Nigra sum sed formosa* (Cc 1r)	Il Conseguente deve cantare le Note nere, come se fossero bianche.	*Plaerunque significat, notas coloratas seu nigras, pro albis canendas esse.* Signifies most of the time that colored or black notes must be sung as whites.
M.40. *Qui se exaltat humiliabitur* (Cc 2v) M.43. *Contraria contrariis curantur* (Cc 2v / Mm 3v) M.42. *Plutonico subiit regna* (Cc 2v) M.41. *Qui se humiliat exaltabitur* (Cc 2v / Nn 1v)	La Risposta deve cantarsi al contrario in maniera tale, che se l'Antecedente ascende, il Conseguente discenda, e se l'Antecedente discende, il Conseguente ascende.	*Hoc est, quantum ascendit nota, tantum descendere illam imagineris, et econtra.* That is, how much a note ascends, as much you will imagine it to descend, and the reverse. *Quamuis hunc canonem in Gallica cantilena,* Languir me fais, *paulo aliter deprehendo, in qua inuestigaui, quod non solum descendentes notae uoce sublata cani debent, sed ipsa quoque cantio etsi tantum quatuor uocum apparet, ex illarumque numero est, quibus supra scriptus est canon,* Qui se humiliat exaltabitur: *Tamen ex quatuor positis insuper quinta artificiose promanat, hoc modo: quatuor uoces ordiuntur cantum, singulae quidem eo sono, quem clauis signata postulat. quinta uero uox pausat duos uulgares tactus, et quinto interuallo infra illam uocem, ex qua deriuatur, orditur. Exempli gratia: praecedens uox orditur in Ffaut: altera uero quae duas pausas habet in bfa♮mi, quinta infra illam canitur, deinde etiam quoties occurrit pausa, sequens non eundem retinet sonum, sed post obseruatam pausam illam, attollitur in sono semper per secundam, idque obseruat ad finem usque.* Although I find this canon in a slightly different form in the French chanson *Languir me fais,* in which I have established that not only should three descending notes be sung at high pitch, but the chanson itself, although it appears to be for only four voices, and is one of those over which is written the canon *Qui se humiliat exaltabitur.* Yet out of the four written voices a fifth emerges as well by artifice, as follows: the four voices begin the song, each at that pitch which the signed clef requires; the fifth voice rests for two ordinary tactus, and begins at the interval of a fifth below that voice from which it is derived. For example: the preceding voice begins on Ffaut: the other that has two rests is sung on b-fa-bquadrum-mi, a fifth below it; then too whenever a rest occurs, the following voice does not keep up the same sound, but after observing the rest is always raised in sound by a second, and observes the rule right to the end.

M.52. *Cantus duarum facierum* (Cc 1r / Ii 3v) M.53. *Tolle moras placido maneant suspiria cantu* (Cc 1r / Ii 3v)	*Si può cantare il Conseguente con le Pause, e senza le Pause, ritenendo però sempre il sospiro, o sia quarto di Battuta, se trovasi scritto nell'Antecedente, affinchè resti compiuta la Battuta.*	*Id est, qui potest cum et sine pausis cantari, attamen ut suspiria tantum maneant quae tactus incolumitati inseruiunt, iuxta uersum:* Tolle moras placido maneant suspiria cantu. This is, that which can be sung with or without pauses, but so that the suspiria should remain that serve the integrity of the tactus according to the verse *Tolle moras placido maneant suspiria cantu* [Take the delays away, let your breath remain calmly in the song].

Table 5

Finck's Expressions
not Cited
by Martini[1]

---

[1] Finck 1556, *Liber Tertius*; Martini 1775.

Gaude cum gaudentibus.
Rejoice with them who rejoice.
EXAMPLE: Josquin, *Missa L'homme armé super voces musicales*, Osanna (Dd 3v)

Hic canon reperitur, quando uni uoci aliquod signum, (et praesertim signum prolationis maioris) additur: reliquae uero uoces in proportione tripla ponuntur, quae tamen iuxta utriusque signi exigentiam cantari possunt.

This canon is found when some sign (and particularly the sign of the *prolatio maior*) is added to one voice; however, the other voices must be put in *proportione tripla*, and can nevertheless be sung according to the requirement of either sign.

Celsa canens imis commuta quadruplicando.
Singing the high notes, exchange them with the lowest, multiplying by four.
In gradus undenos descendant multiplicantes.
Consimilique modo crescant antipodes uno.
They descend eleven steps multiplying, and in the same manner they increase in the opposite direction.
EXAMPLE: Josquin, *Missa Fortuna desperata*, Agnus I (Hh 3v)

Hoc est, numera ab illa nota, quae in Discanto posita est in Ffaut, usque ad undecimum gradum, qui erit Cfaut, in illa claue notam primam colloca, atque eas notas, quae in Canone descendunt, in resolutione ascendere facias: Postea quoque notabis unamquamlibet notam multiplicandam esse per quatuor.

That is, count [descending] from this note which is notated in the Discantus as Ffaut to the eleventh degree which will be Cfaut, place in this degree [clave] the first note and make these notes of the resolution ascend, which in the canon are descending. Then you will also note that each note must be multiplicated by four.

Vae tibi ridenti, nam mox post gaudia flebis.
Woe to you who laugh, for soon after your joys you shall weep.

In hoc uersiculo continentur omnes octo partes orationis, indeque significare uolunt, cantum notatum hoc Canone, ad quemlibet octo tonorum accommodari posse.

In this verse are contained all eight parts of the discourse, by what they want to signify that the chant notated with this canon can be accommodated to any of the eight tones [modes].

I prae, sequar: inquit cancer.
«Go ahead, I will follow», said the crab.

Id est, quando ex postrema cantilenae parte duae uoces se post aliquot pausas sequuntur.

That is, when from the last part of the cantilena two voices follow each other after a few rests.

Vndecies canito pausas linquendo priores.
Sing eleven times omitting the first rests.
EXAMPLE: Josquin, *Missa Gaudeamus*, Et in terra (Ii 1v)

Versus per se planus est, ideo explicatione non indiget.

The verse is clear enough in itself, therefore no explanation is missing.

Luciane Beduschi

Dormiui et soporatus sum.
I have slept and taken my rest.

Id est, quando cantus plurium est partium, et postea in postrema parte aliquid notabile incidit, ibi cum antea praecedentes partes tantum quatuor aut quinque uocum fuerint, tunc adhuc alia uox additur: aut per signum conuenientiae in aliqua uoce significatur, aliquam aliam ex illa sequi debere: Sic Iosquinus composuit Psalmum, in quo iste textus ponitur.

That is, when the work is of many parts, and something notable happens in the last part, then while in the preceding parts there were only four or five voices, another voice is added, or a conventional sign in one of the voices signifies that some other must follow from this one. It is so that Josquin composed a Psalm in which this text is given.

Ranam agit Seriphiam.
He acts the frog of Sephiros.

Vox faucibus haesit.
The voice stuck in the throat.

Hunc Canonem plaerunque usurpant in Missis, in textu: Benedictus qui uenit in nomine domini: *Et notat silendum esse, etiamsi uox adscripta sit.*

This canon is often used in masses, on the text *Benedictus qui venit in nomine domini* and it notes that one should be silent, even though a voice is written.

Da mihi dimidiam lunam, solem, et canis iram.
Give me half a moon, the sun, and the anger of a dog.

Hoc uersiculo utimur, quando cantui nullum est praefixum signum, cum tamen minime carere signis queat. Itaque per lunam intellige hoc signum C, per solem O, et per canis iram, literam .r. quam ueteres sic pinxerunt .z. Habes igitur C tempus imperfectum, et O tempus perfectum, et O2 modum minorem perfectum et caetera. Idem significatur per sequentes uersiculos:

We use this verse when no sign is prefixed to the song, although it should nevertheless not lack a sign. Therefore by the moon, understand this sign C, by the sun O, and by the anger of the dog the letter .r. which the ancients depicted as .2. You then have C, tempus imperfectum and O, tempus perfectum and O2 the minor perfectum mode etc. This is also explained/indicated by the following verses:

Dimidium spherae, spheram, cum principe Romae,
Postulat a nobis totius conditor orbis.
Half a sphere, a sphere, with the beginning of Rome asserts for us the Creator of the whole world.
Quamlibet inspicias notulam qua claue locetur,
Tunc denique socios in eadem concine tentos:
Sed uere prolationes non petunt pausationes, sed sunt signa generis.
Look at every note to see under what clef it is placed; only then sing the comrades held under the same (clef); but truly the prolations do not look for rests, but are signs of the genus.

Hoc est, inspice dictionem intra linearum spacia, aut etiam in ipsis lineis contentam, et quoties tibi litera aliqua occurret, toties duo tempora pro ea pausabis: literae enim pausas denotant. Deinde inspice quamlibet notam, et cuilibet reliquas uoces, quae illi tribuuntur in scala, adde.

That is, examine the expression contained in the spaces between the lines or in these lines, and each time you see another letter, you will pause two breves [*tempora*] for it: the letters indeed denote rests. Then examine any note, and add to it the other *voces* [solmization syllables] that are associated with it in the scale.

Table 5

Verum hoc loco illud obseruare necesse est, illas claues, quae ex scala petendae sunt, non eodem ubique ordine sumi debere, sed in aliquibus media uox: aliquando etiam ultima primo ponitur. Ideo hanc regulam probe teneto: in qua claue nota collocata fuerit, illa clauis uocem cantandam nequaquam suppeditat, si clauis duarum, triumue notarum fuerit: si nota primae uoci competit, reliquas inclusas, ea serie, qua in claui positae sunt, concines: si nota mediam attingit, hanc primo, deinde primam, tandem ultimam: Si nota ultimam attingit, omnes in illa claue sine negotio canes.

It is truly necessary at this point to observe that the clefs [*claves*] that have to be searched from the scale must not be taken in the same order everywhere, but in some the middle *vox*, at times also the last one is put first.

Therefore, hold on to this rule: whatever the clef in which the note is placed, this clef never supplies the *vox* to be sung, if the clef is of two or three notes. If the note accords to the first *vox*, sing together the other ones contained in the series in the order in which they are placed in the clef. If it touches the middle note, [sing] first this one, then the first, and the last. If it touches the last note, sing all of them in this clef without worry.

Desiderium crescit cum spe.
Desire increases with hope.
EXAMPLE: Anon., *Amour parfait madonne hardiesse* (Nn 2v)

Haec itidem cantilena quatuor uocibus composita est. Sed insuper ex illa, cui Canon appositus est, quinta propagatur, et quidem cum textu profertur, estque haec sententia: desiderium crescit cum spe: *prima inchoans, cantum ordine pertexit: altera emergens, quatuor pausat: et undecimam infra hanc orditur, quam deinceps tantisper sequitur, donec textum hunc assequatur,* le desir croist quant et quant lesperance: *Ibi uox illa, quae sequitur, omnes notas tractim et duplo maiori cum mora canit, donec progrediatur eo ubi simul desinant.*

This song likewise has been composed for four voices. But in addition a fifth is produced from the one to which the canon has been appended, and indeed is performed with text, and the sentence is this: *desiderium crescit cum spe*: the first starts, and begins the whole song in order; the second emerges, rests four, and begins the eleventh below it, which it then follows again for as long as it takes to catch up with this text, *Le desir croist quant et quant l'esperance*. There the voice that follows sings all the notes slowly and dwells on them twice as long, until it reaches the point where they cease together.

Table 6

Cherubini's and Ginguené's
Translations of
Martini's List of *Motti o Enigmi*

MARTINI *Esemplare*, pp. xxv-xxvi		CHERUBINI'S *Table de mots latins*	GINGUENÉ *Encyclopédie méthodique*, pp. 199-201
1. *Clama ne cesses*	Ciascun di questi otto Motti, o Enigmi indica, che il Conseguente, o la Parte, che risponde, tralascia le Pause dell'Antecedente, e segue a cantare le sole Note.	Chacun de ces huit mots, ou énigmes, indique que la partie qui repond, chante toutes les notes du Canon en suprimant [*sic*] tous les silences de l'Antécédent.	Chacun de ces *mots* ou énigmes indique que les parties qui répondent doivent négliger les pauses qui se trouvent dans celle qui a proposé le *canon*, & ne chanter que les notes.
2. *Ocia dant vitia*			
3. *Dii faciant sine me non moriar ego*			
4. *Omnia si perdas famam servare memento, Qua semel amissa, postea nullus eris*			
5. *Sperare & prestolari* [*sic*] *multos facit morari*			
6. *Ocia securis insidiosa nocent*			
7. *Tarda solet magnis rebus inesse fides*			
8. *Fuge morulas*			
9. *Misericordias & veritas obviaverunt sibi*	Questi altri Motti, che vengono in appresso fino al Num. 20 significano, che dal Conseguente ne dobbiamo ricavare due altre Parti, che rispondeno, l'una che comincia dalla prima Nota dell'Antecedente, e procede ordinariamente fino al fine; l'altra comincia dall'ultima Nota dell'Antecedente, e proseguisce all'indietro fino alla prima Nota.	Les mots qui se succèdent depuis le n° 9, jusqu'au n° 20, signifient que du Conséquent (*) il doit se former deux autres Parties, l'une qui commence par la première note de l'Antécédent (¹**) en suivant jusqu'à la dernière, et l'autre commençant par la dernière note de l'Antécédent revient en rétrogradant à la première.	Ces douze *mots* signifient que les deux parties qui répondent à la partie proposante, l'une doit commencer à la première note du chant proposé, & aller jusqu'à la fin; l'autre commence à la dernière note, & poursuit toujours en reculant jusqu'à la première.
10. *Justicia & pax se osculatae sunt*			
11. *Nescit vos missa reverti*			
12. *Semper contrarius esto*			
13. *Signa te signa temere me tangis & angis, Romae tibi subito motibus ibit amor*			
14. *Frangenti fidem fides frangatur eidem*			
15. *Roma caput mundi, si veteris, omnia vincit*			
16. *Mitto tibi metulas, erige si dubitas*			
17. *Cancrizat, vel canis more Haebreorum*			
18. *Retrograditur*			
19. *Vadam & veniam ad vos*			
20. *Principium, & finis*			
21. *Symphonizabis*	Il Conseguente risponde all'Unissono.	Le Conséquent repond à l'Unisson.	Répondez à l'unisson.
22. *Omne trinum perfectum*	Che dall'Antecedente si ricavino due Conseguenti, o due Parti, che rispondino, affinchè si formi il Canone a 3. Voci, il quale per lo più vuol essere all'Unissono, o all'Ottava.	Que de l'Antécédent on forme deux Conséquents, dont il résulte un Canon à 3 Parties, le quel Canon, le plus souvent est à l'<u>Unisson</u> ou à l'<u>Octave</u>.	Ceux-ci veulent dire tout simplement que de la partie proposée on doit tirer deux autres parties, qui forment un *canon* à trois voix, & qui prennent ordinairement à l'unisson ou à l'octave.
23. *Trinitas & unitas*			
24. *Trinitatem in unitate veneremur*			
25. *Sit trium seriès una*			
26. *Vidi tres viri qui erant laesi homonem*			

27. *Manet alta mente repostum* 28. *De ponte non cadit, qui cum sapientia vadit*	Possano rispondere all'Antecedente due, tre, e più Voci.	L'Antécédent peut avoir deux, trois Conséquents, et plus qui lui repondent.	Que deux, trois, ou plusieurs voix répondent à la proposition.
29. *Tautum* [sic] *hoc repete, quantum cum aliis sociare videbis* 30. *Non qui inceperit, sed qui perseveraverit* 31. *Itque, reditque frequens*	Una piccola Cantilena, che ritrovasi in una Parte deve repplicarsi fin'a tanto che siano terminate le altre Parti della Composizione.	Une petite phrase de chant dans une des Parties du Canon, doit recommencer autant de fois qu'il en faut pour remplir la durée du Canon dans les autres Parties.	Un petit trait de chant qui est dans une partie doit se répéter jusqu'à ce que les autres parties aient fini de chanter. Il ne s'agit que de distinguer dans le *canon* ce petit trait de chant, & de le continuer, sans l'interrompre, jusqu'à la fin.
32. *Crescit in Duplo, Triplo, &c.* 33. *Decrescit in Duplo, Triplo, &c.*	Il Conseguente deve radoppiare, o triplicare, &c. il valore delle Figure; o diminuirlo la metà, o due terzi.	Le Conséquent doit doubler, ou tripler la valeur des figures notées dans l'Antécédent, ou la diminuer de la moitié, ou de deux tiers.	Le partie qui répond doit doubler au tripler la valeur des notes, ou les diminuer de la moitié, ou des deux tiers, &c.
34. *Dignora sunt priora*	Si devono cantar dal Conseguente le Figure per ordine del loro maggior valore, cioè prima le Massime, indi le Longhe, poscia le Brevi, le Semibrevi, le Minime, le Semiminime, &c.	Le Conséquent doit repondre de manière à suivre par ordre la valeur des figures à commencer par la plus grande et progressivement passer graduellement de celle-ci jusqu'à la plus petite, c'est-à-dire, de la <u>Maxime</u> passer à la <u>Longue</u>, puis à la <u>Breve</u>, ensuite à la <u>Semibreve</u> ou <u>Ronde</u>, après à la <u>Minime</u> ou <u>Blanche</u>, et de celle-ci à la <u>Semiminime</u> ou <u>Noire</u> &c.	La partie qui répond doit chanter les notes dans l'ordre de leur valeur respective, & non dans l'ordre où elles sont notées: c'est-à-dire, les *maximes* d'abord, ensuite les *longues*, puis les *brèves*, les *semi-brèves*, &c.
35. *Descende gradatim* 36. *Ascende gradatim*	Se una Parte forma una piccola Cantilena, questa deve repplicarsi fin tanto che sia teminata la Composizione; e nel repplicarsi deve alzarsi, o abbassarsi un Tuono.	Il peut y avoir dans une partie un passage de nature à être repeté autant de fois qu'il faut pour remplir la durée du chant principal, et qu'en le repetant il soit haussé, ou baissé d'un Ton.	Chaque fois que le chant ou le sujet recommence, il faut descendre ou monter d'un ton.
37. *Et sic de singulis*	Se alla prima Nota dell'Antecedente trovasi segnato il Punto, debbonsi cantare dal Conseguente tutte le altre Note col Punto.	Si la première note de l'Antécédent est marquée avec un point, le Conséquent doit pointer toutes les autres notes.	Si la première note est suivie d'un point, la partie répondante doit chanter en pointant toutes les autres notes.

Table 6

38. *Nigra sum sed formosa* 39. *Caecus non iudicat de colore*	Il Conseguente deve cantare le Note nere, come se fossero bianche.	Le Conséquent doit chanter les notes Noires, comme si elles étaient des Blanches.	La partie qui répond doit chanter les noires comme si c'étoient des blanches.
40. *Qui se exaltat humiliabitur* 41. *Qui se humiliat exaltabitur* 42. *Plutonica subiit regna* 43. *Contraria contrariis curantur* 44. *Qui non est mecum, contra me est* 45. *Duo adversi adverse in unum*	La Risposta deve cantarsi al contrario in maniera tale, che se l'Antecedente ascende, il Conseguente discenda, e se l'Antecedente discende, il Conseguente ascende.	La reponse doit être l'opposé de l'Antécédent, c'est-à-dire que si celui-ci monte, le Conséquent doit descendre, et vice-versa.	On doit chanter la réponse en sens contraire, de manière que si la partie proposante monte, la répondante descend, & si la première descend, la dernière monte.
46. *De Minimis non curat Praetor*	Non si cantano dal Conseguente, benchè scritte nell'Antecedente, nè le Minime, nè le Semiminime.	Le Conséquent ne doit chanter ni les <u>Blanches</u>, ni les <u>Noires</u>, quoiqu'elles soient notées dans l'Antécédent.	La partie répondante ne doit chanter ni les *minimes*, ni les *semi-minimes*, c'est-à-dire, ni les blanches, ni les *noires*, quoi qu'elles soient notées dans la proposition.
47. *Me opportet minui, illum autem crescere*	L'Antecedente diminuisce per metà il valor delle Figure, e il Conseguente lo accresce in quadruplo.	L'Antécédent diminue de moitié la valeur des notes, que le Conséquent a quadruplées.	L'antécédent, ou partie proposante, diminue de moitié la valeur des notes, & la partie répondante les augmente du quadruple.
48. *Qui venit post me, ante me factus est*	Il Conseguente è stato composto prima dell'Antecedente.	Le Conséquent a été composé, avant l'Antécédent.	Le conséquent ou la réponse est fait avant l'antécédent ou la proposition: alors le véritable sujet du canon n'est pas le premier chant qui se fait entendre, c'est celui qui répond.
49. *Exurge in adjutorium mihi*	Il Conseguente risponde all'Unissono.	La reponse est à l'Unisson.	Répondez à l'unisson.
50. *Vous jejuneres le quattr temps*	Il Conseguente deve rispondere dopo il valore di quattro Tempi, cioè di quattro Brevi.		Répondez après la valeur de quatre tems, c'est-à-dire de quatre brèves.
51. *Respice in me: Ostende mihi faciem tuam*	Che il Conseguente canta l'istesse Note dell'Antecedente, ma al contrario voltando la faccia l'uno verso dell'altro.	Le Conséquent execute les mêmes notes de l'Antécédent, mais dans le sens inverse comme si l'un et l'autre se regardaient.	La partie répondante chante les mêmes notes que celle qui propose, mais en sens contraire; de façon que l'une est toujours tournée vers l'autre.

52. *Cantus duarum facierum* 53. *Tolle moras placido maneant suspiria cantu*	Si può cantare il Conseguente con le Pause, e senza le Pause, ritenendo però sempre il sospiro, o sia quarto di Battuta, se trovasi scritto nell'Antecedente, affinchè resti compiuta la Battuta.	Le Conséquent peut chanter avec ou sans les silences marqués dans l'Antécédent, à l'ecception [*sic*] du soupir si l'Antécédent l'a dans sa partie, afin de completer la mesure.	On peut chanter la réponse avec les pauses ou sans les pauses, mais il faut toujours observer le soupir, s'il y en a un écrit dans la proposition, pour que les tems soient toujours complets.
54. *Dum lucem habetis credite in lucem* 55. *Qui sequitur me non ambulat, in tenebris*	Il Conseguente non canta alcuna Nota nera, ma solamente le bianche.	Le Conséquent ne dit aucune note Noire de l'Antécédent, mais seulement celles qui sont Blanches.	La partie qui répond ne chante point les notes noires, mais seulement les blanches.
56. *Intendami chi può, che m'intend'io*	L'annesso Esempio servirà di spiegazione a quest'ultimo Enigma.		M'entendra qui pourra, moi je m'entends.

(*) Le Conséquent est la réponse ou la résolution de l'Antécédent. Il peut y avoir dans un canon plusieurs Conséquents, et leur quantité établit celle des parties.

[1]. (**) On appelle Antécédent la partie qui propose le Canon.

Table 7

François Joseph Fétis's
*Table des Devises ou Inscriptions des
Canons Énigmatiques avec leur Explication*

Des devises ou inscriptions des canons énigmatiques avec leur explication[1]

1.	*Clama ne cesses* (M. 1, C. 1)	Ces huit inscriptions ou devises font connoître que le conséquent répond à toutes les notes de l'antécédent en supprimant les silences.
2.	*Otia dant vitia* (M. 2, C. 2)	
3.	*Dii faciant sine me non moriar ego* (M. 3, C. 3)	
4.	*Omnia si perdas famam servare memento, qua semel emissa: postea nullus eris* (M. 4, C. 4)	
5.	*Sperare et praestolari multos facit morari* (M. 5, C. 5)	
6.	*Otia securis insidiosa nocent* (M. 6, C. 6)	
7.	*Tarda solet magnis rebus in esse fides* (M. 7, C. 7)	
8.	*Fuge morales* (M. 8, C. 8)	
9.	*Misericordias et veritas obviaverunt sibi* (M. 9, C. 9)	Les inscriptions 9 à 22 signifient que le conséquent résout le Canon par mouvement rétrograde. S'il doit y avoir quatre parties, la troisième reprend par mouvement direct, et la quatrième par mouvement rétrograde. Les devises 13, 14, et 15 sont significatives en ce que les lettres forment les mêmes mots, soit qu'on lise de gauche à droite, ou de droite à gauche.
10.	*Justitia et pax se osculatae sunt* (M. 10, C. 10)	
11.	*Nescit vos missa reverti* (M. 11, C. 11)	
12.	*Semper contrarius esto* (M. 12, C. 12)	
13.	*Signa te signa temere me tangis et angis* (M. 13, C. 13)	
14.	*Roma tibi subito motibus ibit amor* (M. 13, C. 13)	
15.	*In girum imus noctu ecce ut consumimur igni*	
16.	*Frangenti fidem fides frangatur eidem* (M. 14, C. 14)	
17.	*Roma caput mundi si veteris, omnia vincit* (M. 15, C. 15)	
18.	*Mitto tibi metulas erige si dubitas* (M. 16, C. 16)	
19.	*Cancrizat, vel canis more haebreorum* (M. 17, C. 17)	
20.	*Retrograditur* (M. 18, C. 18)	
21.	*Vadam et veniam ad vos* (M. 19, C. 19)	
22.	*Principium et finis* (M. 20, C. 20)	
21.	*Symphoniziabis* (M. 21, C. 21)	Le conséquent répond à l'unisson.
24.	*Omne trinum perfectum* (M. 22, C. 22)	De l'antécédent on forme deux conséquents, d'où il résulte un Canon à trois parties, qui est le plus souvent, à l'*Unisson* ou à l'*Octave*.
25.	*Trinitas et unitas* (M. 23, C. 23)	
26.	*Trinitate in unitate veneremur* (M. 24, C. 24)	
27.	*Sit trium series una* (M. 25)	
28.	*Tres in unum*	
29.	*Vidi tres viri qui erant laesi homonem* (M. 26, C. 26)	
30.	*Manet alta mente repostum* (M. 27, C. 27)	L'antécédent peut avoir deux et trois conséquents, et même davantage.
31.	*De ponte non cadit, qui cum sapientia vadit* (M. 28, C. 28)	
32.	*Tantum hoc repete, quantum cum aliis sociare videbis* (M. 29, C. 29)	Une petite phrase de chant doit recommencer à l'une des parties autant de fois qu'il faut pour remplir la durée du Canon.
33.	*Non qui inciperit [sic], sed qui perseveraverit* (M. 30, C. 30)	
34.	*Itque reditque frequens* (M. 31, C. 31)	

---

[1]. Fétis 1824, vol. II, pp. 163-168. Fétis 1846, vol. II, pp. 146-148.

35.	*Crescit* (M. 32, C. 32)	*in duplo, triplo.*	Le conséquent doit doubler ou tripler la valeur des notes de l'antécédent, ou la diminuer de moitié, de deux tiers, etc.
36.	*Decrescit* (M. 33, C. 33)		
37.	*Dignora sunt priora* (M. 34, C. 34)		Le conséquent doit répondre de manière à suivre par ordre la valeur des figures, à commencer par la plus longue et passant graduellement de celle ci jusqu'à la plus petite, c'est-à-dire de la *maxime* à la *longue*; de celle-ci à la *brève*; puis à la *semibrève* ou *ronde*; ensuite à la *minime* ou *blanche*.
38.	*Descende gradatim* (M. 35, C. 35)		Il peut y avoir dans une partie un trait propre à être répété autant de fois qu'il faut pour remplir la durée du Canon, en montant ou descendant successivement d'un ton.
39.	*Ascende gradatim* (M. 36, C. 36)		
40.	*Crescit eundo* (C. 63)		Chaque fois que le Canon recommence, il hausse d'un ton.
41.	*Ascendo ad patrem meum*		
42.	*Decrescit eundo* (C. 64)		À chaque reprise le Canon baisse d'un ton.
43.	*Sol post vesperas declinat*		
44.	*Et sic de singulis* (M. 37, C. 37)		Si la première note de l'antécédent est pointée, le conséquent doit pointer toutes les siennes.
45.	*Nigra sum sed formosa* (M. 38, C. 38)		Le conséquent doit convertir en blanches les notes noires de l'antécédent.
46.	*Cœcus non judicat de colore* (M. 39, C. 39)		
47.	*Dum lucem habetis credite in lucem* (C. 91)		Le conséquent ne dit aucune note noire de l'antécédent, mais seulement celles qui sont blanches.
48.	*Qui sequitur me non ambulat in tenebris* (C. 92)		
49.	*Qui ambulat in tenebris nescit quo vadat*		
50.	*De minimis non curat praetor* (M. 46, C. 46)		Le conséquent ne doit chanter ni les blanches ni les noires de l'antécédent mais seulement les rondes et les notes d'une grande valeur.
51.	*Qui prior canit, et canat ut ipse videt posterior vero pro nigris albas, et contra*		Les notes noires de l'antécédent sont blanches dans le conséquent, et les blanches deviennent noires.
52.	*Qui se exaltat humiliabitur* (M. 40, C. 40)		La réponse doit être l'opposé de l'antécédent, c'est-à-dire que si celui ci monte, le conséquent doit descendre, et *Vice versa*.
53.	*Qui se humiliat exaltabitur* (M. 41, C. 41)		
54.	*Plutonico subiit regna* (M. 42, C. 42)		
55.	*Contraria contrariis curantur* (M. 42, C. 43)		
56.	*Qui non est mecum, contra me est* (M. 44, C. 44)		
57.	*Duo adversi adverse in unum* (M. 45, C. 45)		
58.	*Contrarium tenet iter*		
59.	*Se'l mio compagno vuol meco cantare Per altra strada li convien andare.*		
60.	*Me opportet minui, illum autem crescere* (M. 47, C. 47)		L'antécédent diminue de moitié la valeur des notes que l'antécédent a quadruplées.
61.	*Qui venit post me, ante me factus est* (M. 48, C. 48)		Le conséquent a été composé avant l'antécédent.
62.	*Exurge in adjutorium mihi* (M. 49, C. 49)		La réponse est à l'Unisson.
63.	*Respice in me: ostende mihi faciem tuam* (M. 51, C. 50)		Le conséquent exécute les notes de l'antécédent dans le sens inverse, comme si l'un et l'autre se regardoient.

Table 7

64.	*Cantus duarum facierum* (M. 52, C. 51)	Le conséquent peut chanter avec ou sans les silences de l'antécédent, à l'exception du soupir qui doit être conservé.
65.	*Tolle moras placido maneant suspiria cantu* (M. 53, C. 52)	
66.	*Post unum tempus* (C. 55)	Le conséquent doit répondre après la valeur d'un tems, c'est-à-dire une mesure de ¢ ou de C.
67.	*Vous jeunerez le quatre tems* (M. 50)	Le conséquent répond après la valeur de quatre tems, c'est-à-dire de quatre mesures de ¢ ou C.
68.	*Haec parili modulanda gradu, contraria saltu*	Le conséquent répond aux mouvements diatoniques par mouvement semblable, et aux sauts par mouvement contraire.
69.	*Has gradus aequales, contra dissultus habebit*	
70.	*Ad tonum infra* (C. 56)	Le conséquent répond un ton plus bas.
71.	*Ad tonum supra* (C. 57)	Le conséquent répond un ton plus haut.
72.	*Ad semi-ditonum* (C. 58)	Résolution à la Tierce mineure.
73.	*Ad unissonum* (C. 59)	A l'Unisson.
	Ad diatessaron (C. 59)	A la Quarte supérieure.
	Ad diapason (C. 59)	A l'Octave id.
	Ad ditonum (C. 59)	A la Tierce majeure id.
	Ad duodecimam (C. 59)	A la Douzième id.
	Ad diapente (C. 59)	A la Quinte id.
	Ad diapason diatessaron (C. 59)	A l'Octave de la Quarte id.
	Ad diapason ditonum (C. 59)	A l'Octave de la Tierce id.
	Ad eptachordum (C. 59)	A la Septième id.
	Ad diapason diapente (C. 59)	A l'Octave de la Quinte id.
		Lorsque ces denominations d'intervalles sont précédées de *Sub*, cela indique que l'intervalle est inférieur ou au dessous.
74.	*Ad hypo-diapason* (C. 60)	A l'Octave inférieure.
75.	*Ad diapason intensum* (C. 86)	A l'Octave supérieure.
76.	*Ad hyper diapason*	
77.	*Ad epi-diapason* (C. 65)	
78.	*Ad diapason expensum* (C. 87)	
79.	*Ad homophonum* (C. 69)	A l'Unisson.
80.	*Ad diapason et unissonum vicissim* (c. 85)	A l'Octave supérieure et à l'Unisson alternativement.
81.	*Ad tertiam infra* (C. 91)	A la Tierce inférieure.
82.	*Ad sub-sesqui ditonum* (C. 88)	A la Tierce mineure en dessous.
83.	*Ad hypo-diapente* (C. 67)	A la Quinte inférieure.
84.	*Ad diapente remissum* (C. 71)	
85.	*Ad epi-diapente* (C. 66)	A la Quinte supérieure.
86.	*Ad hyper diapente*	
87.	*Ad diapente expensum* (C. 72)	
88.	*Ad hyper diatessaron* (C. 68)	A la Quarte supérieure.
89.	*Ad eptachordum infra* (C. 80)	A la Septième inférieure.
90.	*Ad septimam infra* (C. 89)	
91.	*Ad nonam* (C. 73)	A la Neuvième supérieure.

92.	*Ad decimam* (C. 90)	A la Dixième supérieure.
93.	*Diapente diapason* C. 76)	Intervalle de Douzième.
	Diapason diapente (C. 76)	
94.	*Ad hypo diapason diapente* (C. 79)	A la Douzième inférieure.
95.	*Ter terni canite vocibus* (C. 74)	De l'antécédent on forme un Canon à 9 voix, qui, ordinairement, est à l'Unisson.
96.	*Congenita haec tria sunt* (C. 75)	Le Canon est à trois voix.
97.	*Ter voce ciemus* (C. 77)	
98.	*Voce ter insonuit* (C. 78)	
99.	*Quatuor vocum*	Canon à quatre voix.
100.	*Quinque vocum*	Canon à cinq voix.
101.	*Sex vocum* (C. 83)	Canon à six voix.
102.	*Tot tempora, tot sunt voces* (C. 85)	Le canon est composé d'autant de voix ou parties qu'il y a de tems ou de mesures.
103.	*Ibit, redibit* (C. 81)	La partie à qui appartiennent ces mots doit exécuter le chant depuis le commencement jusqu'à la fin, et retourner au commencement en chantant la mélodie à reculons.

Padre Martini's
Closed and Enigmatic Canons
with Solutions by
Luigi Cherubini

Canon 1

Vol. 1, Prefazione, p. 1

Repleatur os meum laude, ut cantem gloriam tuam, Psalm 70.8
Sit trium series una

Solution

On trouvera les mots latins, placés à la tête de ce Canon, et leur explication au n° 25 de la Table. Si ces mots indiquent que le Canon est à trois parties, ou Voix, les deux signes § marqués pendant sa durée, l'attestent aussi, car le nombre de ces signes dans un canon établissent la quantité de parties qu'on doit ajouter, à celle qui dit le canon, et marquent en même temps l'endroit où chacune de ces parties doit commencer la réponse au Canon.

Le Père Martini, pour ne pas suivre la route généralement indiquée par l'explication des mots latins et rendre la solution un peu moins facile et plus énigmatique, a combiné ce canon de manière en ce que le <u>1er Conséquent</u> répond à la <u>Quinte</u>, et le <u>2^d Conséquent</u> à l'<u>Octave</u>, supérieures l'une de l'autre à l'<u>Antécédent</u>.

Ce Canon, comme le sont presque tous, est appelé <u>Circulaire</u>, au <u>sans fin</u> parce qu'on peut le recommencer à l'infini.

Latin words will be found placed at the head of this Canon, and their explanation in No. 25 of the Table. If these words indicate that the Canon is in three parts or voices, the two § signs marked throughout its duration prove it also, for the number of these signs in a canon establishes the quantity of parts that must be added to the one that says the canon, and at the same time marks the place where each of these parts must begin the answer to the canon.

In order to avoid the route generally indicated by the explanation of the Latin words, and to make the solution a little less easy and more enigmatic, Padre Martini combined this canon in such a way that the <u>1st consequent</u> answers at the <u>fifth</u>, and the <u>2nd consequent</u> at the <u>octave</u>, both of them above the <u>antecedent</u>.

This canon, as almost all of the canons, is called <u>Circular</u> or <u>Endless</u> because we can restart it ad infinitum.

Padre Martini's Closed and Enigmatic Canons with Solutions by Luigi Cherubini

Luciane Beduschi

Canon 2

Vol. 1, Prefazione, p. 7

Non impedias Musicam, Ecclesiastes 32.5

Solution

Ce Canon, ainsi que l'indiquent les trois signes §, est à quatre parties. Au 1er signe qu'on rencontre, la partie que doit entrer à cet endroit répond au Canon à l'<u>Octave Supérieure</u>; au 2e signe une autre partie répond à la <u>Quinte Inférieure</u>: et, enfin au 3e signe, la dernière partie entre et répond à la <u>Quarte Supérieure</u>.

Ce Canon, négligemment composé, n'est pas exempt de reproches, par la manière dont il est écrit, et dont l'harmonie est traitée.

This canon, as the three § signs indicate, has four parts. At the first sign, the part to start at this place answers to the canon at the <u>upper octave</u>; at the second sign, another part answers at the <u>lower fifth</u>, and finally at the third sign, the last part enters and answers at the <u>upper fourth</u>.

This canon, carelessly composed, is not beyond reproach in respect of manner in which it is written and the harmony treated.

Padre Martini's Closed and Enigmatic Canons with Solutions by Luigi Cherubini

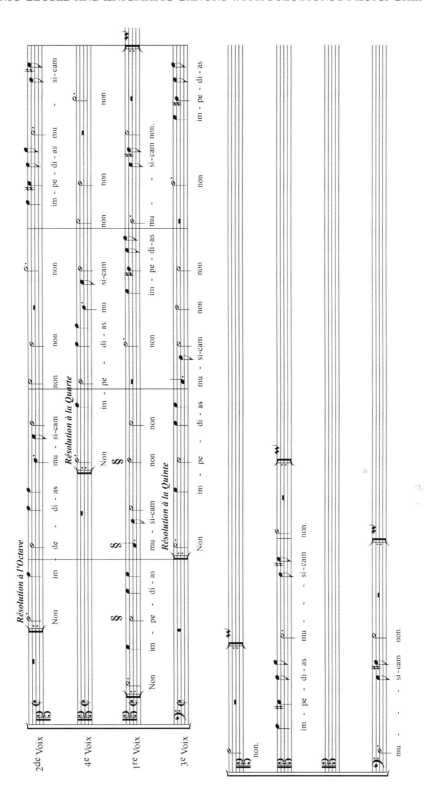

Luciane Beduschi

Canon 3

Vol. 1, Cap. 1, p. 8

Cantate Domino omnis terra, Psalm 95.1
Canon post unum Tempus
Canon 6.7.8 pars si placet

SOLUTION

Le Canon en Clef de Ténor, et celui en Clef d'Alto sont deux Canons différents. Chacun résolut à l'Unisson et si artistiquement composés, qu'on peut les exécuter séparément, et tous les deux en même temps, ce qui produit un Double Canon. Chacun d'eux est à plusieurs parties, comme l'indique assez les mots latins placés à la tête du premier (voyez le nº 55 de la Table), ainsi que les chiffres marqués à la tête du Second.

Quant à cette dernière indication, qui porte <u>6.7.8 pars si placet</u>, c'est-à-dire <u>à 6, à 7, à 8 parties à Volonté</u>, il paraît que le compositeur l'a placée là pour embarrasser davantage ceux qui tenteraient de déchiffrer ces deux canons, car par l'examen que j'en ai fait je me suis assuré que, ni le premier, ni le second ne peuvent produire, chacun à lui seul 8 parties, mais 5 seulement. Or donc, ces chiffres doivent être mis en communauté des deux canons exécutés ensemble. Moyennant cela, j'ai trouvé non seulement que ces canons pouvaient faire naître 8 parties, mais que chacun étant à 5 voix, il en résulte même, comme on va le voir, un tout composé de 10 parties.

Ce canon offre une incorrection dans sa seconde mesure à l'endroit marqué d'une «*», mais elle est légère. Mais elle n'existe plus par la réunion des deux canons.

Padre Martini's Closed and Enigmatic Canons with Solutions by Luigi Cherubini

The canon in tenor clef and the one in alto clef are two different canons. Each one is solved at the unison and so artistically composed that one can execute them separately or both at the same time, which produces a double canon. Each of them is in several parts, as indicated by the Latin words placed at the head of the first (see No. 55 of the Table), as well by the numbers marked at the head of the second.

As for this last indication (<u>6.7.8 pars si placet</u>, that is to say <u>in 6, 7, or 8 parts at will</u>), it seems that the composer placed it there to further confuse those who might try to decipher these two canons, for by the examination I made of them I have ascertained that neither the first nor the second can produce eight parts on its own, but only five. Therefore, these figures must be combined for the two canons executed together. By doing this, I found not only that these canons could produce eight parts, but that as each of them has five voices, the result is even, as we will see, in a total of ten parts.

Ce canon offre une incorrection dans sa seconde mesure à l'endroit marqué d'une « * », mais elle est légère. Mais elle n'existe plus par la réunion des deux canons.

Luciane Beduschi

Premier Canon Ouvert

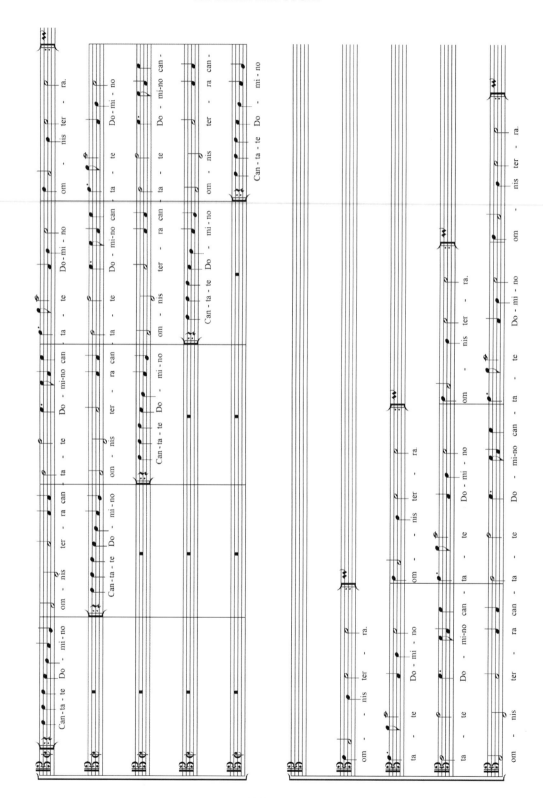

Padre Martini's Closed and Enigmatic Canons with Solutions by Luigi Cherubini

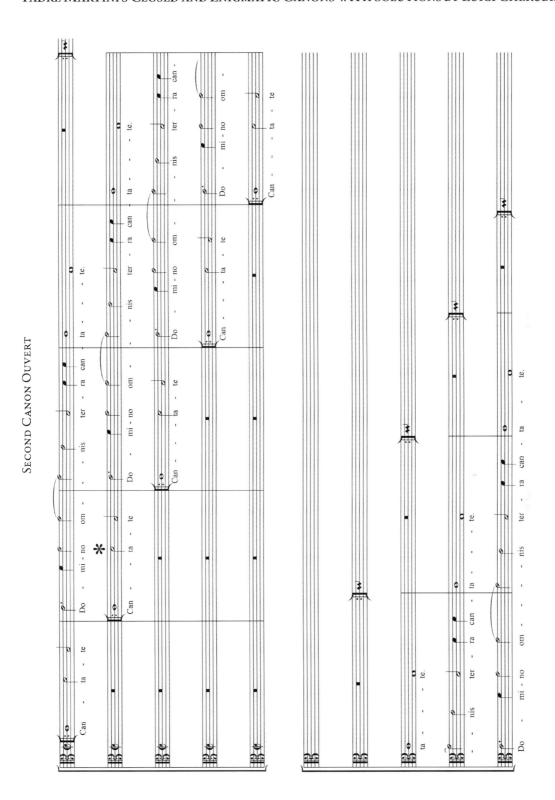

Second Canon Ouvert

Padre Martini's Closed and Enigmatic Canons with Solutions by Luigi Cherubini

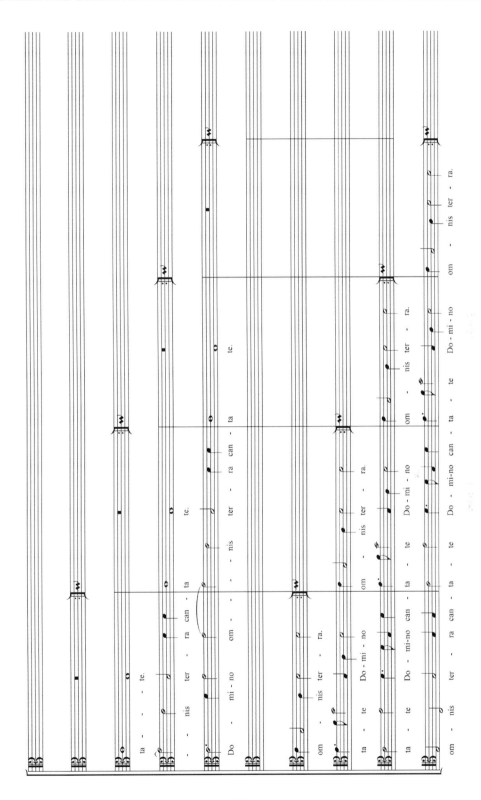

Luciane Beduschi

Canon 4

Vol. i, Cap. i, p. 13

Jubilate Deo in voce exultationis, Psalm 46.2

Solution

Ce Canon n'était pas difficile à déchiffrer. Les paroles renversées, écrites à reculon [sic] au dessus du Canon, donnent exactement, en retournant le livre sens dessus-dessous, la partie du Conséquent, qui, commençant à l'Unisson de l'Antécédent après une mesure de celui-ci, procède ensuite par mouvement contraire. Le Canon est à deux voix, et n'en comporte pas davantage.

This canon was not difficult to decipher. The reversed lyrics written backwards above the canon give exactly, by turning the book upside down, that part of the consequent which starting at the unison after a measure of the antecedent proceeds then by contrary motion. The canon is in two voices, and has no more.

Padre Martini's Closed and Enigmatic Canons with Solutions by Luigi Cherubini

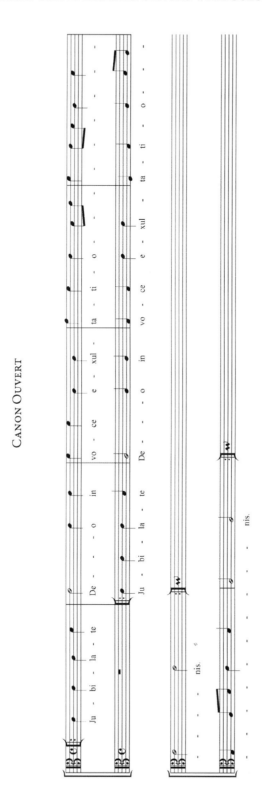

Canon Ouvert

Luciane Beduschi

Canon 5

Vol. I, Cap. II, p. 14

Psallite Domino in cithara, Psalm 97.6
Canon ad Tonum infra / ad Tonum supra

Solution

Les indications, quelles qu'elles soient, étant la Clef qui aide à ouvrir un Canon, celles qui se présentent ici, dont on peut avoir l'explication aux n°s 56, et 57 de la table des mots latins, sont les seuls moyens qui peuvent conduire à la solution de ces deux Canons.

Chaque indication étant toujours le représentant d'un Conséquent, il s'en suit nécessairement, que chacun de ces Canons, en ayant une, l'un et l'autre sont respectivement à deux voix, m'étant bien assuré d'ailleurs qu'ils ne pouvaient en comporter davantage.

En continuant mon examen je me suis assuré aussi, que tous les deux étaient composés exprès pour être exécutés simultanément, sans que le premier puisse se passer du second, et qu'ainsi il en résultait un <u>Double Canon</u> à quatre parties.

As the indications, whatever they may be, are the key that helps to unlock a canon, the ones present here, of which we can find the explanation in Nos. 56 and 57 of the Table of Latin words, are the only means that lead to the solution of these two canons.

Each indication being always the representation of a consequent, it necessarily follows that each of these canons, having one, are both in two voices — I have been assured in fact that they could not have more.

Continuing my examination, I also ascertained that both canons were expressly composed to be performed simultaneously, the first being unable to stand without the second, and thus resulting in a four-part <u>double canon</u>.

Padre Martini's Closed and Enigmatic Canons with Solutions by Luigi Cherubini

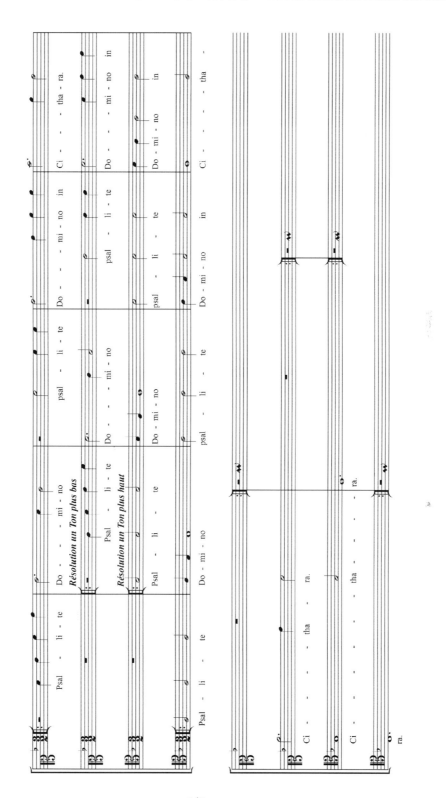

Luciane Beduschi

Canon 6

Vol. I, Cap. II, p. 24

Invocate nomen ejus cantate ei, Psalm 104. 1.2
Manet alta mente repostum

SOLUTION

Les mots latins placés en tête de ce Canon, voyez la Table au n° 27, indiquent qu'il est à plusieurs voix, et le résultat de l'examen que j'en [ai] fait a produit cinq Conséquents tous à l'<u>Unisson</u> de l'Antécédent, en comptant lequel j'ai obtenu en ensemble composé de Six Parties.

The Latin words placed at the head of this canon (see the Table in No. 27) indicate that it is in several voices. The result of the examination I made has shown there to be five consequents all at the <u>unison</u> of the antecedent; counting it I obtained a total of six parts.

Padre Martini's Closed and Enigmatic Canons with Solutions by Luigi Cherubini

Canon Ouvert

Luciane Beduschi

Canon 7

Vol. I, Cap. III, p. 25

Misericordiam et iudicium cantabo tibi Domine, Psalm 100.1
Qui se humiliat exaltabitur
Canon ad Diatessaron

Solution

Ces deux Canons faits pour aller ensemble, ne sauraient se passer l'un de l'autre. Pour me guider dans la recherche de leur solution, j'ai d'abord consulté l'explication des mots latins placés à leur tête, et je l'ai trouvée au n° 41 de la Table.

Continuant ensuite l'examen, je me suis assuré, que ces mots n'ont de rapport qu'avec le premier de ces deux Canons, dont le seul <u>Conséquent</u> qu'il puisse produire, répond à l'<u>Antécédent</u> par mouvement contraire à la <u>Double Octave</u> au-dessus.

À l'égard du Second Canon, la réponse est par mouvement semblable à la <u>Quarte au-dessus</u>.

These two canons, made to work together, cannot function without one another. To guide me in the search for their solution, I first consulted the explanation of the Latin words placed at their head, and I found it in No. 41 of the Table.

Continuing the examination, I made sure that these words have nothing to do with the first of these two canons, whose only possible <u>consequent</u> responds to the antecedent by contrary motion at the upper <u>double-octave</u>.

As for the second canon, the answer is by similar motion at the <u>upper fourth</u>.

Padre Martini's Closed and Enigmatic Canons with Solutions by Luigi Cherubini

Luciane Beduschi

Canon 8

Vol. i, Cap. iii, p. 27

Cantabo Deo Jacob, Psalm 74.9
Canon ad Semi-Ditonum
Symphonizabis

Solution

Voyez d'abord, aux n°s 21 et 58 de la Table, la signification des mots qui sont à la tête de ces deux Canons. Ensuite le signe § placé au-dessous de la première note du premier Canon, indique positivement que le Conséquent commence la réponse en même temps que l'Antécédent.

Quant à ce qui se rapporte au second Canon, comme il n'y avait pas de signe qui marque l'entrée du Conséquent, qui doit répondre à l'Unisson, il fallait en chercher l'endroit, ce que j'ai trouvé, ainsi qu'on le verra par le Canon ouvert.

Ces canons, composés dans un style libre, peuvent, si l'on veut, s'exécuter séparément, toutefois l'effet en est meilleur étant réunis.

First refer, in Nos. 21 and 58 of the Table, to the meaning of the words at the head of these two canons. In addition, the sign § placed below the first note of the first canon indicates without doubt that the consequent begins its answer at the same time as the antecedent.

Coming now onto the second canon, there being no sign marking the entrance of the consequent, which must answer at the unison, it was necessary to look for its place, which I found, as will be seen at the open canon.

These canons, composed in a free style, can, if one likes, be executed separately, but the effect is better if they are combined.

Padre Martini's Closed and Enigmatic Canons with Solutions by Luigi Cherubini

Luciane Beduschi

Canon 9

Vol. I, Cap. IV, p. 28

Cantemus Domino gloriose enim magnificatus est, Exodus 15.1
Canon ad Unissonum, et bis ad Diatessarn. Diapason, et Diapason-Diatessaron

Solution

Ce Canon est à six parties, en comptant l'Antécédent qui est la partie même du Canon, et les mots marqués en tête représentant cinq Conséquents, car le mot bis ajouté au mot <u>Diatessaron</u>, veut dire <u>deux fois à la Quarte</u>. Voyez l'explication de ces mots Gréco-latins au n° 59 de la Table.

This canon is in six parts, including the antecedent, which is the very part of the canon. The words marked at the head represent the five consequents, because the word *bis* added to the word <u>Diatessaron</u> means <u>twice at the fourth</u>. See the explanation of these Greco-Latin words in No. 59 of the Table.

Padre Martini's Closed and Enigmatic Canons with Solutions by Luigi Cherubini

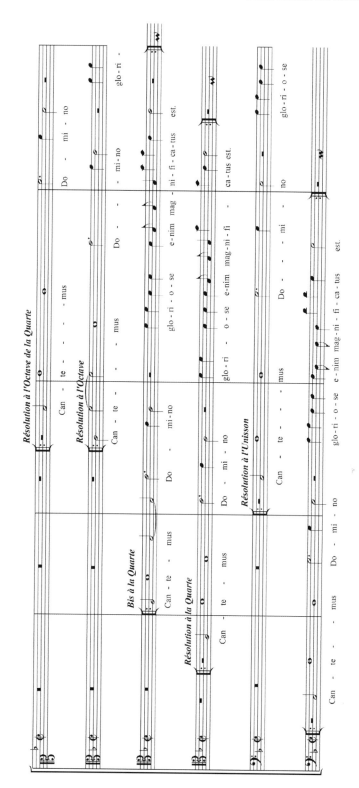

Luciane Beduschi

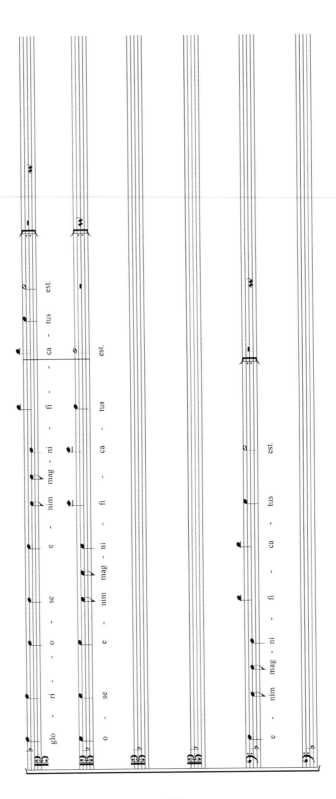

Padre Martini's Closed and Enigmatic Canons with Solutions by Luigi Cherubini

Canon 10

Vol. I, Cap. IV, p. 36

Clangentibus tubis, muri illico coruerunt, Joshua 6.20
Qui querit invenit

Solution

D'après les mots latins placés en tête de ce Canon, il fallait chercher pour trouver; cette recherche a produit un Canon à <u>Six Voix</u> à l'<u>Unisson</u>.

According to the Latin words placed at the head of this canon, one must seek to find; my search found a <u>six-voice</u> canon at the <u>unison</u>.

Luciane Beduschi

Canon Ouvert

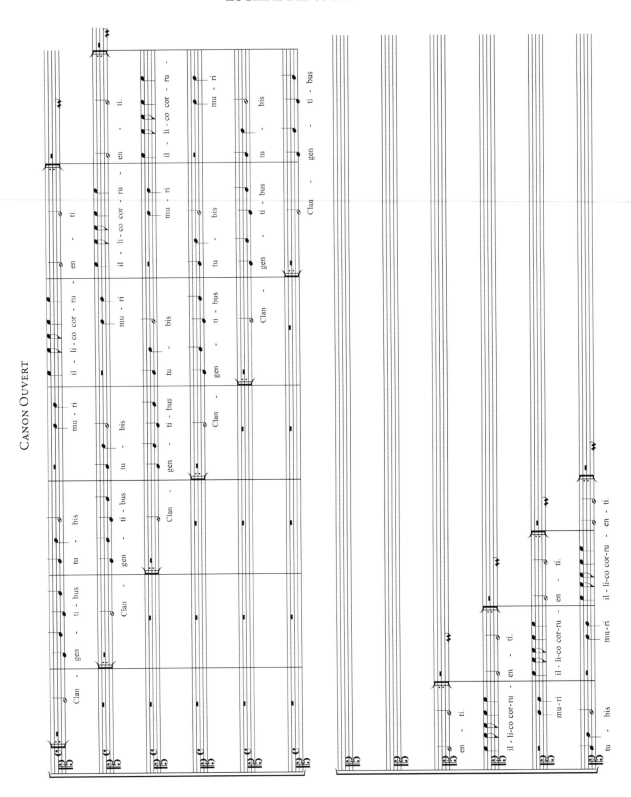

Padre Martini's Closed and Enigmatic Canons with Solutions by Luigi Cherubini

Canon 11

Vol. i, Cap. v, p. 37

Domino canam psallam Domino Deo, Judges 5.3
Tres in unum

Solution

L'Analyse de ce Canon a donné pour résultat trois parties à l'<u>Unisson</u>, comme l'indiquent assez les mots latins marqués en tête, dont la signification se trouve consignée au n° 25 de la Table.

The analysis of this canon resulted in a three-part [canon] at the <u>unison</u>, as indicated by the Latin words marked at the head, whose meaning is recorded in No. 25 of the Table.

Luciane Beduschi

Canon Ouvert

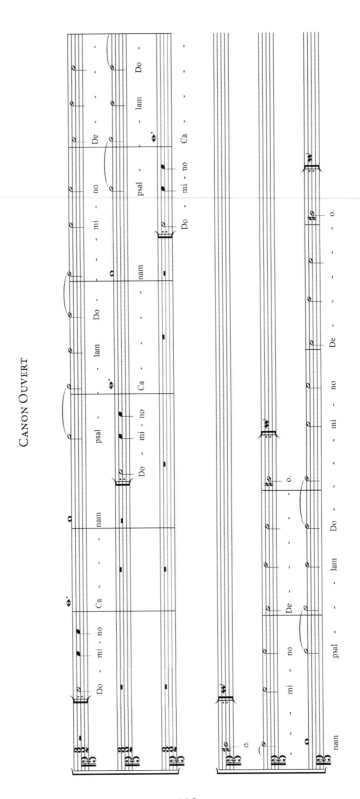

Padre Martini's Closed and Enigmatic Canons with Solutions by Luigi Cherubini

Canon 12

Vol. i, Cap. v, p. 41

Iste est David cui cantabant in choris, I Samuel 29.5
Canon ad Unissonum

Solution

Si ces quatre parties chantent en même temps, sans avoir égard au Canon indiqué par les § que chacune d'elle [sic] renferme, elles produiront un ensemble très correct, quoique à compter de la sixième mesure jusqu'à la fin il ne soit pas assez mélodieux, ni aussi plain, ni autant harmonieux que au commencement. Voyez l'exemple.

Mais en déployant chacun de ces Canons à l'<u>Unisson</u>, on obtiendra un <u>Quadruple Canon</u> formant un ensemble à Seize Parties. Voyez ci-après la partition de ces quatre Canons.

If these four parts sing at the same time, ignoring the canon indicated by the signs § that each of them contains, they will produce a very suitable whole, although from the sixth measure until the end it is not melodious enough, neither as plain nor as harmonious as in the beginning. See the example.

But by deploying each of these canons at the <u>unison</u>, one obtains a <u>quadruple canon</u> forming a total of sixteen parts. See below for the score of these four canons.

Padre Martini's Closed and Enigmatic Canons with Solutions by Luigi Cherubini

Canon Ouvert

Luciane Beduschi

Padre Martini's Closed and Enigmatic Canons with Solutions by Luigi Cherubini

Canon 13

Vol. I, Cap. VI, p. 42

Cantate et exultate et psallite, Psalm 97.4
Canon ad Diatessaron / ad Sub-Diatessaron
Non qui inceperit, sed qui perseveraverit

Solution

Pour avoir l'explication des mots qui sont à la tête de ces deux Canons, consultez, d'abord les n°s 30 et 59 de la Table. Ensuite, les deux clefs placées l'une avant l'autre à chaque Canon indiquent qu'ils sont respectivement à deux voix, et que l'Antécédent de chacun est représenté par la partie dont la clef est marquée la première.

Ces deux Canons séparés, dont la mesure de l'un C *est à quatre temps, et celle de l'autre* ¢ *est à deux temps, sont composés de manière à être exécutés non autrement que simultanément, et pendant que le premier marque quatre temps, le second n'en marque que deux. Il résulte donc de cette réunion, un double Canon à quatre Parties.*

To see the explanation of the words at the head of these two canons, refer to Nos. 30 and 59 of the Table. After this, note that the two clefs placed one before the other at each canon indicate that they are each in two voices; the antecedent of each [canon] is represented by the part whose key is marked first.

These two separate canons, one of which, in C, has a four-beat time signature, and the other of which, in ¢, has two, are composed to be executed in no other way than simultaneously; while the first marks four beats, the second marks only two. From this juxtaposition results a double canon in four parts.

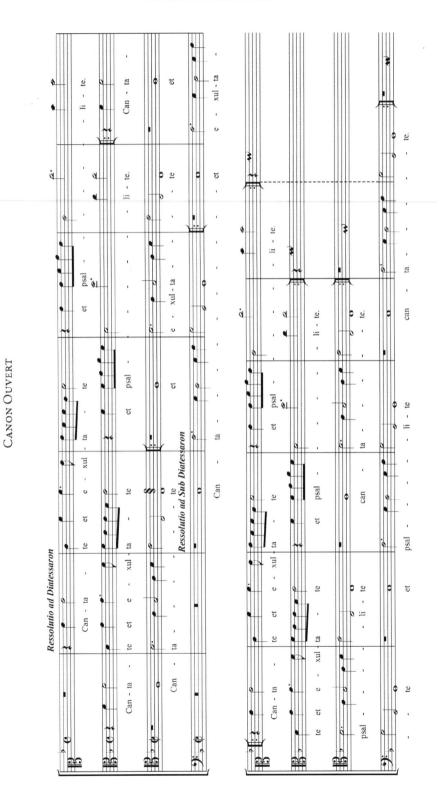

Padre Martini's Closed and Enigmatic Canons with Solutions by Luigi Cherubini

Canon 14

Vol. i, Cap. vii, p. 54

Introite portas eius in confessione atria eius in hymnis, Psalm 99.4
Canon ad Sub-Diatessaron, Sub-Diapason, et Sub-Diapason-Diatessaron

Solution

Par le nombre d'indications, qui sont marquées, en tête du présent Canon, et dont l'explication est consignée au n° 59 de la Table, on est assuré que ce canon est à quatre voix.

Une fois cela déterminé, reste à découvrir l'endroit où chacun de ces conséquents, représentés par les trois indications citées, doit entrer pendant la durée du Canon; c'est ce qu'on verra ci-dessous.

Thanks to the number of indications, which are marked at the head of the present canon and whose explanation is recorded in No. 59 of the Table, we can rest assured that this canon is in four voices.

Having determined this, all that remains to discover is the place where each of these consequents, represented by the three indications mentioned above, must enter throughout the duration of the canon. This is what we will see below.

Luciane Beduschi

Canon Ouvert

Padre Martini's Closed and Enigmatic Canons with Solutions by Luigi Cherubini

Canon 15

Vol. I, Cap. VII, p. 57

Confitemini Dominum in cithara in psalterio decachordo cantate ei, Psalm 32.8
Canon ad Diapason-Ditonum

Solution

Ce Canon, pas difficile à résoudre, est à deux Voix, puisqu'il n'a qu'un seul Conséquent, indiqué par les mots latins marqués au-dessus, dont la signification se trouve au n° 59 de la Table.

This canon, not difficult to solve, is in two voices, since it has only one consequent indicated by the Latin words whose meaning is in No. 59 of the Table.

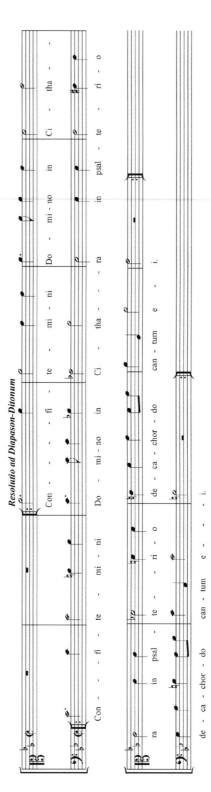

Padre Martini's Closed and Enigmatic Canons with Solutions by Luigi Cherubini

Canon 16

Vol. I, Cap. VIII, p. 58

Cumque caneret psaltes facta est super eum manus Domini, 2 Kings 3.15
Quinque Voc. Post unum Tempus

Solution

<u>Quinque Vocum</u> veut dire à cinq Voix. Voyez ensuite au n° 55 de la Table la signification des mots <u>Post Unum Tempus</u>. Comme il n'y a nulle autre indication relative à l'intervalle auquel chaque Conséquent doit répondre à l'Antécédent, l'analyse de ce Canon a prouvé, que les cinq voix qui le composent sont toutes à l'<u>Unisson</u>.

<u>Quinque Vocum</u> means five voices. Beyond that, refer to No. 55 of the Table for the meaning of the words <u>Post Unum Tempus</u>. There being no other indication as to the interval at which each consequent must answer to the antecedent, the analysis of this canon has proved that the five voices are all at the <u>unison</u>.

Canon Ouvert

Padre Martini's Closed and Enigmatic Canons with Solutions by Luigi Cherubini

Canon 17

Vol. I, Cap. IX, p. 61

In voce exultationis et confessionis sonus epulantis, Psalm 41.5
Canon ad Sub-Diatessaron
Qui post me venit ante me factus est

Solution

Voyez l'explication, aux n°s 48, et 59 de la Table, de tous les mots latins qui sont placés à la tête de ce Canon; d'après ces indications, celui-ci est à deux parties, et le Conséquent précède l'Antécédent, ce dernier étant à une quarte au-dessous de l'autre.

See the explanation in Nos. 48 and 59 of the Table of all the Latin words placed at the head of this canon. According to these indications, the canon is in two parts and the consequent precedes the antecedent, the latter being a fourth below the former.

Luciane Beduschi

Canon Ouvert

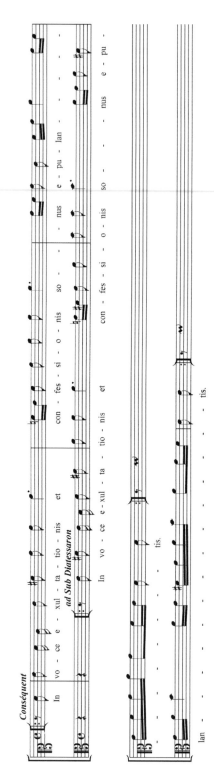

Padre Martini's Closed and Enigmatic Canons with Solutions by Luigi Cherubini

Canon 18

Vol. i, Cap. x, p. 67

Confitebor tibi Domine in gentibus et nomini tuo cantabo, Psalm 41.5
Canon ad Duodeciman. Clama ne cesses
Tertia pars si placet

Solution

La clef qui aide à ouvrir ce canon, est renfermée dans le sens énigmatique des premiers mots latins placés au-dessus. La seconde dénomination latine, et le signe § indiquent premièrement à quel intervalle le Conséquent doit répondre, et ensuite à quel endroit de l'Antécédent il doit entrer. Voyez l'explication de tous les mots qu'on vient de citer aux n°s 1, et 59 de la Table.

Quant aux mots Tertia pars si placet, *qui accompagnent la mélodie notée au-dessous du Canon, ils prouvent d'abord que celui-ci est particulièrement à deux parties, et qu'il ne devient à trois que par l'addition de cette troisième partie, s'il plaît toutefois de l'ajouter, attendu que le Canon peut à la rigueur s'en passer.*

The key that helps to unlock this canon is hidden in the enigmatic sense of the first Latin words placed above it. The second Latin term and the sign § indicate, in turn: the interval at which the consequent must answer, and at what place of the antecedent it must enter. See the explanation of all these words in Nos. 1 and 59 of the Table.

The words *Tertia pars si placet*, which accompany the melody notated below the canon, firstly show that the canon is inherently in two parts, and that it becomes a three-part canon only by the addition of this third part, if one wishes however to add it however one pleases, since the canon may not require it.

Padre Martini's Closed and Enigmatic Canons with Solutions by Luigi Cherubini

Canon 19

Vol. 1, Dissertazione prima, p. 164

Cantabo Domine in vita mea, Psalm 103.3
Canon ad Sub-Diapason
Qui sequitur me non ambulat in tenebris
Clama ne cesses

Solution

Voyez d'abord aux n°ˢ 1, 54, et 59 de la Table, l'explication des mots latins qui précèdent ces deux canons composés de manière à être exécutés en même temps, et à former par leur association un Double Canon à quatre parties. D'après ces indications la solution n'était pas difficile à obtenir.

First, see Nos. 1, 54, and 59 of the Table for the explanation of the Latin words that precede these two canons composed to be executed at the same time, and to form by their association a double four-part canon.

By following these indications, the solution was not difficult to obtain.

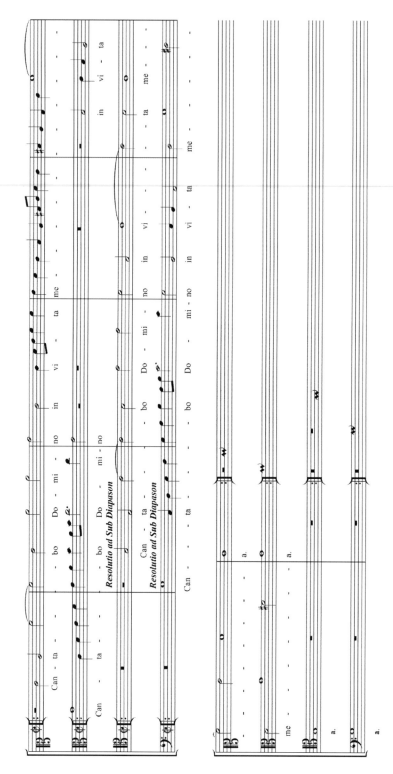

Padre Martini's Closed and Enigmatic Canons with Solutions by Luigi Cherubini

Canon 20

Vol. I, Cap. X, p. 74

Omnis terra adoret te et canat tibi, Psalm 65.4
Canon ad Unisson, ad Hypo-Diapason, et Hyper-Diatessaron

Solution

Puisque ce Canon porte avec lui trois indications, dont l'explication se trouve aux n°s 60 et 61 de la Table, il est par conséquent à Quatre Parties.

On va voir par l'ouverture suivante de ce Canon, qu'il est composé en style libre, et que d'ailleurs il est un peu négligemment traité.

Since this canon carries with it three indications — explained in Nos. 60 and 61 of the Table — it is therefore in four parts.

We will see from the opening of this canon that it is composed in a free style, and that moreover it is a little carelessly treated.

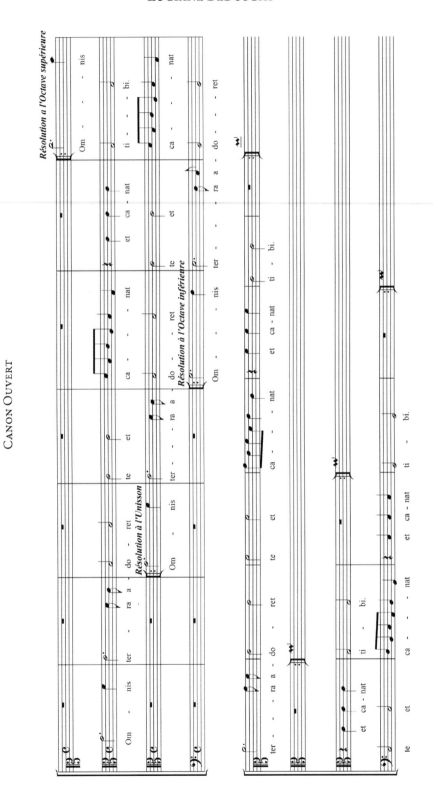

Padre Martini's Closed and Enigmatic Canons with Solutions by Luigi Cherubini

Canon 21

Vol. i, Cap. vi, p. 53

Cantate Domino psalmum dicite nomini ejus cantate, Psalm 67.4
Canon ad Unisson, et bis Ad Diapente. Crescit eundo
Canon ad Duodeciman

Solution

Consultez avant tout la Table, aux n°s 63, et 59, pour savoir ce que signifient les Indications Latines qui accompagnent ces Canons. Les mots, <u>Crescit eundo</u> sont applicables à ces deux Canons, puisque l'un, et l'autre sont faits pour être exécutés simultanément. Le <u>bis</u> ajouté au mot, <u>Ad Diapente</u>, indique que cette réponse au Canon, doit être dite deux fois à cet Intervalle.

Quoique le signe qui marque la mesure de chaque Canon ne soit pas le même, cela n'empêche pas que la mesure de l'un ne coïncide avec la mesure de l'autre, et qu'elles ne se trouvent d'accord pour marcher ensemble ; car pendant que la première marque un <u>Temps</u>, ou une <u>Mesure</u> selon sa valeur, la seconde en fait autant selon la sienne. De toutes ces notions il résulte un Double Canon à Six parties, comme on va le voir par l'ouverture de ces deux Canons réunis.

Consult the Table in Nos. 63 and 59 to know what the Latin indications that accompany these canons mean. The words <u>*Crescit eundo*</u> are applicable to these two canons, since they are made to be executed simultaneously. The <u>*bis*</u> added to the word <u>*Ad Diapente*</u> indicates that this answer to the canon must be stated twice at this interval.

Although the signs indicating the time signature of each canon are not the same, this does not prevent the meter of one from coinciding with the meter of the other, and [does not mean] that they cannot agree to work together: while the first marks one <u>beat</u>, or one <u>measure</u> according to its value, the second does as much according to its own. All these indications produce a double canon in six parts, as we will see in the opening of these two combined canons.

Padre Martini's Closed and Enigmatic Canons with Solutions by Luigi Cherubini

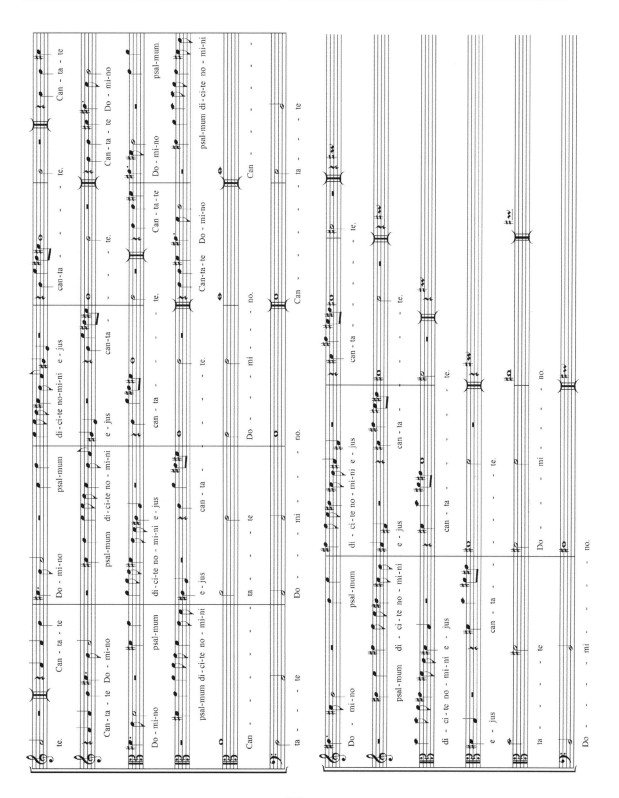

Luciane Beduschi

Canon 22

Vol. 1, Dissertazione prima, p. 83

Laudabo nomen Dei cum cantico, Psalm 68.31
Canon ad Sub-Diatessaron, ad Epi-Diapason, et Epi-Diapente

Solution

Les trois indications marquées au-dessus du canon représentent trois Conséquents, lesquels réunis à l'Antécédent forment un ensemble à quatre voix. La première opération à faire pour déchiffrer ce Canon, est de consulter la table aux n°s 59, 65, et 66 afin de connaître la signification des trois indications ci-dessus. Cette connaissance une fois acquise, ce qui reste à faire est aisé à trouver.

The three indications above the canon represent three consequents, which when combined with the antecedent form a total of four voices. The first step to deciphering this canon is consulting Nos. 59, 65, and 66 of the Table to see the meaning of the three indications. Having acquired that understanding, what remains to be done is easy to find.

Padre Martini's Closed and Enigmatic Canons with Solutions by Luigi Cherubini

Luciane Beduschi

Canon 23

Vol. II, Prefazione, p. i

Incipe Menalios mecum mea tibia versus, Theocritus
Sit trium series una

SOLUTION

Ce Canon est à trois voix à l'Unisson; les mots latins marqués à sa tête l'indiquent assez: voyez le n° 25 de la Table. La Solution du reste est par trop facile, pour me croire obligé d'en dire davantage.

This canon is in three voices at the Unison; the Latin words at its head indicate this clearly: see No. 25 of the Table. The solution of what remains is too easy for me to feel obliged to say more.

Padre Martini's Closed and Enigmatic Canons with Solutions by Luigi Cherubini

Canon Ouvert

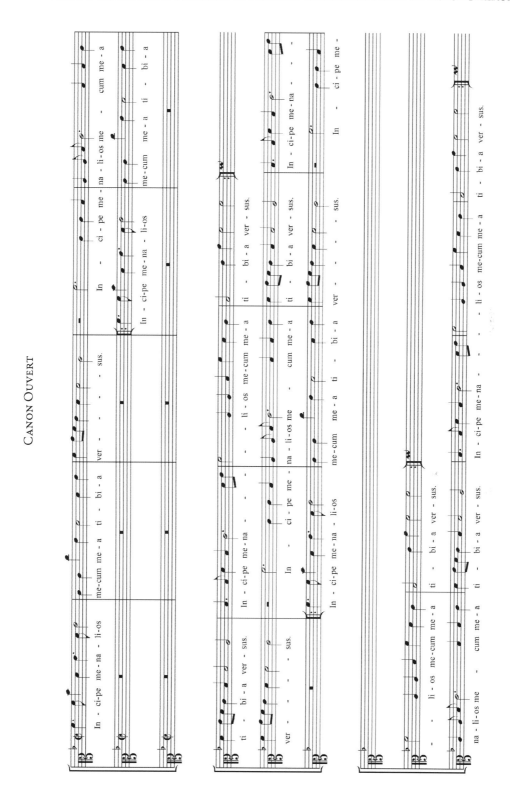

Luciane Beduschi

Canon 24

Vol. 1, Dissertazione seconda, p. 334

Hymnum novum cantemus Deo nostro, Judith 16.15
Canon ad Sub-Diapason

Solution

Ces deux Canons peuvent s'exécuter séparément; réunis ils forment un Double Canon à quatre voix. L'indication <u>Ad Sub Diapason</u>, voyez-en la signification au nº 59 de la Table, se rapporte à chacun de ces deux Canons.

These two canons can be executed separately; together, they form a double canon in four voices. The indication <u>*Ad Sub Diapason*</u> (see the meaning in No. 59 of the Table) applies to each of these two canons.

Padre Martini's Closed and Enigmatic Canons with Solutions by Luigi Cherubini

Canon Ouvert

Résolutions à l'Octave inférieure

Luciane Beduschi

Canon 25

Vol. I, Cap. XI, p. 80

Cantate Domino et benedicite nomini eius, Psalm 95.2
Canon ad Homophonum, vel ad Equisonum

Solution

Ce Canon, qui porte avec lui deux Indications, (Voyez les n°s 69 et 70 de la Table), n'est qu'à deux Voix, attendu que c'est par l'une, ou bien par l'autre de ces Indications que le Conséquent peut également répondre à l'Antécédent.

This canon, which comes with two indications (see Nos. 69 and 70 of the Table), has only two voices, since it is by one or by the other of these indications that the consequent can answer to the antecedent.

Padre Martini's Closed and Enigmatic Canons with Solutions by Luigi Cherubini

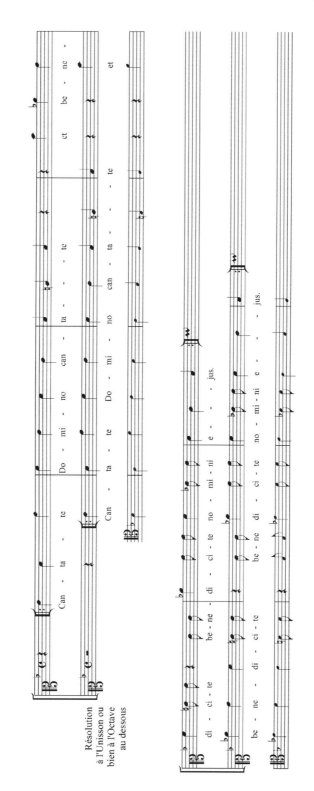

Luciane Beduschi

Canon 26

Vol. I, Cap. XI, p. 75

Regna terrae cantate Deo, Psalm 67.33
Canon Decrescit eundo ad Hypo-Diapente / ad Hyper-Diatessaron

Solution

Voyez d'abord la Table aux n°s 64, 67, et 68, pour connaître la signification des Indications dont ces Canons sont précédés.

Les mots latins, <u>Decrescit eundo</u> se rapportent également à l'un et l'autre Canon, qui tous les deux sont composés pour être chantés en même temps, et dont il résulte un double Canon à quatre voix, ainsi qu'on pourra s'en convaincre en voyant la partition suivante.

Refer first to Nos. 64, 67, and 68 of the Table to learn the meaning of the indications that precede these canons.

The Latin words <u>*Decrescit eundo*</u> also refer to both canons, which are composed to be executed at the same time. This results in a double canon in four parts — as we can see for ourselves by examining the score.

Padre Martini's Closed and Enigmatic Canons with Solutions by Luigi Cherubini

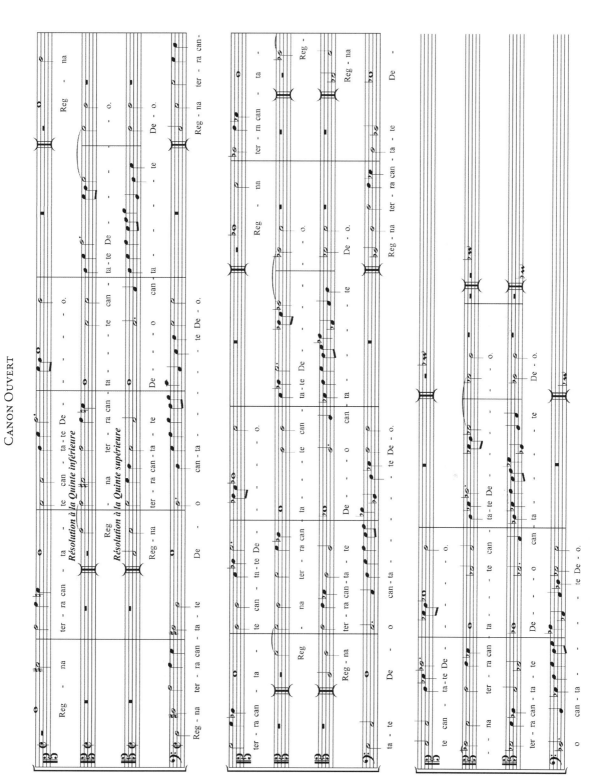

Luciane Beduschi

Canon 27

Vol. II, Prefazione, p. xx

Argentum carmen strepens Phrygiis numeris sonabo, Anacreon
Canon ad Unissonum, et bis ad Eptacordum / Canon ad Diapason

SOLUTION

Il faut, premièrement, consulter la Table au n° 59, pour s'instruire de ce que signifient les indications placées autour de ces Canons, qui sont faits de manière à marcher ensemble. Le mot <u>bis</u> marqué à côté de la seconde indication du premier Canon, veut dire que celui-ci produit deux réponses à cet intervalle.

Il résulte enfin de tout cela deux <u>Antécédents</u>, et quatre <u>Conséquents</u>, ce qui donne un Double Canon à Six parties.

First, consult No. 59 of the Table to learn what is meant by the indications placed on these canons, which are made to fit together. The word <u>bis</u> marked next to the second phrase in the first canon means that it produces two answers at this interval.

All this ultimately produces two <u>antecedents</u> and four <u>consequents</u>, yielding a double canon in six parts.

Padre Martini's Closed and Enigmatic Canons with Solutions by Luigi Cherubini

Luciane Beduschi

Canon 28

Vol. I, Cap. VIII, p. 60

Lauda Jerusalem Dominum canet Deum tuum Sion, Psalm 147.1
Canon ad Diapente remissum, et ad Nonam, et Diapente expansum
Nec mihi, nec tibi, sed dividatur

SOLUTION

 Les auteurs anciens, et le Père Martini, n'ayant pas donné, à ma connaissance, l'explication du sens énigmatique renfermé dans les mots latins Nec Mihi *&c. placés en première ligne de ce Canon, il fallait malgré l'absence de ce guide, déchiffrer ce même Canon, dont je suis venu à bout, aidé par les autres indications latines, l'explication desquelles est consignée aux n*os *71, 72, et 73 de la Table.*

 Ces indications Ad Diapente remissum *&c., étant au nombre de trois, et représentant autant de Conséquents, il s'ensuit qu'en comptant l'Antécédent il résulte de cette addition un ensemble à quatre voix.*

 En revenant au sens caché de l'énigme, je pense que celui-ci se rapporte à la désunion, ou à l'incohérence qui règne dans la succession des Tons, toujours croissante, entre l'Antécédent, et les Conséquents.

 En effet le canon lui-même étant composé de deux phrases, chacune dans un Ton différent montant de l'une, à l'autre à la distance d'un degré majeur, produit avec les Conséquents qui l'imitent fidèlement un enchaînement de Tons étrangers au Ton principal, et qui force l'Antécédent, ainsi que les Conséquents de recommencer la première phrase du Canon, toujours un Ton plus haut de la seconde.

 Ce canon devient à la longue inexécutable, quand même on le transposerait d'une quinte plus bas en le commençant.

Padre Martini's Closed and Enigmatic Canons with Solutions by Luigi Cherubini

As ancient authors and Padre Martini have not, to my knowledge, given an explanation of the enigmatic meaning contained in the Latin words *Nec Mihi* etc. written in the first line of this canon, it was necessary to decipher it. Despite the lack of their guidance I succeeded with the aid of other Latin indications, whose explanations of them are recorded in Nos. 71, 72, and 73 of the Table.

The indications *Ad Diapente remissum* etc., being three and representing as many consequents, imply that adding the antecedent results in a total of four voices.

Returning to the hidden meaning of the enigma, I think that this one relates to the disunity, or to the incoherence that reigns in the succession of keys always increasing between the antecedent and the consequent.

Indeed the canon itself is composed of two sentences, each in a different key, ascending one major second from one to the other. This means that the consequents, which faithfully imitate these sentences, produce a sequence of keys foreign to the main one. This forces both the antecedent and the consequents to always restart the first sentence of the canon one tone higher than the second sentence.

This means that the canon ultimately becomes unperformable, even if starting it transposed down a lower fifth.

Luciane Beduschi

Canon Ouvert

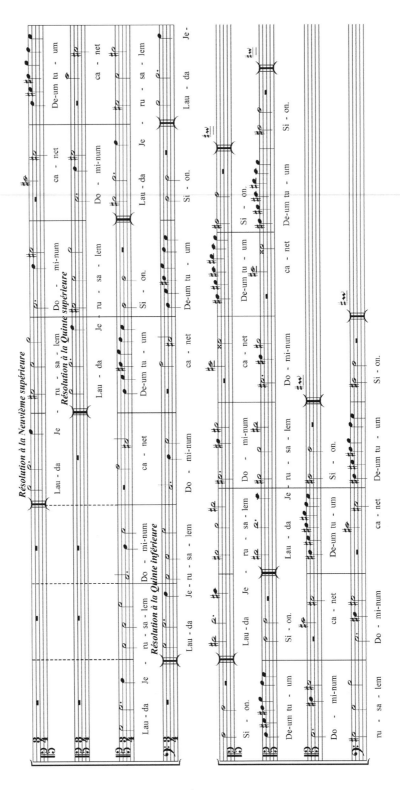

Padre Martini's Closed and Enigmatic Canons with Solutions by Luigi Cherubini

Canon 29

Vol. 1, Dissertazione seconda, p. 165

Cantate Domino in cymbalis modulamini illi psalmum novum, Judith 16.2
Me pente, me tesseris phones

Solution

Les anciens auteurs ne m'ont fourni non plus l'explication du sens énigmatique des mots latins qui précèdent ce Canon. Le Père Martini cependant, dans son Histoire de la Musique dit que, <u>Pente</u>, signifie, <u>Distance de Cinq Voix ou Sons</u>; et que <u>Tessera</u>, veut dire, <u>Distance de Quatre Sons</u>.

D'après ce guide j'ai cherché la Solution du Canon, et l'ayant trouvée j'ai pensé, que le sens énigmatique de ces mots latins <u>Mepente</u> &c., devait s'expliquer ainsi: <u>Le Conséquent doit répondre d'abord à la quinte de l'Antécédent, et ensuite à la quarte</u>.

Le travail que j'ai fait pour déchiffrer ce Canon, m'a convaincu que, par la manière dont il est composé, il ne peut produire qu'un seul Conséquent, ce qui donne un ensemble à deux parties.

Here again, the ancient authorities have not provided me with the explanation of the enigmatic sense of the Latin words that precede this canon. Padre Martini however, in his History of Music, says that <u>Pente</u> means a <u>distance of five voices or sounds</u>; and that <u>Tessera</u> means a <u>distance of four sounds</u>.

According to this guide, I sought the solution of the canon, and having found it I thought that the enigmatic sense of these Latin words <u>Mepente</u> etc. must be explained as follows: <u>the consequent must answer first at the fifth of the antecedent, and then at the fourth</u>.

The work I have done to decipher this canon has convinced me that, by the way it is composed, the canon can only produce one consequent, yielding a two-part whole.

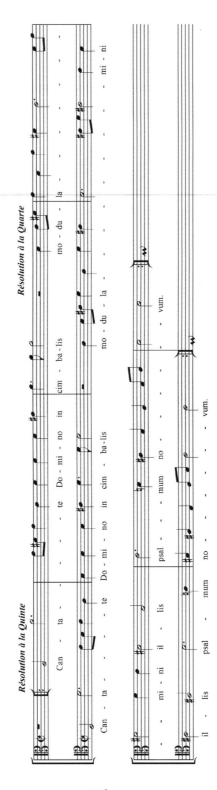

Padre Martini's Closed and Enigmatic Canons with Solutions by Luigi Cherubini

Canon 30

Vol. 1, Dissertazione terza, p. 335

Psallite Deo nostro, Psalm 46.6
Omne trinum perfectum

Solution

L'explication des mots latins qui précèdent ce Canon, est consignée au n° 22 de la Table. Nul doute, d'après cela, qu'il ne soit à trois voix, et à l'<u>Unisson</u>, ainsi qu'on le verra dans la partition ci-dessous.

Je n'ai ensuite d'autres remarques à faire à l'égard de ce Canon, sinon que sa composition est négligemment traitée, et, si j'ose le dire, fautive même dans les dernières mesures, soit par l'arrangement des parties, soit par la manière dont les accords sont renversés.

The explanation of the Latin words that precede this canon is recorded in No. 22 of the Table. This explanation leaves no doubt that the canon has three voices at the <u>unison</u>, as it will be seen in the score below.

I do not therefore have any further remarks regarding this canon, except that its composition is careless and, if I may say so, even faulty in the last bars, in terms of the arrangement of the parts and in the way the chords are inverted.

Luciane Beduschi

Canon Ouvert

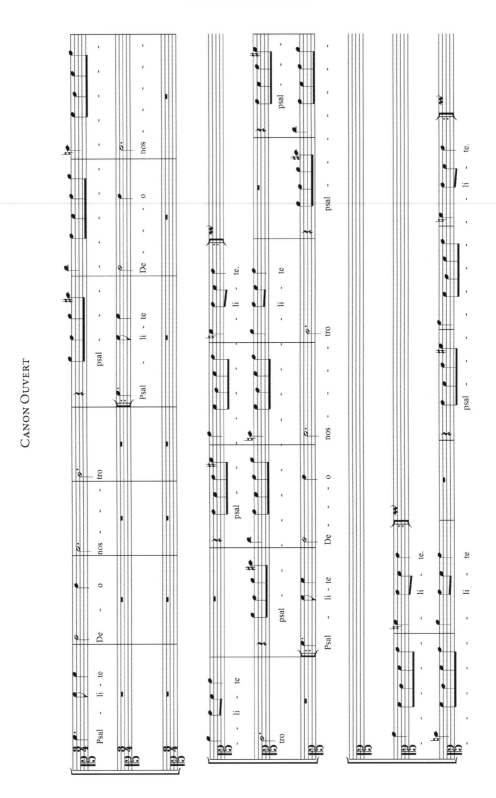

Padre Martini's Closed and Enigmatic Canons with Solutions by Luigi Cherubini

Canon 31

Vol. I, Dissertazione terza, p. 446

Sumite psalmum date tympanum psalterium incundum cum cithara, Psalm 80.2
Canon ad Unissonum

Solution

 En examinant attentivement ces trois Canons, je me suis assuré d'abord, que l'indication <u>Ad Unissonum</u> *(à l'Unisson) placée en tête du premier, devait d'appliquer de même aux deux autres, et qu'ensuite chacun de ces Canons étant à deux voix, et composés tous les trois de manière à être exécutés en même temps, il en résulterait un Triple Canon à Six parties.*

 Pour faire marcher le troisième Canon avec les deux autres, dont la mesure est différente, il faut avant tout, examiner la valeur de ce signe ¢. *Lorsque le signe* C *est barré une seule fois* ¢ *sa valeur diminue de moitié; et quand il est barré deux fois* ¢ *elle est réduite à un quart.*

 Pour lors les figures de notes, dans la prolation de la mesure dont il s'agit ici, en suivant cette progression décroissant à l'égard de leurs valeurs respectives, il s'en suivra que la <u>Blanche</u> *égalera la valeur d'une* <u>Croche</u> *de la mesure* C, *et la* <u>Noire</u> *celle d'une* <u>Double Croche</u> *de la même mesure. De cette façon leur deux mesures* C *et* ¢ *se correspondront et pourront marcher ensemble parfaitement, ainsi qu'on va s'en convaincre par l'ouverture de ces trois Canons réunis à la page suivante.*

Luciane Beduschi

In carefully examining these three canons, I first made sure that the phrase *Ad Unissonum* (at the unison), placed at the head of the first, also applied to the other two, and, having done this, that each of these canons had two voices and were composed to be performable at the same time, the result being a six-part triple canon.

To make the third canon work with the other two (its time signature being different), it is necessary first of all to examine the value of this sign ₵. When the sign C is crossed once ₡, its value decreases by half, and when it is crossed twice ₵, it is reduced to a quarter.

Thus, if we retain the proportional relationships of the time signatures in question here, the progressive shortening of the respective durations of the rhythmic values means that a <u>half note</u> will equal the value of an <u>eighth note</u> of the time signature C, and the <u>quarter note</u> the value of a <u>sixteenth note</u>. In this way the two time signatures ₡ and ₵ will correspond to each other and can work together perfectly, as we can see for ourselves on the following page by looking at the opening of these three combined canons.

Padre Martini's Closed and Enigmatic Canons with Solutions by Luigi Cherubini

Canon Ouvert

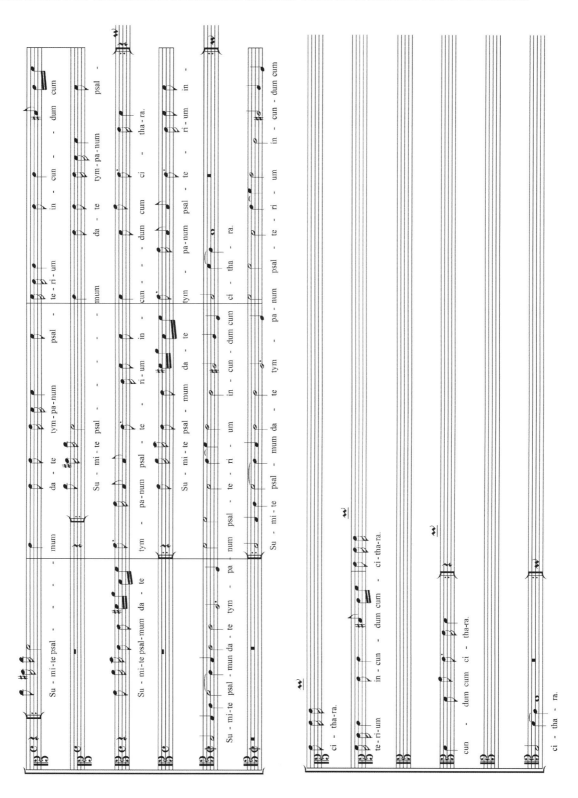

Luciane Beduschi

Canon 32

Vol. ii, Cap. i, p. 1 A

A Musis Heliconiadibus incipiamus canere, Hesiod
Ter terni canite vocibus

SOLUTION

Les mots latins Ter terni *&c., voyez le n° 74 de la Table, établissent un Canon à 9 voix, le travail que j'ai fait pour le déchiffrer, m'a prouvé que les neuf voix ne pouvaient se répondre autrement qu'à l'Unisson.*

The Latin words *Ter terni* etc., see No. 74 of the Table, establish a 9-voice canon. The work I have done to decipher it proved to me that the nine voices could only answer to each other at the unison.

Padre Martini's Closed and Enigmatic Canons with Solutions by Luigi Cherubini

Canon Ouvert

Luciane Beduschi

Padre Martini's Closed and Enigmatic Canons with Solutions by Luigi Cherubini

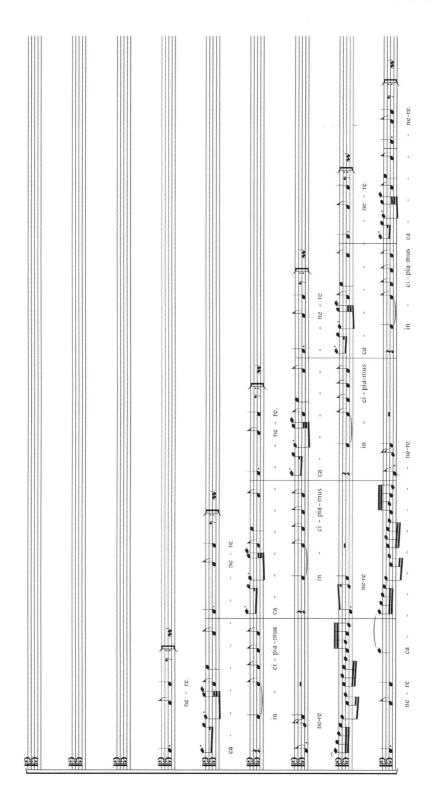

Luciane Beduschi

Canon 33

Vol. ii, Cap. i, p. 6

Cignorum instar varii modi sunt accinendi, Pratinas
Congenita haec tria sunt

Solution

L'explication des mots latins Congenita *&c., consignée au nº 75 de la Table, fait connaître que le présent Canon est à trois voix; et l'examen que j'ai fait de ce même Canon m'a procuré que ces trois voix se succèdent à l'Unisson.*

The explanation of the Latin words *Congenita* etc., recorded in No. 75 of the Table, reveals that the present canon is in three voices; and the examination I made of the same canon assured me that these three voices succeed one another at the unison.

Padre Martini's Closed and Enigmatic Canons with Solutions by Luigi Cherubini

Canon Ouvert

Luciane Beduschi

Canon 34

Vol. II, Cap. II, p. 7

Jovi patri canendo oblectant, Hesiod
Justitia et Pax se osculatae sunt

Solution

L'Indication latine, marquée au-dessus de ce Canon, se trouve avec son explication au n° 10 de la Table. D'après cela ce Canon s'exécute en même temps en avant, et en arrière, ce qui lui donne le surnom de Retrograde, *ou de* Cancarizzato. *Il est à deux parties, et n'en comporte guère un plus grand nombre.*

The Latin indication marked above this canon and its explanation are in No. 10 of the Table. It indicates that this canon is executed forwards and backwards at the same time, which gives to it the nickname of *Retrograde* or *Cancarizzato*. It is in two parts, and does not involve a greater number.

Padre Martini's Closed and Enigmatic Canons with Solutions by Luigi Cherubini

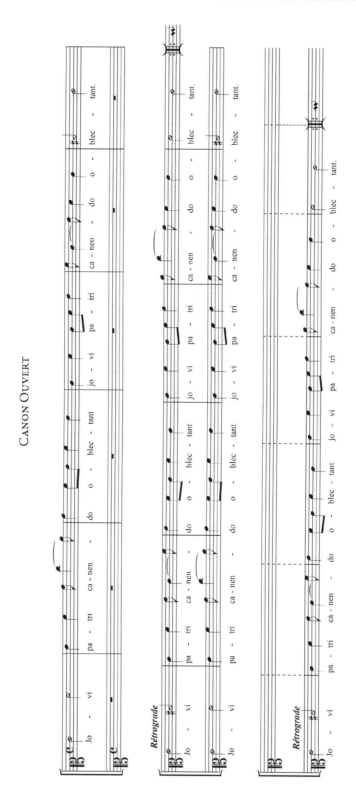

Luciane Beduschi

Canon 35

Vol. ii, Cap. ii, p. 30

Cano Peana magnum Deum Apollinem, Epigr. Poet. Graec., Lib. i.
Canon ad Diapente, Diapason, et Diapason-Diapente

Solution

Les indications, au nombre de trois, en tête de ce Canon (voyez leur signification au n° 59 de la Table) établissent trois Conséquents, qui joints à l'Antécédent forment un Canon à quatre Voix.

The indications, numbering three, at the head of this canon (see their meaning in No. 59 of the Table) establish three consequents, which together with the antecedent form a four-voice canon.

Padre Martini's Closed and Enigmatic Canons with Solutions by Luigi Cherubini

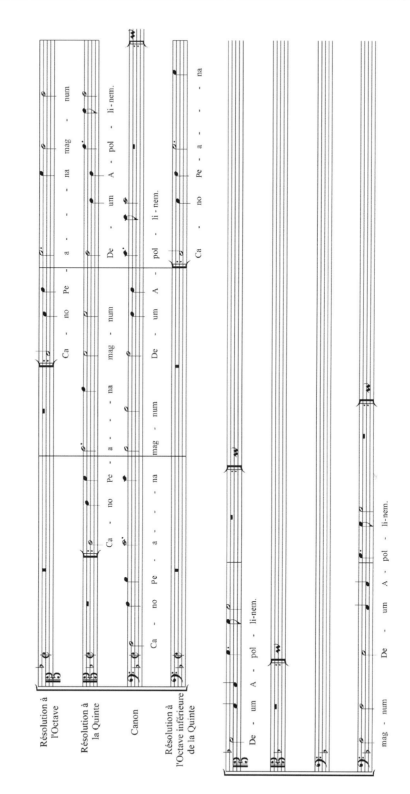

Luciane Beduschi

Canon 36

Vol. II, Cap. III, p. 31

Canam semideorum quorum audiunt opera poetae, Homer
Canon ad Sub-Diapason-Diapente, ad Sub-Diapason, Sub-Diapente

Solution

Un égal nombre d'indications qu'au Canon précédent, la signification desquelles est consignée au n° 59 de la Table, fait que celui-ci est de même à quatre voix. Il ne restait, d'après cela autre chose à faire pour le déchiffrer, sinon qu'à établir chaque Conséquent qui lui est affecté; c'est ce qu'on verra ci-après à l'ouverture de ce Canon.

An equal number of indications to the previous canon, the meaning of which is recorded in No. 59 of the Table, means that this canon also is in four voices. Nothing therefore remained to be done to decipher the canon, except to establish each consequent attached to it, which can be seen below at the opening of this canon.

Padre Martini's Closed and Enigmatic Canons with Solutions by Luigi Cherubini

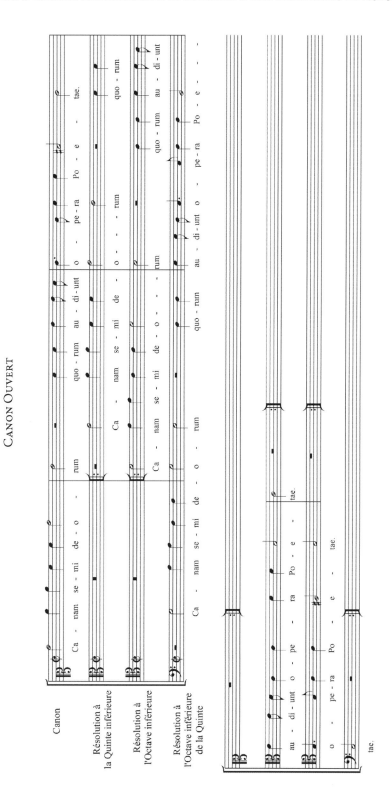

Luciane Beduschi

Canon 37

Vol. ii, Cap. iii, p. 40

Sirenum cantus delectant, Homer

SOLUTION

Comme ce Canon ne porte avec lui nulle indication qui puisse guider à le déchiffrer, c'est à force de travail qu'il a fallu atteindre ce but. C'est donc par un examen scrupuleux que je suis parvenu à m'assurer que ce Canon est susceptible de deux aspects, offrant chacun un artifice particulier.

Le premier de ces deux aspects présente un ensemble à trois voix, formé par deux Conséquents à l'unisson de l'Antécédent, comme on va le voir ci-après.

Le second aspect, offre ce même canon exécuté d'abord par l'Antécédent tel qu'il est, et ensuite continué par lui par mouvement contraire transposé à la quinte supérieure. Les Conséquents répondent également à l'Unisson, et l'artifice, sous ce second aspect, est tel, qu'il produit des Conséquents jusqu'au nombre de cinq, lesquels, en comptant l'Antécédent forment un ensemble à Six parties.

As this canon carries no indication that can guide us to decipher it, it was work that enabled this goal to be reached. It was through a scrupulous examination that I managed to assure myself that there are two possible versions of this canon, each with its own characteristics.

The first of these two facets consists of a total of three voices, formed by two consequents at the unison with the antecedent, as we will see below.

The second facet consists of the same canon executed by the antecedent: first as it is, and then as continued by contrary motion transposed at the upper fifth. The consequents answer at the unison, and the skill shown in this second facet is such that it produces consequents up to the number of five, which, counting the antecedent, form a six-part whole.

Padre Martini's Closed and Enigmatic Canons with Solutions by Luigi Cherubini

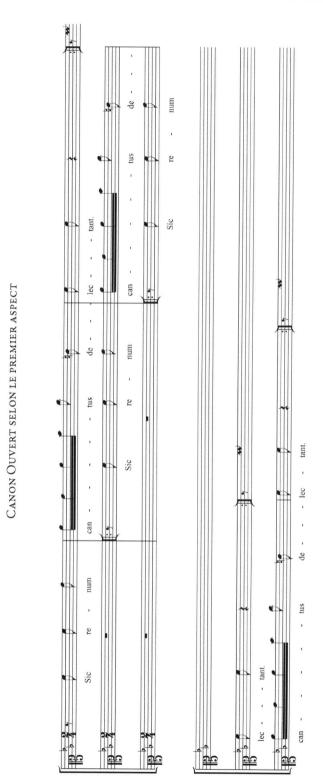

Canon Ouvert selon le premier aspect

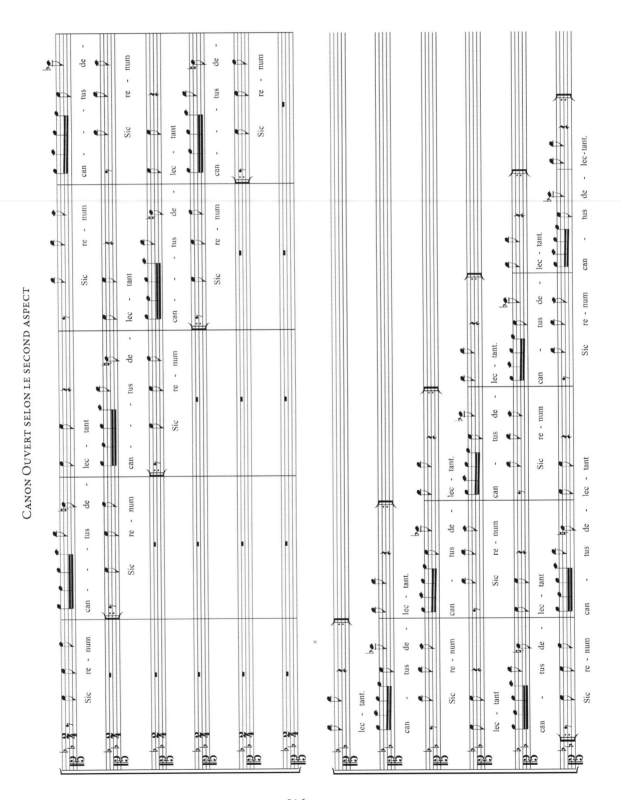

Padre Martini's Closed and Enigmatic Canons with Solutions by Luigi Cherubini

Canon 38

Vol. II, Cap. IV, p. 41

Tebana bella cantus Troiana cantat alter, Anacreon
Ter voce ciemus
Voce ter insonuit

Solution

D'après les mots latins <u>Ter Voce</u> *&c., qu'on trouvera marqués avec leur signification aux n°s 77, et 78 de la Table, la solution de ces deux Canons est très aisée. L'un, et l'autre étant à trois voix, et composés pour être chantés simultanément, il résulte de tout cela un double Canon à Six Parties.*

Taking into account the Latin words <u>Ter Voce</u> etc., which we will find their meaning in Nos. 77 and 78 of the Table, the solution of these two canons is very easy. Since both are in three voices and composed to be sung simultaneously, the result is a double six-part canon.

Luciane Beduschi

Canon Ouvert

Padre Martini's Closed and Enigmatic Canons with Solutions by Luigi Cherubini

Canon 39

Vol. II, Cap. v, p. 58

Carmine cunctos mortales mulcent, Homer
Canon ad Hypo-Diapason-Diapente

Solution

L'explication des mots tracés aux dessus [sic] de ce Canon est au n° 79 de la Table. Par l'effet de cette indication, qui ne désigne qu'un seul Conséquent, ce Canon est à deux Voix.

The explanation of the words written above this canon is in No. 79 of the Table. As a result of this indication, which designates only one consequent, this canon has two voices.

Luciane Beduschi

Canon Ouvert

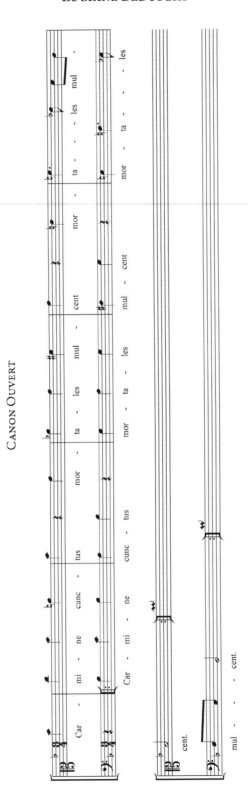

Padre Martini's Closed and Enigmatic Canons with Solutions by Luigi Cherubini

Canon 40

Vol. II, Cap. IV, p. 57

Hymnum canunt demulcent que nationes hominum, Homer
Canon 4 vocib. et 8 voc. si placet
Qui deprimit se, altissimo fit altior

Solution

Lest mots latins, Qui deprimit *&c., ont la même signification, que ceux qui sont placés dans la Table depuis le n° 40, jusqu'à et compris le n° 45; consultez leur explication. À l'égard ensuite de ceux placés à côté du Canon, ils indiquent que celui-ci peut être à 4 voix, ou à 8 voix si l'on veut.*

D'après l'explication des premiers mots latins, le Conséquent répond à la Quinte *ou à la* Douzième *de l'Antécédent, en procédant toujours par* mouvement contraire.

Pour que ce même Canon puisse s'exécuter à huit voix, il faut que l'Antécédent après avoir dit le Canon par mouvement droit, le redise par mouvement contraire, et que le Conséquent après avoir d'abord répondu par mouvement contraire, continue le canon par mouvement droit. Le Canon ainsi établi par les quatre premières parties, les quatre autres suivront exactement le même ordre : d'où il résulte que les Antécédents deviennent des Conséquents, et que ceux-ci à leur tour deviennent des Antécédents.

The Latin words, Qui deprimit etc., have the same meaning as those placed in the Table from No. 40 up to and including No. 45; refer to these for an explanation. The words placed next to the canon indicate that it can have four voices, or eight voices if desired.

The explanation of the first Latin words reveals that the consequent answers at the fifth or at the twelfth of the antecedent, always proceeding by contrary motion.

For this canon to be performed in eight voices, the antecedent, after having stated the canon in straight motion, must repeat it in contrary motion, and the consequent, after having first answered in contrary motion, must continue the canon in straight motion. The canon thus established by the first four parts, the other four will follow exactly the same order: antecedents become consequents, and these in turn become antecedents.

Luciane Beduschi

Canon Ouvert à 4 Parties

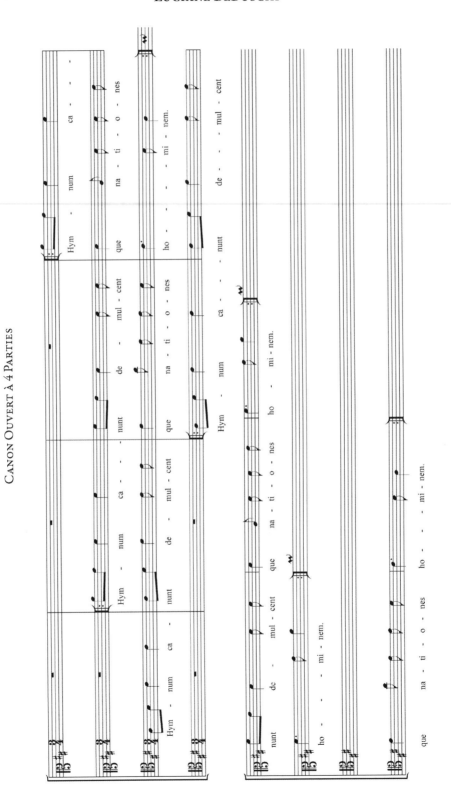

Padre Martini's Closed and Enigmatic Canons with Solutions by Luigi Cherubini

Canon Ouvert à 8 Parties

Luciane Beduschi

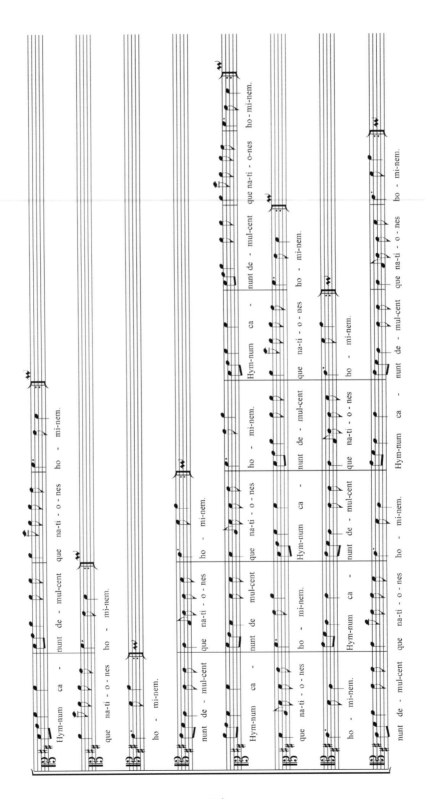

Padre Martini's Closed and Enigmatic Canons with Solutions by Luigi Cherubini

Canon 41

Vol. ii, Cap. v, p. 85

Dulcis repente nostro erumpit ore cantus, Anacreon
Canon ad Eptachordum infra, vel ad tonum supra
Ad Diapente

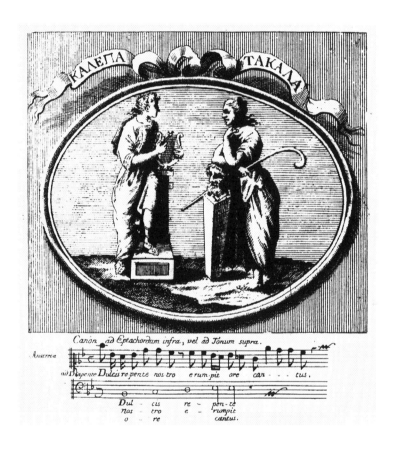

Solution

  Avant tout on doit consulter la Table aux n°s 80, et 57 pour avoir l'explication des mots latins écrits *au-dessus du Premier Canon, et au n° 59 pour connaître celle de l'indication marquée au-dessus du Second Canon.*
  Quant au mot Vel, *qui fait partie de la première inscription, cela veut dire que le Conséquent peut répondre soit à l'un soit à l'autre intervalle.*
  À l'égard ensuite du signe de la mesure du Second Canon, ainsi retourné ↄ *on doit supputer chaque note dans cette mesure, comme ayant la moitié de la valeur de celle qu'elle représente par sa figure, de façon qu'une* <u>Ronde</u> *vaudra*

une Blanche, celle-ci une Noire et la Pause une demie Pause. Ainsi cette mesure retournée de la sorte, moyennant la réduction de la valeur des notes, répond exactement à la mesure du premier Canon.

De cette manière les deux Canons marcheront simultanément, et les paroles du second Canon écrites les unes au-dessus des autres, indiquent que la Phrase, dont il est composé, doit être dite dans l'Antécédent, et dans le Conséquent autant de fois que les paroles ont de lignes, pendant quoi le premier canon recommence à plusieurs reprises afin de remplir la durée du second.

Ces deux Canons réunis offrent dans la première mesure une harmonie fort nue, et même fautive, puisque les deux parties font entendre l'effet mal déguisé de deux octaves, et de deux quintes qu'on n'excuse, en quelque sorte, que parce qu'on ne pouvait faire autrement par rapport à l'imitation canonique, et à ses conséquences.

Voyez l'ouverture de ces deux Canons réunis à la page suivante.

Before all else, consult the Table in Nos. 80 and 57 for an explanation of the Latin words written above the first canon, and in No. 59 for an explanation of the indication marked above the second canon.

The word *Vel*, which is part of the first inscription, means that the consequent can answer either at one or at the other interval.

As for the time signature of the second canon, turned in this way ↄ, the necessary calculation is that each note in this measure has half of the value of what its figure represents, so that a whole note will be worth a half note, a half note will be a black note, and a whole rest will be a half rest. This time signature turned in this way, by reducing the value of the notes, corresponds exactly to the time signature of the first Canon.

This allows the two canons to move simultaneously, and the words of the second canon, written one above the other, indicate that the sentence of which it is composed must be stated in the antecedent and repeated in the consequent for as many times as the lyrics have lines, during which the first canon repeats several times in order to fill the duration of the second.

These two canons combined offer a very bald harmony in their first measure; indeed, even faulty, since the two parts lead us to hear the poorly disguised effect of two octaves and two fifths, which one somehow excuses only because one could not do otherwise in relation to canonical imitation and its consequences.

See the opening of these two canons combined on the following page.

Padre Martini's Closed and Enigmatic Canons with Solutions by Luigi Cherubini

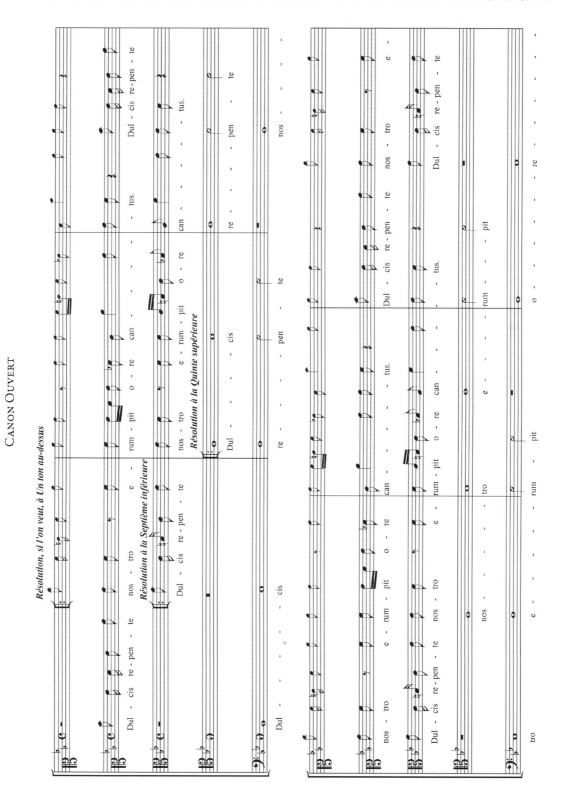

Luciane Beduschi

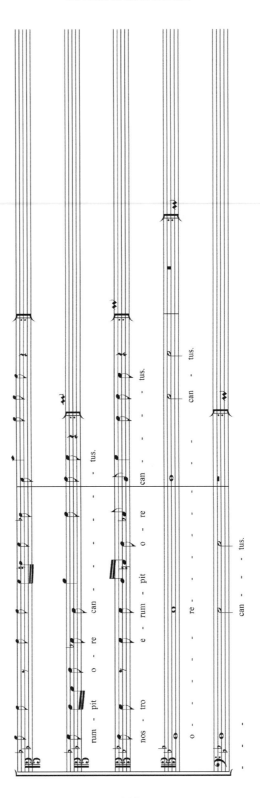

Padre Martini's Closed and Enigmatic Canons with Solutions by Luigi Cherubini

Canon 42

Vol. II, Cap. VI, p. 86

Canoris tibiis emittebant cantum, Hesiod
Canon ibit, redibit
Canon ad Tonum, infinit, et finit

Solution

On trouve l'explication des mots <u>Ibit</u> &c., et du Canon <u>ad Tonum</u> &c. aux n°s 81, et 82 de la Table. Moyennant cela la solution n'est pas embarrassante. On verra à l'Ouverture de ce Canon, que tout cela s'exécute en même temps, soit sous le rapport des deux chants, qui produisent un ensemble à trois voix, soit sous celui des signes de la mesure, l'un différent de l'autre, et dont nous avons déjà eu des exemples, dans quelques-uns des Canons précédents.

The explanation of the words *<u>Ibit</u>* etc., and *Canon <u>ad Tonum</u>* etc. can be found in Nos. 81 and 82 of the Table. With the explanation, the solution is not difficult. We will see at the opening of this canon that all this is carried out at the same time, both in terms of the two melodies, which produce a total of three voices, and in terms of the time signatures, the one different from the other — of which we have already had examples in some of the preceding canons.

Luciane Beduschi

Canon Ouvert

Padre Martini's Closed and Enigmatic Canons with Solutions by Luigi Cherubini

Canon 43

Vol. II, Cap. VI, p. 102

Tibia vero cantabunt mihi pastores duo, Theocritus
Canon ad Sub-Diapason, vel ad Unisson

SOLUTION

Ce Canon, selon l'indication qui est au-dessus, est à deux voix, le Conséquent répond à l'<u>Octave Inférieure</u>, ou bien à l'<u>Unisson</u>, si on l'aime mieux.

This canon, according to the indication above it, is in two voices. The consequent answers at the <u>lower octave</u>, or at the <u>unison</u>, if preferred.

Padre Martini's Closed and Enigmatic Canons with Solutions by Luigi Cherubini

Canon 44

Vol. II, Cap. VII, p. 123

Obloquitur numeris septem discrimina vocum et hic septem calida nervis, Virgil

Solution

Lorsqu'un Canon n'est accompagné d'aucune indication, ses Conséquents, s'il est susceptible d'en avoir plusieurs, répondent à l'Antécédent communément à <u>l'Unisson</u>; toutefois ils peuvent aussi répondre à tout autre intervalles. Mais après avoir examiné attentivement le présent Canon, je me suis assuré que les Conséquents répondent tous à l'Unisson. Que ce même Canon, ensuite soit à Sept Voix, les paroles sur lesquelles il est composé l'indiquent positivement.

When a canon is not accompanied by any indication, its consequents, if it is likely to have more than one, answer the antecedent at the <u>unison</u>; however, they can also answer at any other interval. Nevertheless, after carefully examining the present canon, I concluded that all the consequents answer at the unison. The words on which it is composed indicate without doubt that this canon is in seven voices.

Canon Ouvert

Luciane Beduschi

234

Padre Martini's Closed and Enigmatic Canons with Solutions by Luigi Cherubini

Luciane Beduschi

Padre Martini's Closed and Enigmatic Canons with Solutions by Luigi Cherubini

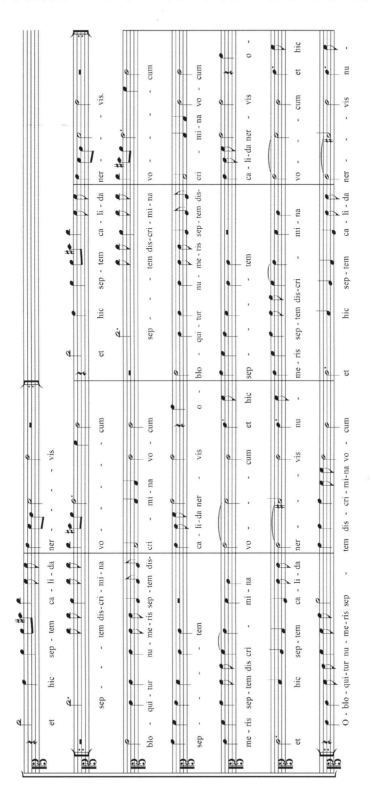

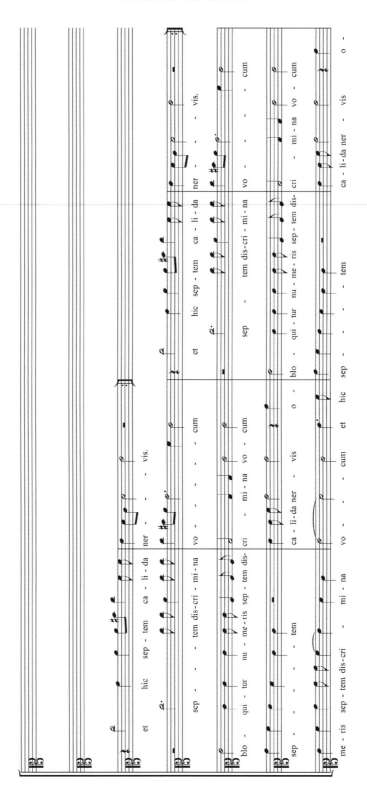

Padre Martini's Closed and Enigmatic Canons with Solutions by Luigi Cherubini

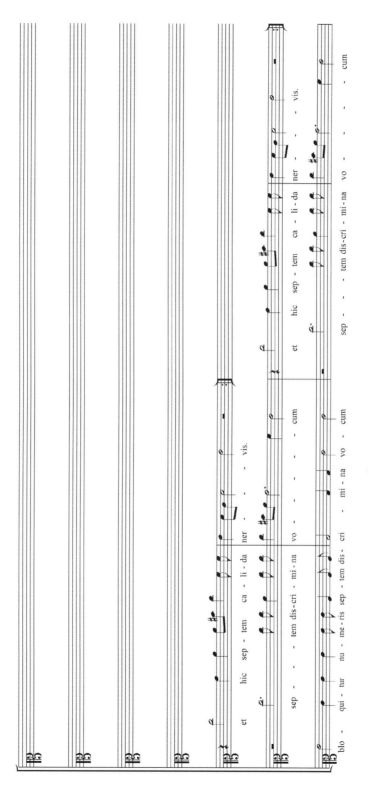

Luciane Beduschi

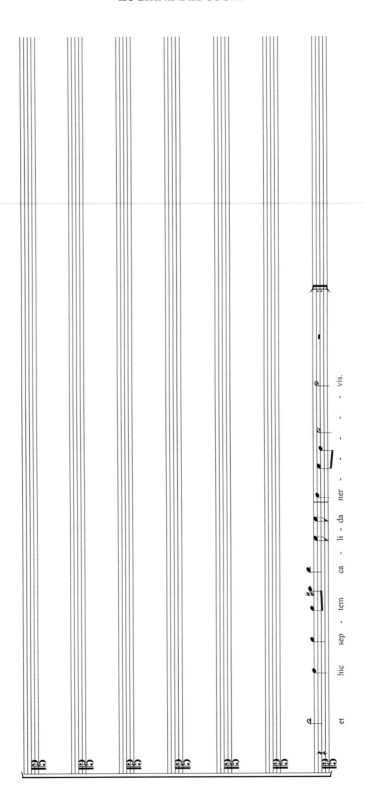

Padre Martini's Closed and Enigmatic Canons with Solutions by Luigi Cherubini

Canon 45

Vol. II, Cap. VII, p. 103

Concentus reciprocos voce modulabantur, Sophocles
Canon ad Sub-Diapason
Canon ad Diapason

SOLUTION

Consultez la Table au n° 59 pour connaître la signification des deux Indications marquées en tête de ces Canons. Chacun de ceux-ci étant accompagné d'une seule indication, n'a qu'un seul Conséquent; ainsi l'un et l'autre sont à deux voix: et comme ces deux Canons sont faits pour être exécutés en même temps, il résulte de cette réunion un Double Canon à quatre parties.

See the Table in No. 59 for the meaning of the two indications written at the head of these canons. Each one, being accompanied by a single indication, has only one consequent, meaning both are in two voices; as these two canons are made to be performed at the same time, this produces a four-part double canon.

Luciane Beduschi

Canon Ouvert

Padre Martini's Closed and Enigmatic Canons with Solutions by Luigi Cherubini

Canon 46

Vol. II, Cap. VIII, p. 124

Placent convivia et oblectant cantus, Hesiod
Canon ad Hypo-Diapason. Bis dicitur
Canon ad Hyper-Diapason
Otia dant vitia

Solution

Voyez d'abord la Table au n° 60, touchant la première indication du premier Canon, et aux n°ˢ 61, et 2 à l'égard des deux indications du Second Canon. Quant au mots Bis dicitur, *ils signifient qu'on doit dire deux fois le premier Canon, et puis s'arrêter; cette condition, jointe aux signes ⌒ qu'on rencontre dans l'étendue de ces deux Canons composés pour marcher simultanément, fait que le Double Canon qui en résulte n'est point circulaire, mais il est terminé. Chacun de ces Canons étant à deux voix, leur réunion forme un ensemble à quatre parties.*

First refer to No. 60 of the Table for the first indication of the first canon, and Nos. 61 and 2 for the two indications above the second canon. As for the words *Bis dicitur*, they mean that we must play the first canon twice and then stop; this condition, together with the signs ⌒ that are found throughout both canons (which are composed to work simultaneously), means that the resulting double canon is not circular, but 'finished'. As each of these canons is in two voices, their combination produces a four-part whole.

Padre Martini's Closed and Enigmatic Canons with Solutions by Luigi Cherubini

Canon 47

Vol. II, Cap. IX, p. 142

Certamine et tripudio et cantu memores exilarant, Homer

Solution

Le mot grec marqué au-dessus du premier Canon veut dire <u>Deux</u>; celui tracé sur le Second, signifie <u>Doubles</u>. L'examen que j'ai fait de ces Canons m'a prouvé, que ces deux indications renferment le même sens, puisqu'elles constituent l'un et l'autre Canon à deux voix, dont celle qui est le Conséquent répond à l'<u>Unisson</u>. Ces deux Canons, faits pour être exécutés en même temps, produisent un double Canon à quatre parties. La mesure $\frac{6}{4}$ qui intervient à la fin du Second Canon, comme elle est binaire, elle doit aller en même temps que celle marquée ₵, ainsi qu'on va le voir ci-dessous.

The Greek word written above the first canon means '<u>two</u>'; the one written above the second signifies '<u>doubled</u>'. The examination I have made of these canons has convinced me that these two indications have the same meaning; they specifies that both canons are in two voices, of which the one that is the consequent answers at the <u>unison</u>. These two canons, composed to be performed at the same time, produce a double four-part canon. The $\frac{6}{4}$ measure that occurs at the end of the second canon, being a simple meter, must match the one marked ₵, as we will see below.

Luciane Beduschi

Canon Ouvert

Padre Martini's Closed and Enigmatic Canons with Solutions by Luigi Cherubini

Canon 48

Vol. II, Cap. VIII, p. 141

Hilari merum bibentes bromium patrem canamus, [Anacreon]

Solution

Les Clefs, marquées au nombre de quatre, en tête de chaque Canon indiquent clairement que l'un et l'autre sont respectivement à quatre parties, et comme, par l'examen que j'en ai fait, ces deux Canons sont de nature à être exécutés conjointement, il résulte de cette réunion un Double Canon à 8 Voix.

On a déjà observé précédemment, que quand un Canon n'était accompagné d'aucune indication, qui précisât à quel intervalle les Conséquents doivent répondre, ceux-ci résolvaient ordinairement le Canon à l'Unisson, mais ce n'est pas ici de même, car ayant bien inspecté les deux Canons actuels, je me suis assuré que le premier a un Conséquent qui

*lui répond à l'*Unisson*, et deux autres qui lui répondent à la* Quarte Inférieure*: et que le Second a un Conséquent qui lui répond également à l'*Unisson*, et deux autres qui lui répondent à la* Douzième Supérieure*.*
    Voyez la partition de ces deux Canons à la page suivante.

    The four clefs at the head of each canon clearly indicate that they are in four parts. As my study of them shows that these two canons are of a kind to be performed together, it follows that the result is a double canon in eight voices.

    It has been previously observed that, when a canon is not accompanied by any indication that specifies at what interval the consequents must answer, it is usually resolved at the unison, but this is not the case here. Having thoroughly inspected these two canons, I have ascertained that the first has a consequent that answers at the <u>unison</u>, and two others that answer at the <u>lower fourth</u>; the second canon has a consequent that also answers at the <u>unison</u>, and two others that answer at the <u>upper twelfth</u>.

    See the score of these two canons on the next page.

Padre Martini's Closed and Enigmatic Canons with Solutions by Luigi Cherubini

Luciane Beduschi

Padre Martini's Closed and Enigmatic Canons with Solutions by Luigi Cherubini

Canon 49

Vol. II, Cap. IX, p. 184

Utinam pulchra fiam eburnea Lyra, Carcinus
Canon 6 Voc. ad Diapente
Contraria contrariis curantur

Solution

Voyez les n⁰ˢ 83, 59, et 43 pour l'explication de tous les mots écrits au-dessus de ce Canon. Il a déjà été question aux Canons 13ᵉ, 31ᵉ, et 42ᵉ, où elles ont été employées, des mesures ₵ et ₵ combinées avec la mesure ₵; il est donc inutile de reparler ici de leur valeur respective, comparée avec la mesure à quatre temps, et l'on va voir leur emploi à l'égard du présent Canon, dans l'ouverture de celui-ci, qu'on va voir ci-dessous.

See Nos. 83, 59, and 43 for the explanation of all the words written above this canon. Measures ₵ and ₵ combined with measure ₵ have already been discussed in Canons 13ᵗʰ, 31ᵗʰ and 42ⁿᵈ, where they are used. There is therefore no need to repeat here the explanation about their respective values compared with the four-beat measure. We will see their use in the present canon by looking at its opening bellow.

Luciane Beduschi

Canon Ouvert

Canon 50

Vol. II, Dissertazione prima, p. 187

Cithara sonante plaudo, Anacreon
Canon ad Unisson, et ad Sub-Diapason
Omne trinum perfectum
Non qui inceperit, sed qui perseveraverit
Cantus duarum facierum

SOLUTION

Les mots tracés au-dessus de chacun de ces deux Canons, sont consignés avec leur explication aux n°s 22, 59, et 51 de la Table. Le premier Canon est à trois, et le second à deux Voix; le Conséquent de celui-ci, quoique l'Intervalle auquel il doit répondre ne soit pas indiqué, fait sa réponse <u>ad Diapason</u>, c'est-à-dire à l'<u>Octave Supérieure</u>. Tout cela produit un <u>Double Canon</u> à Cinq Parties.

The words written above each of these two canons are recorded, along with their explanation, in Nos. 22, 59, and 51 of the Table. The first canon is in three voices and the second in two voices; the consequent, although the interval at which it must answer is not indicated, answers *<u>ad Diapason</u>*, that is to say at the <u>upper octave</u>. All this produces a <u>double</u> five-part <u>canon</u>.

Luciane Beduschi

Canon Ouvert

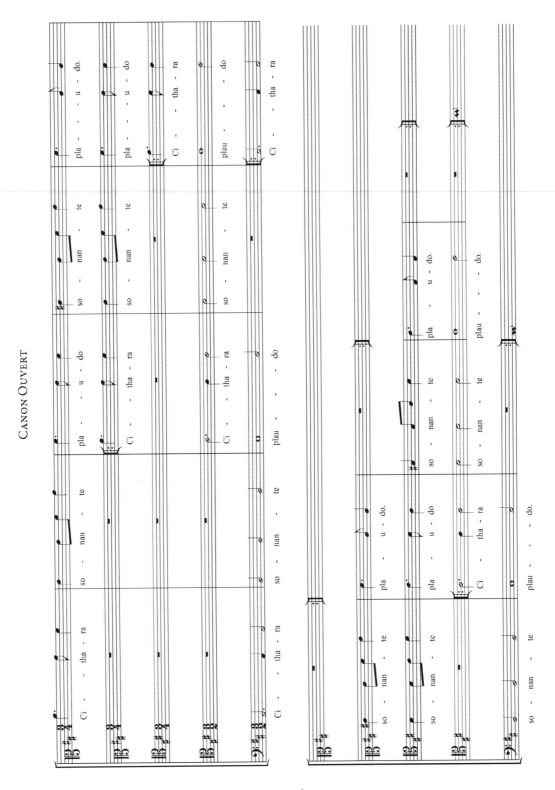

Padre Martini's Closed and Enigmatic Canons with Solutions by Luigi Cherubini

Canon 51

Vol. II, Dissertazione prima, p. 228

Tibio Phebe lex attributa est cantus, Homer
Canon ad Diapason, et Unissonum vicissim
Tot tempora, tot sunt voces

Solution

Consultez, avant tout, la Table aux n⁰ˢ 84, et 85, afin de connaître la signification des mots placés au-dessus du Canon. D'après l'explication du n° 85, ce Canon est à huit voix, puisqu'il renferme huit temps, ou mesures. Toutes ces indications suffisent pour ne pas éprouver d'embarras à le déchiffrer.

First consult the Nos. 84 and 85 of the Table to know the meaning of the words placed above the canon. In line with the explanation of No. 85, this canon is in eight voices, since it has eight beats, or measures. All these clues are sufficient to avoid difficulties in decipherment.

Luciane Beduschi

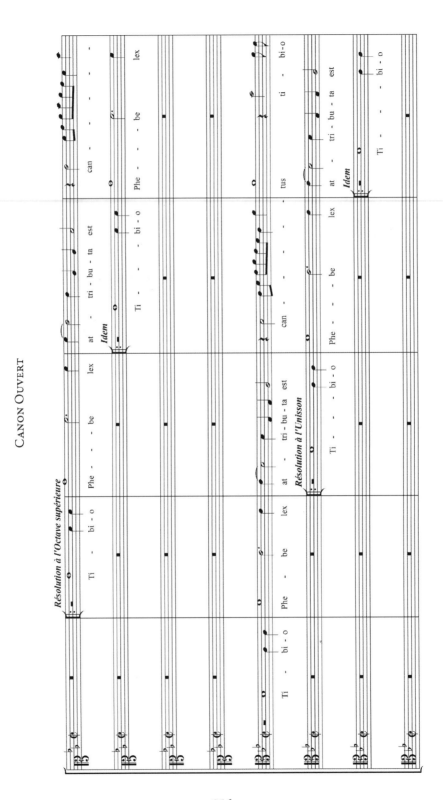

Padre Martini's Closed and Enigmatic Canons with Solutions by Luigi Cherubini

Luciane Beduschi

Padre Martini's Closed and Enigmatic Canons with Solutions by Luigi Cherubini

Canon 52

Vol. II, Dissertazione seconda, p. 229

Dulce meum carmen est et cum fistula modulor, Theocritus
Canon ad Sub-Diatessaron
Canon ad Diapente
Canon ad Diapente

Solution

Au n° 59 de la Table on trouvera l'explication des mots qui accompagnent ces trois Canons; chaque indication représente un Conséquent, or, comme chacun de ces trois Canons ne porte avec lui qu'une seule indication, il est évident que tous les trois sont respectivement à deux voix: et puisque ces Canons sont de nature à être exécutés en même temps, il résulte de cette association un triple Canon à Six parties.

No. 59 of the Table contains the explanation of the words that accompany these three canons. Each indication represents a consequent; since each of these three canons carries only one indication, it is evident that all three are in two voices. Given that these canons are written to be performed at the same time, it follows that they combine to create a triple canon in six parts.

Luciane Beduschi

Canon Ouvert

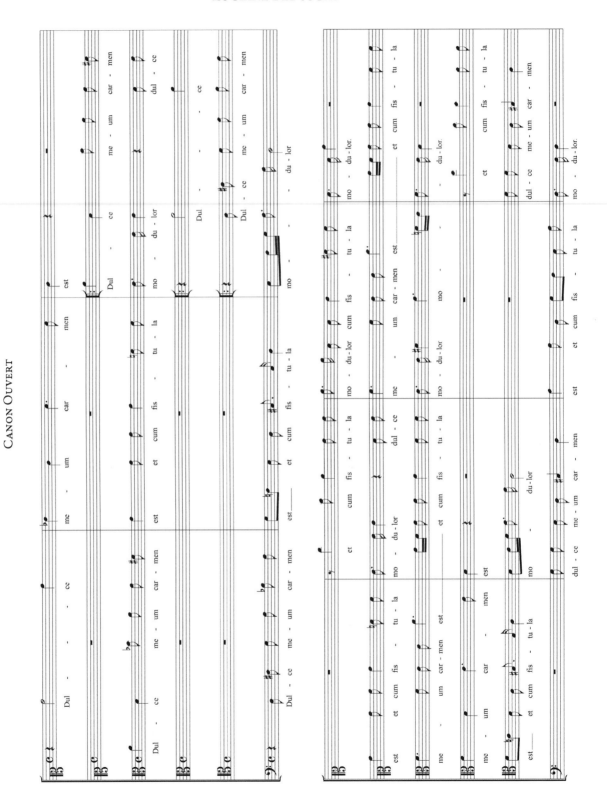

Padre Martini's Closed and Enigmatic Canons with Solutions by Luigi Cherubini

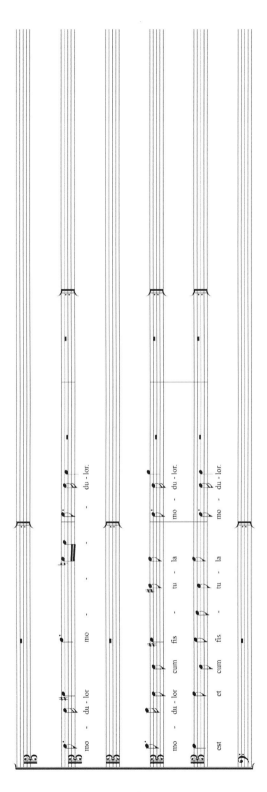

Luciane Beduschi

Canon 53

Vol. II, Dissertazione seconda, p. 279

Charum genus est cantorum, Homer
Canon 12 Voc. ad Unissonum, et ad Diapente
Contraria contrariis curantur
6 Voc. Canon cancrizat

Solution

Le premier Canon est à 12 voix; quant à l'égard des indications qui le précèdent, voyez la Table aux n° 59 *et* 43 *pour connaître leur désignation. Le Second Canon* Cancarizat [sic], *c'est-à-dire, qui de la fin revient au commencement en marchant à reculons, est à Six Voix; et comme ce Canon ne porte aucune autre indication les Conséquents répondent tous à l'Unisson. Ces Canons faits pour être réunis, forment en Double Canons à 18 parties.*

The first canon is in twelve voices. For information about the indications that precede it, and to know their meaning, see the Table, Nos. 59 and 43. The second canon *cancarizat* [sic], that is to say, walks backwards from the end back towards the beginning, is in six voices. As it has no other indication, the consequents all respond at the unison. These canons, written to be combined, form a double canon in eighteen parts.

Padre Martini's Closed and Enigmatic Canons with Solutions by Luigi Cherubini

Canon Ouvert

Luciane Beduschi

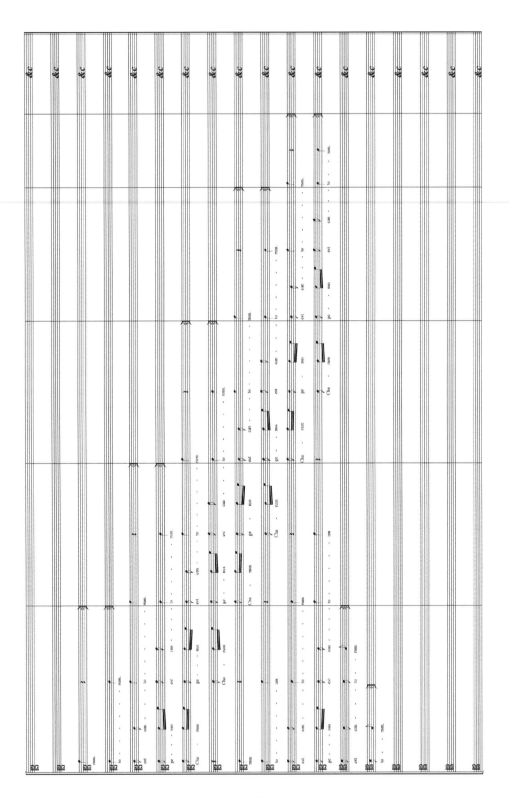

Padre Martini's Closed and Enigmatic Canons with Solutions by Luigi Cherubini

Canon 54

Vol. II, Dissertazione terza, p. 280

Tibia et fistula canebat bubulcus, Theocritus
Canon ad Diapason-Diapente
Plutonica subiit regna
Tertia pars si placet

Solution

Ce qu'il importe de connaître avant tout, c'est la signification des mots tracés au-dessus du Canon, qu'on trouvera aux n°ˢ 76, et 42. Ce Canon est à deux voix, il sera à trois, si l'on y ajoute la partie Ad Libitum *écrite au-dessous, mais dont il peut se passer.*

What you need to know first is the meaning of the words written above the canon, which will be found in Nos. 76 and 42. This canon is in two voices; it will be in three if we add the <u>*Ad Libitum*</u> part written below, but this is not necessary.

Canon Ouvert

Padre Martini's Closed and Enigmatic Canons with Solutions by Luigi Cherubini

Canon 55

Vol. II, Dissertazione terza, p. 326

Incipientes que canunt Deae et finientes carmen, Hesiod
Canon ad Diapason intensum
Canon ad Diapason expansum

Solution

On verra l'explication des mots latins ci-dessus aux nos 86, et 87 de la Table. Chacun de ces Canons est à deux voix, n'ayant qu'une seule indication, qui représente un seul Conséquent. Comme ces deux Canons sont combinés pour être réunis l'un à l'autre, et que les deux différents signes ¢ et ¢ de la mesure sont à leur tour susceptibles à marcher de concert, ainsi que plusieurs Canons précédents l'ont démontré, il résulte de tout cela un double Canon à quatre parties.

We will see that Nos. 86 and 87 of the Table provide the explanation of the Latin words above. Each of these canons is in two voices, having only one indication, which represents a single consequent. Since these two canons are to be combined with each other, and the two different time signature signs ¢ and ¢ are likely to function in tandem, as several previous canons have shown, we may deduce that this is a double canon in four parts.

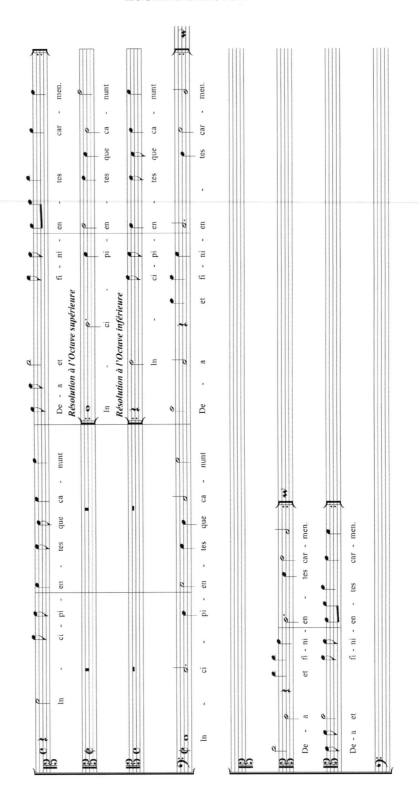

CANON OUVERT

Padre Martini's Closed and Enigmatic Canons with Solutions by Luigi Cherubini

Canon 56

Vol. III, Prefazione, p. xi

Vicissim canebat dulci Voce
Canon ad unissonum

Solution

Le mot <u>Ad Unissonum</u>, qui veut dire Unisson, appartient aux deux Canons, qui chacun n'ayant un seul Conséquent, l'un et l'autre sont respectivement à deux voix. Exécutés en même temps, ils produisent un Double Canon à quatre parties.

The word <u>Ad Unissonum</u>, which means unison, belongs to both canons. Since each of them has only one consequent, both are in two voices. When performed at the same time, they produce a four-part double canon.

Luciane Beduschi

Canon Ouvert

Canon 57

Vol. III, Prefazione, p. xx

Canoros domi personat modos
Canon ad unissonum

Solution

Ce Canon n'ayant qu'un seul Conséquent qui répond à l'Unisson, est à deux voix.

This canon, which has only one consequent that answers at the unison, is in two voices.

Luciane Beduschi

Canon Ouvert

Padre Martini's Closed and Enigmatic Canons with Solutions by Luigi Cherubini

Canon 58

Vol. III, Cap. I, p. 1

Numeros Jonicos illis modulatur, Platon
Canon ad Sub-Diapason
Canon ad Sub-Diapason

Solution

L'explication des indications ci-dessus, se trouve au nº 59 de la Table. Chaque Canon ne portant avec lui qu'une seule indication, qui constitue un seul Conséquent, l'un, et l'autre sont à deux voix. Pour lors ces deux Canons étant réunis forment un Double Canon à quatre parties.

The explanation of the indications above can be found in No. 59 of the Table. Since each canon carries with it only one indication, which indicates a single consequent, both are in two voices. When combined, these two canons form a double canon in four parts.

Luciane Beduschi

Canon Ouvert

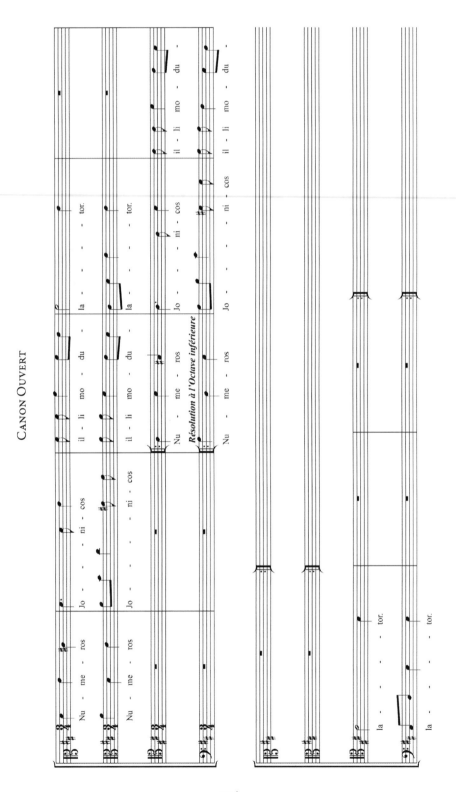

Padre Martini's Closed and Enigmatic Canons with Solutions by Luigi Cherubini

Canon 59

Vol. III, Cap. I, p. 24

Canebant Tibia suorum docti concentuum numeros, Atheneo
Canon ad Sub-Sesquiditonum
Canon ad Unissonum

Solution

Le signe § marqué sur la première note du premier Canon, indique que le Conséquent commence au même temps que l'Antécédent, à l'Intervalle dont on aura l'explication au n° 88 de la Table. Le signe pareil, qu'on rencontre dans l'étendu du Second Canon, indique de même que le Conséquent commence la réponse à l'Unisson à partir de cet endroit. Chacun de ces deux Canons étant à deux voix, exécutés tous les deux en même temps, donnent pour résultat un double Canon à quatre parties.

The sign § marked on the first note of the first canon indicates that the consequent begins at the same time as the antecedent, at the interval explained in No. 88 of the Table. The same sign, found during the second canon, similarly indicates that the consequent begins the response at the unison from that place. As each of these two canons are in two voices, both performed at the same time, the result is a double four-part canon.

Luciane Beduschi

Canon Ouvert

Padre Martini's Closed and Enigmatic Canons with Solutions by Luigi Cherubini

Canon 60

Vol. III, Cap. II, p. 25

Vicissim canebant dulci voce, Iliad
Canon ad Sub-Diapason
Canon ad Diapason

Solution

La seule indication dont est revêtu le premier Canon prouve qu'il est à deux voix. La même remarque a lieu au sujet du Second Canon. Voyez ensuite la Table au n° 59 pour savoir ce que veulent dire l'une et l'autre indication. Ainsi que le Canon précédent, celui-ci est double, et forme un ensemble à quatre parties.

The single indication pertaining to the first canon proves that it is in two voices. The same applies to the second canon. See the Table, No. 59, to find out what each indication means. As with the previous canon, this is a double canon which forms a four-part whole.

Padre Martini's Closed and Enigmatic Canons with Solutions by Luigi Cherubini

Canon 61

Vol. III, Cap. II, p. 90

Die tota placabant carmine Phoebum, Plutarch
Canon ad Diapason

Solution

Une seule indication; produisant un seul Conséquent, fait que ce Canon est à deux voix, dont celle qui fait la réponse au Canon, est à l'<u>Octave Supérieure</u>. D'après cela la solution n'est pas difficile à obtenir.

This canon, with one single indication meaning a single consequent, is in two voices, of which the one that answers to the canon is at the <u>upper octave</u>. With this knowledge the solution is not difficult to obtain.

Canon Ouvert

Luciane Beduschi

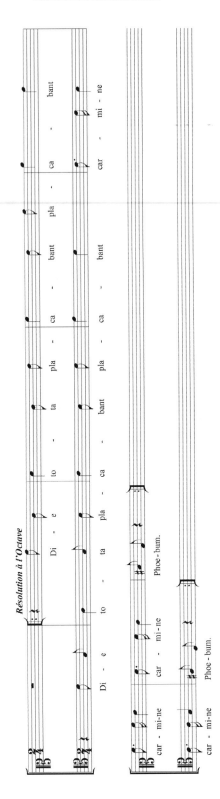

Padre Martini's Closed and Enigmatic Canons with Solutions by Luigi Cherubini

Canon 62

Vol. III, Cap. III, p. 91

Per multa canunt mendacia vates, Plutarch
Canon ad Sub-Diatessaron; Sub-Diapason et ad Sub-Diapason-Diatessaron

SOLUTION

Les trois indications qui se présentent en tête de ce Canon, forment trois Conséquents qui constituent, en comptant l'Antécédent, un ensemble à quatre parties. Voyez la Table au n° 59 pour avoir l'explication de ces trois indications.

The three indications that appear at the head of this canon form three consequents, which creates, by counting the antecedent, a total of four parts. See No. 59 of the Table for an explanation of these three indications.

Luciane Beduschi

Canon Ouvert

Padre Martini's Closed and Enigmatic Canons with Solutions by Luigi Cherubini

Canon 63

Vol. III, Cap. III, p. 148

Cantibus ad Lyram utendum
Canon 4 Voc.

Solution

Ce Canon, selon les mots <u>4 Vocum</u> dont il est accompagné, est à quatre voix; et comme il ne porte avec lui d'autre indication que celle-là, ces quatre parties doivent être toutes à l'Unisson, et elles le sont effectivement.

This canon, as indicated by the words <u>4 Vocum</u> that accompanies it, is in four voices. Since it carries no other indication besides this one, these four parts must all be at the unison, and indeed they are.

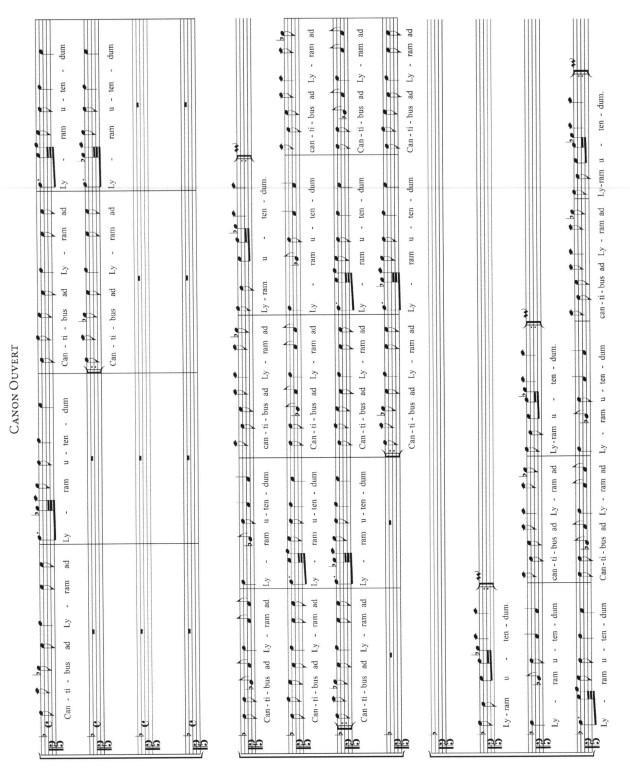

Padre Martini's Closed and Enigmatic Canons with Solutions by Luigi Cherubini

Canon 64

Vol. III, Cap. IV, p. 149

Musarum lepido semper ore canitur, Nicander
Canon ad Tonum
3ª Pars si placet

Solution

Consultez la Table au nº 57 pour avoir la signification du mot latin marqué en tête de ce Canon qui, par cela même qu'il n'est accompagné que d'une seule indication, est à deux voix. Si à ces deux parties, on ajoute la partie <u>Ad Libitum</u> écrite au-dessous du Canon, celui-ci pour lors sera à trois voix.

Consult the Table in No. 57 for the meaning of the Latin word marked at the head of this canon, which, by the very fact that it is accompanied by only one indication, is in two voices. If we add the *<u>Ad Libitum</u>* part written below the canon to these two parts, this canon will then be in three voices.

Luciane Beduschi

Padre Martini's Closed and Enigmatic Canons with Solutions by Luigi Cherubini

Canon 65

Vol. III, Cap. v, p. 170

Invenere illum Cithara oblectantem, Illiad
Canon ad Septimam infra [3a. pars.]

Solution

Ce que j'ai dit au sujet de la solution du Canon précédent, ou 64ᵉ, peut s'appliquer au présent Canon, à l'exception cependant, qu'à l'égard de celui-ci, il faut interroger la Table au n° 89 pour connaître l'intervalle auquel le Conséquent doit répondre, et que son entrée est positivement indiquée à l'endroit où se trouve marqué le signe §.

What I said about the solution of the previous canon, the 64th, may apply to the present canon, except that, with respect to this one, we have to examine the No. 89 of the Table to know the interval at which the consequent must answer, and that its entry is positively indicated at the place where the sign § is marked.

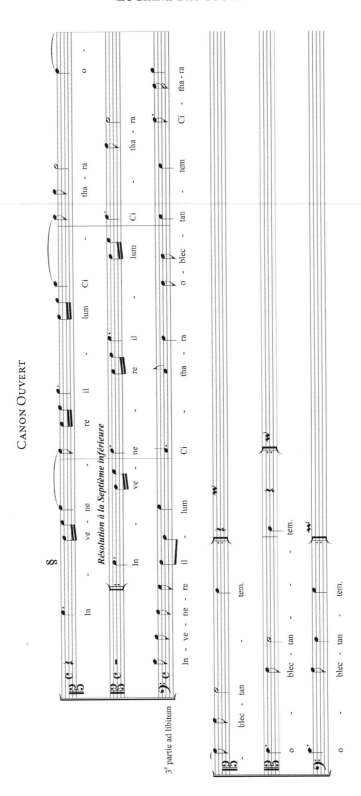

Padre Martini's Closed and Enigmatic Canons with Solutions by Luigi Cherubini

Canon 66

Vol. III, Cap. VI, p. 198
Musarum incunda lyra
Canon ad unissonum
3ª Pars si placet

SOLUTION

Ce Canon est à deux voix, parce qu'il n'a qu'un seul Conséquent répondant à l'Unisson; il sera à trois, si on lui associe la partie Ad Libitum.

This canon is in two voices, because it has only one consequent responding at the unison. It will be in three voices if we add the *Ad Libitum* part.

Luciane Beduschi

Padre Martini's Closed and Enigmatic Canons with Solutions by Luigi Cherubini

Canon 67

Vol. III, Cap. VI, p. 268

Non enim usitatos prius cantus afferimus sed illibatum exordimur hymnum
Canon ad Decimam et ad Sub-Diapente
4ª pars si placet

SOLUTION

Les deux indications qui paraissent au-dessus du Canon forment deux Conséquents qui établissent ce même Canon à trois voix; en ajoutant la partie Ad Libitum, *qui vient ensuite, le Canon sera à quatre voix. L'explication des deux indications citées, est consignée aux n°s 59, et 90 de la Table.*

The two indications that appear above the canon form two consequents, establishing a three-voice canon; by adding the *Ad Libitum* part, the canon will be in four voices. The explanation of the two indications is reported in Nos. 59 and 90 of the Table.

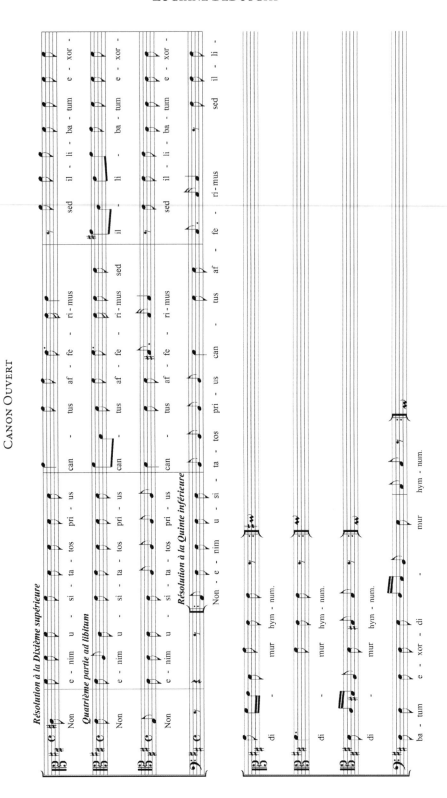

Padre Martini's Closed and Enigmatic Canons with Solutions by Luigi Cherubini

Canon 68

Vol. III, Cap. VII, p. 269

Cantus afferimus sed illibatum exordimur hymnum
Canon ad 3ª infra
Canon ad Unissonum

Solution

Le premier Canon est à deux voix, ainsi que le second; le Conséquent du premier répond à la <u>Tierce Inférieure</u> en commençant en même temps que l'Antécédent, comme le signe § placé sur la première note de celui-ci l'indique. Le Conséquent du Second Canon répond à l'Unisson, et n'entre qu'après son Antécédent, à l'endroit qu'on verra désigné dans l'ouverture de ces deux Canons. Leur réunion produit un Double Canon à quatre parties.

The first canon is in two voices, as is the second canon. The consequent of the first canon responds at the <u>lower third</u>, starting at the same time as the antecedent, as the sign § placed on its first note indicates. The consequent of the second canon responds at the unison, and enters only after its antecedent, at the place which will be designated in the opening of these two canons. Putting them together produces a four-part double canon.

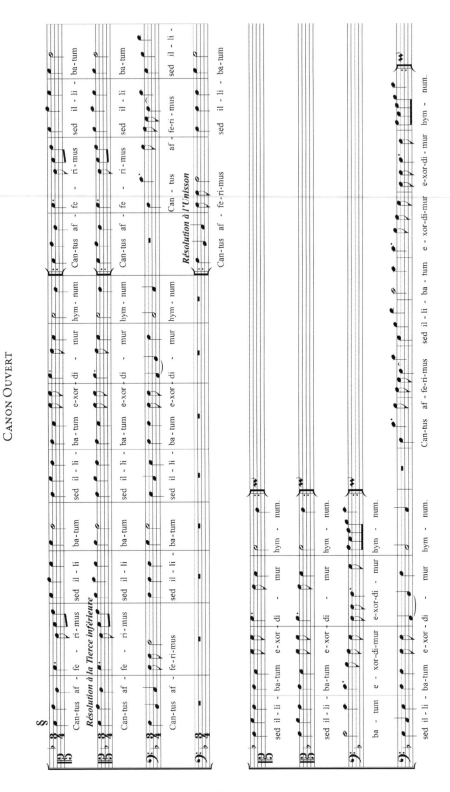

Padre Martini's Closed and Enigmatic Canons with Solutions by Luigi Cherubini

Canon 69

Vol. III, Cap. VII, p. 369

Sumpto Monaulo Hymenaeum accinebam
Canon ad unissonum
3ª pars si placet

Solution

Le Canon est à deux, parce qu'il n'a qu'un seul Conséquent, représenté par l'unique indication dont il est précédé; il est à trois voix, en lui associant la 3ᵉ partie Ad Libitum. J'ai copié fidèlement le mot <u>Ad Unissonum</u>, de la vignette de laquelle j'ai extrait ce Canon, mais cette indication est fausse, car de quelque manière que je me sois pris, je n'ai jamais pu combiner cette réponse à l'<u>Unisson</u>, ni avec l'Antécédent, ni avec la 3ᵉ partie Ad Libitum, ce dont on pourra s'assurer, si l'on veut prendre la peine d'en entreprendre l'analyse. Il est donc à présumer, que le Père Martini s'est trompé par distraction en marquant une indication par une autre, ou bien c'est la personne qui a gravé ce Canon qui a commis la faute. Il fallait rectifier cette erreur, en cherchant le véritable intervalle de la réponse; je crois l'avoir trouvé en plaçant cette réponse à <u>la Septième inférieure</u>, qui offre, sous le rapport de la mélodie et de l'harmonie, la plus exacte correction, et se combine parfaitement avec l'Antécédent ainsi qu'avec la partie Ad Libitum, comme on le verra dans la partition suivante.

The canon is in two parts because it has only one consequent represented by the single indication that precedes it; it is in three voices, adding the third part *Ad Libitum*. I faithfully copied the word <u>Ad Unissonum</u> from the vignette from which I extracted this canon, but this tag is false, because however I have attempted it, I have never been able to combine this answer at the <u>unison</u>, neither with the antecedent, nor with the third part *Ad Libitum* — which can be proven, if we want to take the trouble to carry out the analysis. It is therefore to be presumed that Padre Martini was inadvertently mistaken in confusing two indications, or that it was the person who engraved the canon who committed the fault. It was necessary to rectify this error by seeking the true interval of the answer. I think I found it by placing the answer at the <u>lower seventh</u>, which offers the most exact correction in terms of melody and harmony, and combines perfectly with the antecedent as well as with the *Ad Libitum* part, as we will see in the following score.

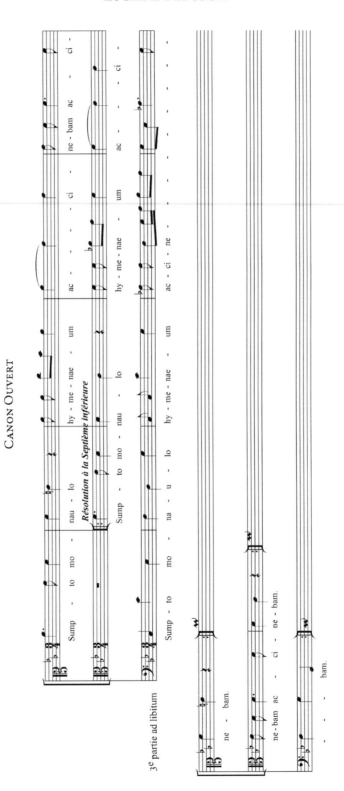

Padre Martini's Closed and Enigmatic Canons with Solutions by Luigi Cherubini

Canon 70

Vol. III, Cap. VIII, p. 370

Tibiarum atque lyrae cantus musicus
Canon ad Unissonum
Canon ad Sub-Diapason

Solution

Toute autre recherche pour déchiffrer ces Canons, doit être précédée par celle qui donne la connaissance de la signification des deux indications latines; on l'obtiendra ayant recours à la Table au n° 59. Chacun de ces deux Canons est à deux voix, et leur association produit un Double Canon à quatre parties.

Any attempt at deciphering these canons must be preceded by that information which gives the meaning of the two Latin indications; this will be obtained in No. 59 of the Table. Each of these two canons is in two voices, and their combination produces a four-part double canon.

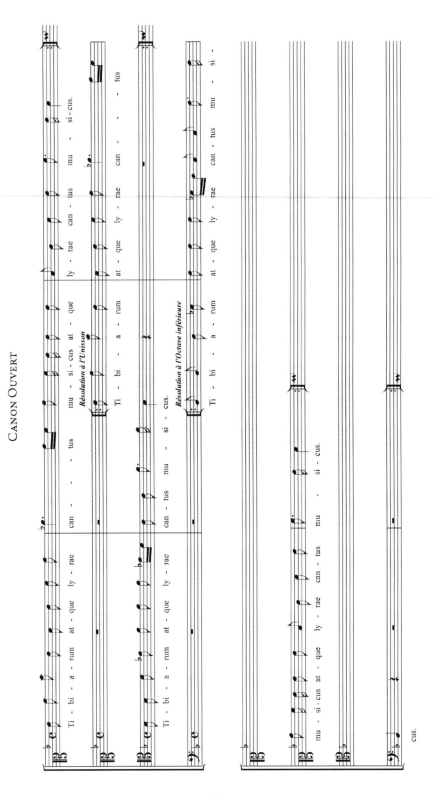

Padre Martini's Closed and Enigmatic Canons with Solutions by Luigi Cherubini

Canon 71

Vol. III, Cap. VIII, p. 415

Citharam pulsare aut Tibias inflare dacuisti
Canon 5ᵉ Vocibus

Solution

Comme nulle autre indication, que celle qu'il est à Cinq Voix, n'accompagne ce Canon, ces cinq voix sont naturellement à l'Unisson.

Since no other indication accompanies this canon besides the one specifying that it is in five voices, these five voices are naturally at the unison.

Luciane Beduschi

Canon Ouvert

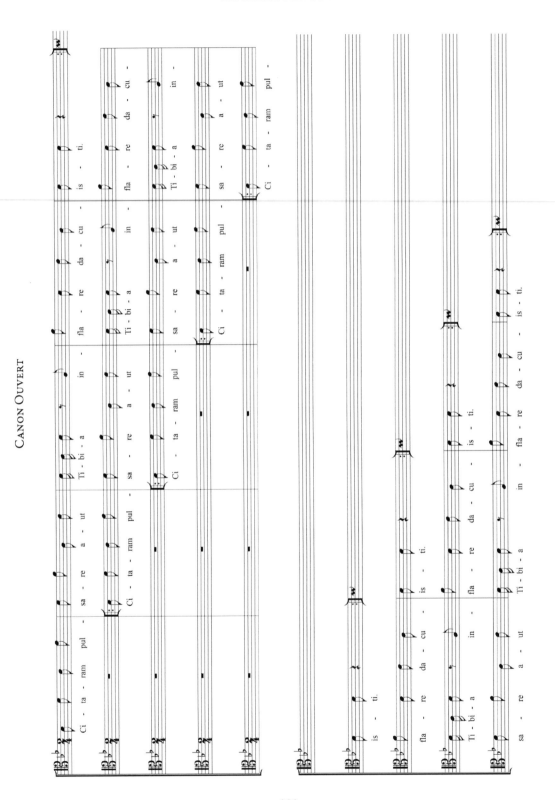

Padre Martini's Closed and Enigmatic Canons with Solutions by Luigi Cherubini

Canon 72

Vol. III, Dissertazione, p. 419

Tibiis virgo quidem caricos canit modos
Canon ad Sub-Diapente

Solution

Le mot latin qu'on voit marqué au-dessus de ce Canon, et dont on aura l'explication au n° 59 de la Table, étant le seul Conséquent que peut avoir ce même Canon, fait que celui-ci est à deux voix. Le reste est aisé à trouver.

The Latin word that we see written above this canon, and of which we will have the explanation in No. 59 of the Table, is the only consequent that this canon can have. This means it is in two voices. The rest is easy to find.

Luciane Beduschi

Canon Ouvert

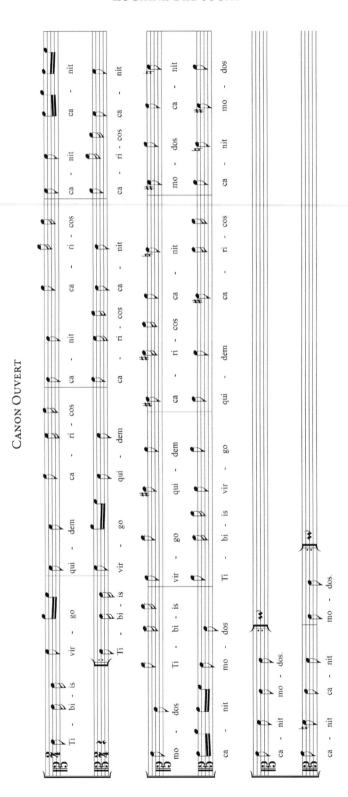

List of Canons in Cherubini's Collection

Canon 1, vol. I. Prefazione, p. 1
Repleatur os meum laude, ut cantem gloriam tuam, Psalm 70.8
Sit trium series una
3 voices, 1 resolution

Canon 2, vol. I. Prefazione, p. 7
Non impedias Musicam, Ecclesiastes 32.5
4 voices, 1 resolution

Canon 3, vol. I. Cap. I, p. 8
Cantate Domino omnis terra, Psalm 95.1
Canon post unum Tempus
Canon 6.7.8 pars si placet
5 voices / 5 voices / 10 voices double-canon, 3 resolutions

Canon 4, vol. I. Cap. I, p. 13
Jubilate Deo in voce exultationis, Psalm 46.2
2 voices double-canon, 1 resolution

Canon 5, vol. I. Cap. II, p. 14
Psallite Domino in cithara, Psalm 97.6
Canon ad Tonum infra / ad Tonum supra
4 voices double-canon, 1 resolution

Canon 6, vol. I. Cap. II, p. 24
Invocate nomen ejus cantate ei, Psalm 104. 1.2
Manet alta mente repostum
6 voices, 1 resolution

Canon 7, vol. I. Cap. III, p. 25
Misericordiam et iudicium cantabo tibi Domine, Psalm 100.1

Qui se humiliat exaltabitur
Canon ad Diatessaron
4 voices double-canon, 1 resolution

Canon 8, vol. I. Cap. III, p. 27
Cantabo Deo Jacob, Psalm 74.9
Canon ad Semi-Ditonum
Symphonizabis
4 voices double-canon, 1 resolution

Canon 9, vol. I. Cap. IV, p. 28
Cantemus Domino gloriose enim magnificatus est, Exodus 15.1s
Canon ad Unissonum, et bis ad Diatessaron. Diapason, et Diapason-Diatessaron
6 voices, 1 resolution

Canon 10, vol. I. Cap. IV, p. 36
Clangentibus tubis, muri illico coruerunt, Joshua 6.20
Qui querit invenit
6 voices, 1 resolution

Canon 11, vol. I. Cap. V, p. 37
Domino canam psallam Domino Deo, Judges 5.3
Tres in unum
3 voices, 1 resolution

Canon 12, vol. I. Cap. V, p. 41
Iste est David cui cantabant in choris, 1 Samuel 29.5
Canon ad Unissonum
16 voices, 1 resolution

Canon 13, vol. I. Cap. VI, p. 42
Cantate et exultate et psallite, Psalm 97.4
Canon ad Diatessaron / ad Sub-Diatessaron
Non qui inceperit, sed qui perseveraverit
4 voices double-canon, 1 resolution

Canon 14, vol. I. Cap. VII, p. 54
Introite portas eius in confessione atria eius in hymnis, Psalm 99.4

List of Canons in Cherubini's Collection

Canon ad Sub-Diatessaron, Sub-Diapason, et Sub-Diapason-Diatessaron
4 voices, 1 resolution

Canon 15, vol. I. Cap. VII, p. 57
Confitemini Dominum in cithara in psalterio decachordo cantate ei, Psalm 32.8
Canon ad Diapason-Ditonum
2 voices, 1 resolution

Canon 16, vol. I. Cap. VIII, p. 58
Cumque caneret psaltes facta est super eum manus Domini, 2 Kings 3.15
Quinque Voc.
Post unum Tempus
5 voices, 1 resolution

Canon 17, vol. I. Cap. IX, p. 61
In voce exultationis et confessionis sonus epulantis, Psalm 41.5
Canon ad Sub-Diatessaron
Qui post me venit, ante me factus est
2 voices, 1 resolution

Canon 18, vol. I. Cap. X, p. 67
Confitebor tibi Domine in gentibus et nomini tuo cantabo, Psalm 41.5
Canon ad Duodeciman
Clama ne cesses
Tertia pars si placet
2 voices / 3 voices double-canon, 2 resolutions

Canon 19, vol. I. Dissertazione prima, p. 164
Cantabo Domine in vita mea, Psalm 103.3
Canon ad Sub-Diapason
Qui sequitur me non ambulat in tenebris
Clama ne cesses
4 voices double-canon, 1 resolution

Canon 20, vol. I. Cap. X, p. 74
Omnis terra adoret te et canat tibi, Psalm 65.4
Canon ad Unisson, ad Hypo-Diapason, et Hyper-Diatessaron
4 voices, 1 resolution

Canon 21, vol. I. Cap. VI, p. 53
Cantate Domino psalmum dicite nomini ejus cantate, Psalm 67.4
Canon ad Unisson, et bis Ad Diapente
Crescit eundo
Canon ad Duodeciman
6 voices double-canon, 1 resolution

Canon 22, vol. I. Dissertazione prima, p. 83
Laudabo nomen Dei cum cantico, Psalm 68.31
Canon ad Sub-Diatessaron, ad Epi-Diapason, et Epi-Diapente
4 voices, 1 resolution

Canon 23, vol. II. Prefazione, p. I
Incipe Menalios mecum mea tibia versus, Theocritus
Sit trium series una
3 voices, 1 resolution

Canon 24, vol. I. Dissertazione seconda, p. 334
Hymnum novum cantemus Deo nostro, Judith 16.15
Canon ad Sub-Diapason
4 voices double-canon, 1 resolution

Canon 25, vol. I. Cap. XI, p. 80
Cantate Domino et benedicite nomini eius, Psalm 95.2
Canon ad Homophonum, vel ad Equisonum
2 voices, 1 resolution

Canon 26, vol. I. Cap. XI, p. 75
Regna terrae cantate Deo, Psalm 67.33
Canon Decrescit eundo ad Hypo-Diapente / ad Hyper-Diatessaron
4 voices double-canon, 1 resolution

Canon 27, vol. II. Prefazione, p. xx
Argentum carmen strepens Phrygiis numeris sonabo, Anacreon
Canon ad Unissonum, et bis ad Eptacordum / Canon ad Diapason
6 voices double-canon, 1 resolution

List of Canons in Cherubini's Collection

Canon 28, vol. I. Cap. VIII, p. 60
Lauda Jerusalem Dominum canet Deum tuum Sion, Psalm 147.1
Canon ad Diapente remissum, et ad Nonam, et Diapente expansum
Nec mihi, nec tibi, sed dividatur
4 voices, 1 resolution

Canon 29, vol. I. Dissertazione seconda, p. 165
Cantate Domino in cymbalis modulamini illi psalmum novum, Judith 16.2
Me pente, me tesseris phones
2 voices, 1 resolution

Canon 30, vol. I. Dissertazione terza, p. 335
Psallite Deo nostro, Psalm 46.6
Omne trinum perfectum
3 voices, 1 resolution

Canon 31, vol. I. Dissertazione terza, p. 446
Sumite psalmum date tympanum psalterium incundum cum cithara, Psalm 80.2
Canon ad Unissonum
6 voices triple-canon, 1 resolution

Canon 32, vol. II. Cap. I, p. 1 A
A Musis Heliconiadibus incipiamus canere, Hesiod
Ter terni canite vocibus
9 voices, 1 resolution

Canon 33, vol. II. Cap. I, p. 6
Cignorum instar varii modi sunt accinendi, Pratinas
Congenita haec tria sunt
3 voices, 1 resolution

Canon 34, vol. II. Cap. II, p. 7
Jovi patri canendo oblectant, Hesiod
Justitia et pax se osculatae sunt
2 voices, 1 resolution

Canon 35, vol. II. Cap. II, p. 30
Cano Peana magnum Deum Apollinem, Epigr. Poet. Graec., Lib. I.

Canon ad Diapente, Diapason, et Diapason-Diapente
4 voices, 1 resolution

Canon 36, vol. II. Cap. III, p. 31
Canam semideorum quorum audiunt opera poetae, Homer
Canon ad Sub-Diapason-Diapente, ad Sub-Diapason, Sub-Diapente
4 voices, 1 resolution

Canon 37, vol. II. Cap. III, p. 40
Sirenum cantus delectant, Homer
3 voices / 6 voices, 2 resolutions

Canon 38, vol. II. Cap. IV, p. 41
Tebana bella cantus Troiana cantat alter, Anacreon
Ter voce ciemus
Voce ter insonuit
6 voices double-canon, 1 resolution

Canon 39, vol. II. Cap. V, p. 58
Carmine cunctos mortales mulcent, Homer
Canon ad Hypo-Diapason-Diapente
2 voices, 1 resolution

Canon 40, vol. II. Cap. IV, p. 57
Hymnum canunt demulcent que nationes hominum, Homer
Canon 4 vocib. et 8 voc. si placet
Qui deprimit se, altissimo fit altior
4 voices / 8 voices double-canon, 2 resolutions

Canon 41, vol. II. Cap. V, p. 85
Dulcis repente nostro erumpit ore cantus, Anacreon
Canon ad Eptachordum infra, vel ad tonum supra
Ad Diapente
5 voices double-canon, 1 resolution

Canon 42, vol. II. Cap. VI, p. 86
Canoris tibiis emittebant cantum, Hesiod
Canon ibit, redibit

List of Canons in Cherubini's Collection

Canon ad Tonum, infinit, et finit
3 voices double-canon, 1 resolution

Canon 43, vol. II. Cap. VI, p. 102
Tibia vero cantabunt mihi pastores duo, Theocritus
Canon ad Sub-Diapason, vel ad Unisson
2 voices, 1 resolutions

Canon 44, vol. II. Cap. VII, p. 123
Obloquitur numeris septem discrimina vocum et hic septem calida nervis, Virgil
7 voices, 1 resolution

Canon 45, vol. II. Cap. VII, p. 103
Concentus reciprocos voce modulabantur, Sophocles
Canon ad Sub-Diapason
Canon ad Diapason
4 voices double-canon, 1 resolution

Canon 46, vol. II. Cap. VIII, p. 124
Placent convivia et oblectant cantus, Hesiod
Canon ad Hypo-Diapason. Bis dicitur
Canon ad Hyper-Diapason
Otia dant vitia
4 voices double-canon, 1 resolution

Canon 47, vol. II. Cap. IX, p. 142
Certamine et tripudio et cantu memores exilarant, Homer
4 voices double-canon, 1 resolution

Canon 48, vol. II. Cap. VIII, p. 141
Hilari merum bibentes bromium patrem canamus
8 voices double-canon, 1 resolution

Canon 49, vol. II. Cap. IX, p. 184
Utinam pulchra fiam eburnea Lyra, Carcinus
Canon 6 Voc. ad Diapente
Contraria contrariis curantur
6 voices triple-canon, 1 resolution

Canon 50, vol. II. Dissertazione prima, p. 187
Cithara sonante plaudo, Anacreon
Canon ad Unisson, et ad Sub-Diapason
Omne trinum perfectum
Non qui inceperit, sed qui perseveraverit
Cantus duarum facierum
5 voices double-canon, 1 resolution

Canon 51, vol. II. Dissertazione prima, p. 228
Tibio Phebe lex attributa est cantus, Homer
Canon ad Diapason, et Unissonum vicissim
Tot tempora, tot sunt voces
8 voices, 1 resolution

Canon 52, vol. II. Dissertazione seconda, p. 229
Dulce meum carmen est et cum fistula modulor, Theocritus
Canon ad Sub-Diatessaron
Canon ad Diapente
Canon ad Diapente
6 voices triple-canon, 1 resolution

Canon 53, vol. II. Dissertazione seconda, p. 279
Charum genus est cantorum, Homer
Canon 12 Voc. ad Unisson, et ad Diapente.
Contraria contrariis curantur
6 Voc. Canon cancrizat
18 voices double-canon, 1 resolution

Canon 54, vol. II. Dissertazione terza, p. 280
Tibia et fistula canebat bubulcus, Theocritus
Canon ad Diapason-Diapente
Plutonica subiit regna
Tertia pars si placet
2 voices / 3 voices double-canon, 2 resolutions

Canon 55, vol. II. Dissertazione terza, p. 326
Incipientes que canunt Deae et finientes carmen, Hesiod
Canon ad Diapason intensum

List of Canons in Cherubini's Collection

Canon ad Diapason expansum
4 voices double-canon, 1 resolution

Canon 56, vol. III. Prefazione, p. XI
Vicissim canebat dulci Voce
Canon ad unissonum
4 voices double-canon, 1 resolution

Canon 57, vol. III. Prefazione, p. XX
Canoros domi personat modos
Canon ad unissonum
2 voices, 1 resolution

Canon 58, vol. III. Cap. I, p. 1
Numeros Jonicos illis modulatur, Platon
Canon ad Sub-Diapason
Canon ad Sub-Diapason
4 voices double-canon, 1 resolution

Canon 59, vol. III. Cap. I, p. 24
Canebant Tibia suorum docti concentuum numeros, Atheneo
Canon ad Sub-Sesquiditonum
Canon ad Unissonum
4 voices double-canon, 1 resolution

Canon 60, vol. III. Cap. II, p. 25
Vicissim canebant dulci voce, Illiad
Canon ad Sub-Diapason
Canon ad Diapason
4 voices double-canon, 1 resolution

Canon 61, vol. III. Cap. II, p. 90
Die tota placabant carmine Phoebum, Plutarch
Canon ad Diapason
2 voices double-canon, 1 resolution

Canon 62, vol. III. Cap. III, p. 91
Per multa canunt mendacia vates, Plutarch

Canon ad Sub-Diatessaron; Sub-Diapason et ad Sub-Diapason-Diatessaron
4 voices, 1 resolution

Canon 63, vol. III. Cap. III, p. 148
Cantibus ad Lyram utendum
Canon 4 Voc.
4 voices, 1 resolution

Canon 64, vol. III. Cap. IV, p. 149
Musarum lepido semper ore canitur, Nicander
Canon ad tonum
3a pars si placet
2 voices / 3 voices, 2 resolutions

Canon 65, vol. III. Cap. V, p. 170
Invenere illum Cithara oblectantem, Illiad
Canon ad Septimam infra [3a pars]
2 voices / 3 voices double-canon, 2 resolutions

Canon 66, vol. III. Cap. VI, p. 198
Musarum incunda lyra
Canon ad unissonum
3a pars si placet
2 voices / 3 voices double-canon, 2 resolutions

Canon 67, vol. III. Cap. VI, p. 268
Non enim usitatos prius cantus afferimus sed illibatum exordimur hymnum
Canon ad Decimam et ad Sub-Diapente
4a pars si placet
3 voices / 4 voices double-canon, 2 resolutions

Canon 68, vol. III. Cap. VII, p. 269
Cantus afferimus sed illibatum exordimur hymnum
Canon ad 3a infra
Canon ad Unissonum
4 voices double-canon, 1 resolution

List of Canons in Cherubini's Collection

Canon 69, vol. III. Cap. VII, p. 369
Sumpto Monaulo Hymenaeum accinebam
Canon ad unissonum
3a pars si placet
2 voices / 3 voices double-canon, 2 resolutions

Canon 70, vol. III. Cap. VIII, p. 370
Tibiarum atque lyrae cantus musicus
Canon ad Unissonum
Canon ad Sub-Diapason
4 voices double-canon, 1 resolution

Canon 71, vol. III. Cap. VIII, p. 415
Citharam pulsare aut Tibias inflare dacuisti
Canon 5e Vocibus
5 voices, 1 resolution

Canon 72, vol. III. Dissertazione, p. 419
Tibiis virgo quidem caricos canit modos
Canon ad Sub-Diapente
2 voices, 1 resolution

Letter Sent by the French Musicologist Henry Expert (1863-1952) to the Administrator of the National Library in Paris on 10 June 1924[1]

---
[1]. The original in French, not reproduced here, is kept now at the BnF with the manuscript of Cherubini's collection.

Among musicians in ancient times — from the 15th to 18th centuries — pieces in strict imitation were in great favor, which we call canons. In their extraordinary number blossomed the most subtle enquiries in counterpoint. Some canons were enigmatic — so much so that their difficulty in interpretation defies the ingenuity of the most skilled readers.

Among the latter group are the canons that Padre Martini placed in vignettes etched at the beginning and end of the chapters of the *Storia della musica* (1757, 1770, 1781).

In the early years of the 19th century, Cherubini solved all these enigmas and formed a collection of the 72 most curious pieces, which he was pleased to show to amateurs of this kind of virtuosity, but which he never published, jealously keeping them for himself. Fétis alone obtained four of them, which can be read in his *Traité du Contrepoint et de la Fugue*[1].

After Cherubini's death, his precious collection disappeared and was thought to be lost.

In 1911-1912, in the Hôtel Drouot, the furniture of one of Cherubini's granddaughters was sold. There were also two piles of books; besides works by Cherubini, these contained scores by Méhul, Boieldieu, Halévy, etc., most of them autographed for Cherubini.

A music librarian, Mr. Costa-Borgna, bought these last remnants of the composer's library and had the rare luck to find, in his own hand, and calligraphed with love *Padre Martini's Closed and Enigmatic Canons... with solutions by L. Cherubini, followed by other Canons of various authors, solved by Fétis*.

The authenticity of this truly great autograph, with respect both to form and content, seem to me incontestable. The characteristic tremor seen in Cherubini's writing in the last twenty years of his life is already manifest here. The calligraphic portions can be attributed beyond doubt by comparing them to the facsimile of the *Canoni composti da L. Cherubini e copiati di sua propria mano per il suo caro Halevy*[2], published in March 1834 in the *Gazette musicale de Paris*[3]. Finally, the essential characteristics of the master's notation are present and evident.

As the title indicates, Cherubini added several canons by other authors, solved by his friend Fétis, to his collection of Martini's canons.

These remarkable pieces take up the last twenty-four pages of the manuscript. They are written in the same hand as Fétis used in the *Biographie des musiciens* (I identified the handwriting). This new autograph makes the collection even more valuable.

---

[1]. Fétis 1824.
[2]. BnF, MS-1695 (11).
[3]. *Gazette musicale de Paris*, I/supplement to no. 10 (9 March 1834).

Mr. Costa-Borgna is asking three thousand francs for this volume. I consider this sum to be very modest when considering the significance of this manuscript, which would place it among the gems of the Bibliothèque nationale's musical treasures.

Please be assured, dear sir, of my devoted respect.

Henry Expert

Librarian of the Conservatoire national de musique et de déclamation

P.S. Mr. Conta-Borgna lives at 1 rue du Pont-de-Lodi.

I am attaching to this report the manuscript with which he has been kind enough to trust me.

Plates

PLATE 1: Paris manuscript, *Canons Fermés et Énigmatiques du Père Martini. Extraits des Vignettes qui ornent son Histoire de la Musique; avec les solutions de ces Canons, par L. Cherubini, suivis par d'autres Canons de différents auteurs, résolus par Fétis*, BnF, VMB.MS.1 (1), p. 3r.

PLATE 2: Brussels manuscript, *Trente cinq canons résolus | par Fétis ms autographe*, KBR 4957, p. 1.

Critical Notes

Cherubini sometimes uses texts in his solutions whose spelling is very different from that of the original riddle. I have chosen Cherubini's notation. Cherubini does not make systematic use of custos. I have not added any custos that are not present in the original. All the words highlighted in the explanations of the solutions are in Cherubini's original.

Canon 1
Martini's designations for what Cherubini refers to «Circulaire» and «sans fin» are probably «canone circolare» or «infinito». See MARTINI, *Esemplare*, p. xxi.

Canon 3
Cherubini writes: «Each of them is in several parts, as indicated by the Latin words placed at the head of the first (see No. 55 of the Table), as well by the numbers marked at the head of the second». The expression No. 55 of the Table, *Post unum Tempus*, which appears at the beginning of the first canon, indicates that «The consequent answers one beat later, i.e. one measure of cut time or common time». What Cherubini probably means is that the simple presence of these expressions «Post unum Tempus» and «Canon 6. 7. 8. pars si placet» indicates the existence of consequents.

Martini offers four different solutions for this canon. None is identical to Cherubini's.

Canon 7
Contrary to what Cherubini indicates, the answer is at the lower octave.

It truly is similar motion that Cherubini suggests, not parallel motion, to allow the transposition of a 4th in the consequent of the second canon.

Canon 10
«Coruerunt» in the riddle and Martini's solution.

Canon 14
«Eius» in the riddle.

Canon 15
«Detachordo» in Cherubini.

Canon 16
«Psaltet» in Cherubini.

Canon 20
«et Iper Diatessaron» in Martini' solution and in the *Storia della musica* riddle.
«et ad Hyper Diapason» in Cherubini' solution and his copy of the riddle.
Martini proposes an identical solution.

Canon 21
5th voice, tenor clef in common time: Cherubini indicates a rest after the repeat barline, just before the custos.

Canon 25
Cherubini writes: «This canon, which comes with two indications (see Nos. 69 and 70 of the Table), has only two voices, since it is by one or by the other of these indications that the consequent can answer to the antecedent». This is because the word «vel» indicates «or alternatively».

In Cherubini's optional solution, last bar: B-flat quaver-note is missing in the original.

Canon 28
3/4 in Cherubini.

The expression 'Nec Mihi, Nec Tibi, sed dividetur' appears in Obrecht, IJO 32, *Nec mihi nec tibi sit, sed dividatur*: *Nec mihi nec tibi, sed dividatur* (Let it me neither mine nor thine, but divide it) (I Kings 3.26).

Cherubini writes: «Returning to the hidden meaning of the enigma, I think that this one relates to the disunity, or to the incoherence that reigns in the succession of keys always increasing between the antecedent and the consequent. Indeed, the canon itself is composed of two sentences, each in a different key, ascending one major second from one to the other. This means that the consequents, which faithfully imitate these sentences, produce a sequence of keys foreign to the main one. This forces both the antecedent and the consequents to always restart the first sentence of the canon one tone higher than the second sentence. This means that the canon ultimately becomes unperformable, even if starting it transposed down a lower fifth». Cherubini is probably referring to the second realization: instead of restarting a major third higher with each new realization, he had also considered starting a fifth lower with each new realization.

CRITICAL NOTES

Martini's and Cherubini's solutions differ radically. Martini does not propose transpositions for every new realization. He suppresses instead the entire second part of the canonic line in the 3rd and 4th consequents[1].

Canon 29

Cherubini writes: «Padre Martini however, in his History of Music, says that <u>Pente</u> means a <u>distance of five voices or sounds</u>; and that <u>Tessera</u> means a <u>distance of four sounds</u>». See MARTINI, *Storia della Musica*, vol. I, pp. 506-507.

Canon 30

Martini proposes an identical solution.

Canon 37

The second facet proposed by Cherubini is identical to a solution sketched by Martini in his original and not published in 2018.

Canon 39

«Cunctos» in Martini.

Canon 40

«Hominum» and «demulcentque» in Martini.

Cherubini writes: «The Latin words, *Qui deprimit* etc., have the same meaning as those placed in the Table from No. 40 up to and including No. 45; refer to these for an explanation. The words placed next to the canon indicate that it can have four voices, or eight voices if desired».

In the original riddle, these words are placed above the canon and not next to it as in Cherubini's transcription.

Martini proposes an 8-voice solution quite different from Cherubini's.

Canon 45

Bass line, bass clef, 2nd measure: in his copy of the riddle, Cherubini writes one minim G, but in the solution, he writes two crotchets G instead.

---

[1]. These comparisons have been made with Martini's original, not with the 2018 edition, where Martini's original is not faithfully reproduced. In this canon e.g., the edition keeps the second part of the canonic line for all the consequent parts.

Canon 46
Martini's designations to which Cherubini refers are probably 'canone infinito' (or 'circolare') and 'canone finito' — this last one for what Cherubini has named «terminé». See Martini, *Esemplare*, p. xxi.

Canon 48
Martini proposes an identical solution.

Canon 51
In his transcription of the enigma, Cherubini does not indicate «Non qui inceperit, sed qui perseveraverit». This phrase refers to the second canon. Martini proposes three other solutions. Cherubini's solution is identical to Martini's first The canon has an alla breve time signature. One counts for it eight quarter-notes per measure but it also counts eight measures for the entire canonic line.

Canon 53
Retrograde canon.

Canon 58
«Illis» and «modulatur» in Martini.

Canon 62
«Permulta» in Martini.

Canon 65
The indication «3ᵉ partie ad libitum» is not in the enigma. Besides writing this indication in his solution, Cherubini also writes «3ᵃ pars» in his copy of the riddle, next to the second canonic line.

Canon 66
«Iucunda» in Martini.

Canon 67
«Hymnum» in Martini.

Canon 69
F. Böhme proposed an identical solution.

Bibliography

Primary Sources

Aaron 1516
Aaron, Pietro. *Libri tres de institutione harmonica*, Bologna, Benedetto di Ettore, 1516.

Angleria 1622
Angleria, Camillo. *Regola del Contrapunto, e della musical Compositione. Nella quale si tratta breuemente di tutte le consonanze, e dissonanze coi suoi esempi à due, trè, e quattro voci. Della cognitione de' Tuoni; secondo l'uso moderno, e la regola agli organisti per suonare trasportato in vari luoghi bisognosi. Con due Ricercari l'vno à 4: e l'altro à 5. dell'autore, & un Ricercare, e Canoni à 2. 3. e 4. da cantarsi in vari modi del Signor Gio. Paolo Cima, al quale la presente Opera è dedicata*, Milan, Giorgio Rolla, 1622.

Bononcini 1673
Bononcini, Giovanni Maria. *Musico Prattico che breuemente dimostra il modo di giungere alla perfetta cognizione di tutte quelle cose, che concorrono alla composizione de i Canti, e di ciò che all'Arte del Contrapunto si ricerca*, Bologna, Giacomo Monti, 1673.

Bontempi 1695
Bontempi, Angelini. *Historia mvsica, nella quale si ha piena cognitione della teorica, e della pratica antica della mvsica harmonica; secondo la dottrina de' Greci […] e come dalla teorica, e dalla pratica antica sia poi nata la pratica moderna, che contiene la scientia del contrapunto*, Perugia, Costantini, 1695.

Cerone 1613
Cerone, Pietro. *El Melopeo y maestro*, Naples, Gargano & Nucci, 1613.

Cerreto 1601
Cerreto, Scipione (Napolitano). *Della Prattica musica vocale, et strumentale, opera necessaria a coloro, che di Musica si dilettano*, Naples, Giacomo Carlino, 1601.

Fétis 1824
Fétis, François-Joseph. *Traité du contrepoint et de la fugue contenant l'exposé analytique des règles de la composition musicale depuis deux jusqu'à huit parties réelles, […] par F.-J. Fétis […]*, 2 vols., Paris, Michel Ozi et C.ie, [1824].

Fétis 1846
Id. *Traité du contrepoint et de la fugue, contenant l'exposé analytique des règles de la composition musicale depuis deux jusqu'à huit parties réelles. Ouvrage divisé en deux parties. La première traitant du contrepoint simple*

et de ses applications dans l'imitation, le canon et les divers styles. La deuxième, des contrepoints doubles et de la fugue. Nouvelle édition. Revue Corrigée et Augmentée d'un grand nombre d'Exemples, 2 vols., Paris, E. Troupenas et cie., 1846.

FINCK 1556
FINCK, Hermann. *Practica musica*, Wittenberg, Rhaw, 1556.

FORKEL 1801
FORKEL, Johann Nicolaus. *Allgemeine Geschichte der Musik. 2*, Leipzig, Schwickert, 1801.

FRAMERY – GINGUENÉ 1791
FRAMERY, Nicolas-Étienne – GINGUENÉ, Pierre-Louis. *Encyclopédie méthodique, ou par ordre de matières; par une société de gens de lettres, de savans et d'artistes, précédée d'un Vocabulaire universel, servant de table à tout l'ouvrage, ornée des portraits de MM. Diderot & d'Alembert, premiers éditeurs de l'Encyclopédie. Musique. 1*, Paris, Panckoucke, 1791.

GLAREAN 1547
GLAREAN, Heinrich. *Dodecachordon*, Basel, Petri, 1547.

HEYDEN 1540
HEYDEN, Sebald. *De arte canendi*, Nuremberg, Schoenig, 1540.

LANFRANCO 1533
LANFRANCO, Giovanni Maria. *Scintille di musica*, Brescia, Lodovico Britannico, 1533.

MARTINI 1757, 1770, 1781
MARTINI, Giovanni Battista. *Storia della Musica*, 3 vols., Bologna, Lelio dalla Volpe, 1757, 1770, 1781.

MARTINI 1774/1775
ID. *Esemplare, o sia Saggio fondamentale pratico di contrappunto sopra il canto fermo*, 2 vols., Bologna, Lelio dalla Volpe, 1774, 1775.

ORTIGUE 1860
ORTIGUE, Joseph d'. *Dictionnaire liturgique, historique et théorique de plain-chant et de musique religieuse, au Moyen Âge et dans les temps modernes*, Paris, J.-P. Migne, 1860.

ROSSI 1618
ROSSI, Giovanni Battista. *Organo de cantori per intendere da se stesso ogni passo difficile che si trova nella musica, et anco per imparare contrapunto*, Venice, Gardano, 1618.

ROUSSEAU 1768
ROUSSEAU, Jean-Jacques. *Dictionnaire de musique*, Paris, Vve Duchesne, 1768.

Bibliography

Rousseau 1779
Id. *A Complete Dictionary of Music consisting of A copious Explanation of all Words necessary to a true Knowledge and Understanding of Music, translated from the Original French of J. J. Rousseau by William Waring*, London, Murray, 1779.

Tigrini 1588
Tigrini, Oratio. *Il compendio della musica nel quale brevemente si tratta dell'Arte del Contrapunto, diviso in quatro libri*, Venice, Ricciardo Amadino, 1588.

Zacconi 1596
Zacconi, Lodovico. *Prattica di musica utile et necessaria si al compositore per comporre i canti suoi regolatamente, si anco al cantore per assicurarsi in tutte le cose cantabili: divisa in quattro libri; Ne i quali si tratta delle cantilene ordinarie, de tempi de prolationi, de proportioni, de tuoni, et della convenienza de tutti gli istrumenti musicali*, Venice, Bartolomeo Carampello, 1596.

Secondary Sources

Arias 1989
Arias, Enrique Alberto. 'Cerone and His Enigmas', in: *Anuario Musical*, no. 44 (1989), pp. 85-114.

Beduschi 2007
Beduschi, Luciane. 'Survivance du canon énigmatique au xixe siècle: le cas de Sigismund Neukomm', in: Schiltz 2007, pp. 445-455.

Beduschi 2021
Ead. 'Luigi Cherubini's Solutions for Padre Martini's Closed and Enigmatic Canons: An Unpublished (and Overlooked) Pedagogical Collection', in: *Luigi Cherubini: A Multifaceted Composer at the Turn of the 19th Century*, edited by Massimiliano Sala, Turnhout, Brepols, 2021 (Studies on Italian Music History, 14), pp. 325-350.

Blackburn 2001
Blackburn, Bonnie. 'Aaron [Aron], Pietro [Piero]', in: *Grove Music Online*, 2001, <https://www.oxfordmusiconline.com/grovemusic>, accessed December 2023.

Blackburn 2012
Ead. 'The Corruption of One is the Generation of the Other: Interpreting Canonic Riddles', in: *Journal of The Alamire Foundation*, iv/2 (2012), pp. 182-203.

Blackburn – Holford-Strevens 2002
Ead. – Holford-Strevens, Leofranc. 'Juno's Four Grievances: The Taste for the Antique in Canonic Inscriptions', in: *Musikalische Quellen – Quellen Zur Musikgeschichte: Festschrift für Martin Staehelin zum 65. Geburtstag*, edited by Jürgen Heidrich, Hans Joachim Marx and Ulrich Konrad, Göttingen, Vandenhoek & Ruprecht, 2002, pp. 159-174.

BRUMANA 2001
BRUMANA, Biancamaria. 'Bontempi [Angelini, Angelini-Bontempi], Giovanni Andrea', in: *Grove Music Online*, 2001, <https://www.oxfordmusiconline.com/grovemusic>, accessed December 2023.

BUSI 1891
BUSI, Leonida. *Il padre G. B. Martini. Musicista, letterato del secolo XVIII*, Bologna, N. Zanichelli, 1891, [reprint Bologna, A. Forni, 1969].

CATALOGUE DES LIVRES 1817
Catalogue des livres de la bibliothèque de feu P.-L. Ginguené [...], Paris, Marlin, 1817.

CATALOGUE GÉNÉRAL 1760
Catalogue Général par ordre chronologique des ouvrages composés par moi, Marc-Louis-Charles-Zenobi-Salvador Cherubini né a [sic] *Florence le 14 Septembre de l'année 1760*.

COLLINS 1992
COLLINS, Denis. *Canon in Music Theory from c.1550 to c.1800*, Ph.D. Diss., 2 vols., Stanford (CA), Stanford University, 1992.

DELLA CROCE 1986
DELLA CROCE, Vittorio. *Cherubini e i musicisti italiani del suo tempo*, 2 vols., Turin, Eda, 1986.

FINCK 2008
FINCK, Hermann. *Canon*, Buenos Aires, Eduardo Sohns Libros de Musica, 2008.

HABERL 2000
HABERL, Dieter. *Bischöfliche Zentralbibliothek Regensburg. Thematischer Katalog der Musikhandschriften, Kataloge bayerischer Musiksammlungen. 7: Bibliothek Franz Xaver Haberl, Manuskripte BH 6001 bis BH 6949*, Munich, G. Henle, 2000.

LAMLA 1997
LAMLA, Michael. 'Canons on Artistic Prints in the 16th and 17th Centuries', in: *Music Fragments and Manuscripts in the Low Countries: Alta Capella – Music Printing in Antwerp and Europe in the 16th Century*, edited by Eugeen Schreurs and Henri Vanhulst, Leuven, Alamire Foundation, 1997, pp. 479-510.

LAMLA 2003
ID. *Kanonkünste im barocken Italien, insbesondere in Rom*, 3 vols., Berlin, dissertation.de, 2003.

LOWINSKY 1989
LOWINSKY, Edward E. 'Music on Titian's Bacchanal of the Andrians: Origin and History of the Canon per tonos', in: *Music in the Culture of Renaissance and other Essays. 1*, edited by Bonnie Blackburn, Chicago-London, The University of Chicago Press, 1989, pp. 316-320.

Bibliography

Mann – Wilson – Urquhart 2001
Mann, Alfred – Wilson, J. Kenneth – Urquhart, Peter. 'Canon', in: *Grove Music Online*, 2001, <https://www.oxfordmusiconline.com/grovemusic>, accessed December 2023.

Martini 2018
Martini, Giovanni Battista. *Canoni della Storia della musica*, critical edition by Alberto Zanotelli, Padua, Centro studi Antoniani, 2018.

Méthode de Chant 1803
Méthode de Chant, Paris, Imprimerie du Conservatoire, [1803].

New Senfl edition 2023
New Senfl edition 4, Motetten für sechs und acht Stimmen, Kanons par Ludwig Senfl, edited by Scott L. Edwards, Stefan Gasch and Sonja Tröster, Vienna, Hollitzer Verlag, 2023 (Denkmäler der Tonkunst in Österreich, 163.4).

Notice 1845
Notice des manuscrits musicaux autographes de la musique composée par feu M.-L.-C.-Z.-S. Cherubini..., Paris, Chez les Principaux éditeurs de musique, 1845.

Schiltz – Blackburn 2007
Canons and Canonic Techniques, 14th-16th Centuries: Theory, Practice, and Reception History. Proceedings of the International Conference (Leuven, 4-6 October 2005), edited by Katelijne Schiltz and Bonnie J. Blackburn, Leuven-Dudley, Peeters Publishers, 2007 (Leuven Studies in Musicology).

Schiltz 2015
Schiltz, Katelijne. *Music and Riddle Culture in the Renaissance, with a Catalogue of Enigmatic Canonic Inscriptions by Bonnie J. Blackburn*, Cambridge, Cambridge University Press, 2015.

Schnoebelen 1979
Schnoebelen, Anne. *Padre Martini's Collection of Letters in the Civico museo bibliografico musicale di Bologna*, New York, Pendragon, 1979.

Wuidar 2007
Wuidar, Laurence. *Canons énigmes et hiéroglyphes musicaux dans l'Italie du 17e siècle*, Bruxelles, Peter Lang, 2007.

Index of Names

A

Aaron, Pietro 12-13, 36, 39, 59-61, 87, 103
Agostino, Lodovico 43
Albrechtsberger, Johann Georg 1
Anacreon 1, 308, 310
Angleria, P. Camillo 12, 42, 59-61 98, 104
Athenaeus 311

B

Baini, Giuseppe 1
Basili, Andrea 1, 2
Blackburn, Bonnie xii-xiii, 17-18, 37, 86
Böhme, August Julius Ferdinand 3, 326
Boieldieu, François-Adrien 317
Bononcini, Giovanni Maria 35
Bontempi, Giovanni Andrea Angelini 12, 14, 24, 31, 33, 38, 43-45, 59-61, 63, 87, 91, 95-97, 100, 103
Brumel, Antoine 18
Busi, Giuseppe 2
Busi, Leonida 2-3

C

Capalti, Francesco 1
Carcinus 1
Cardoso, Manuel 12, 93
Cerone, Pietro 12, 14, 17, 22-26, 28-34, 36, 38-39, 41-42, 45, 56-57, 59-61, 86-87, 89, 91, 93, 97-101, 103
Cerreto, Scipione 23, 35, 54, 57
Cervellini, Giuseppe 1
Champion, Charles Antoine 1
Cherubini, Luigi xi-xiv, 3, 5-9, 12-13, 23-26, 28-33, 37-40, 43, 47, 52-57, 59, 61-62, 74, 83, 86, 104, 315, 317, 323-326
Chiti Carletti, Girolamo 2, 26
Cima, Paolo 42, 61

D

De Silva, Andreas 95

E

Expert, Henry xi-xii, 5, 56, 62, 318

F

Felipe III, King of Spain 22
Fétis, François-Joseph xiii, xiv, 2, 5, 13, 47, 52-57, 59, 62-63, 317
Finck, Hermann xiv, 12, 14-25, 28, 30, 36-39, 42, 44-45, 59-61, 86-99, 103
Flaminio, Giovanni Antonio 13
Floncel, Albert François 47
Forkel, Johann Nicolaus 52, 62
Framéry, Nicolas-Étienne 61
Frescobaldi, Girolamo 43

G

Garat, (Dominique) Pierre (Jean) 47
Gargano, Juan Bautista 22
Ghiselin, Johannes 23
Ginguené, Pierre-Louis xiii-xiv, 8, 13, 32-33, 47-52, 61-62
Glarean, Heinrich [Heinrich Loriti] 12, 14, 18, 24, 31, 59-61, 87, 92, 99
Gombert, Nicolò 40
Gossec, François-Joseph 47
Guichard, François 47
Gumpelzhaimer, Adam 35

Index of Names

H
Haberl, Franz Xaver 2
Halévy, Fromental 317
Hesiod 1, 308-310
Heyden, Sebaldo 23, 34-35
Homer 1, 308, 310

I
Ingegneri, Marc'Antonio 23
Isaac, Henricus 12

J
Josquin (Lebloitte dit) des Prez [Desprez; del Prato] 12, 18-19, 23, 26, 37-38, 86-87, 91, 93-94, 97, 100, 102, 113-114

L
Lamla, Michael xiii, 22, 43
Lanfranco, Giovanni Maria 35
Langlé, Honoré 47
La Rue, Pierre de 96
Lobo de Borja, Alonso 12, 24, 26, 86, 91

M
Martini, Giovanni Battista xi-xiv, 1-3, 5, 7-9, 11-26, 28-45, 47-57, 59-63, 74, 83, 86-87, 89, 92, 94-95, 98-99, 101-102, 317, 323, 325-326
Méhul, Étienne-Nicolas 47, 317
Memo, Andrea 1
Mensa, Diego 23
Metallo, Grammatio [Grammatico] 23
Montanos, Francisco de 23
Morales, Cristóbal de 17
Morosini, Giuseppe 2
Moulu [Molu], Pierre 39, 103
Mouton, Giovanni 12, 14, 37, 99, 102, 104
Mozart, Wolfgang Amadeus 2, 83

N
Nanino, Giovanni Maria 23-25, 28, 30, 54, 56-57, 86-87, 89, 92, 97, 99
Napoleon I, Bonaparte, Emperor 47
Neukomm, Sigismund Ritter von xi-xii
Nicander 312
Nucci, Lucrecio 22

O
Obrecht, Jacob 62
Ockeghem, Johannes 18, 39
Orto, Marbriano [Marbianus] de 18

P
Palestrina, Giovanni Pierluigi da 23, 39, 92
Paolucci, Giuseppe 2
Petrarca, Francesco xi
Petri, Heinrich 14
Pipelare, Matthaeus 37, 101
Plantade, Charles-Henri 47
Plato 1, 311
Plutarch 1, 311
Porta, Costanzo 39-40, 82-83
Pratinas 1
Pythagoras 1

R
Riccieri, Giovanni Antonio 43
Rodio, Rocco 23
Rolla, Giorgio 42
Rore, Cipriano de 23, 54, 57
Rossi, Giovanni Battista 12, 14, 24, 30-31, 34-37, 39-43, 45, 51, 59-61, 92, 100-102, 104
Rousseau, Jean-Jacques 48-49
Rovello 23

S
Sabbatini, Luigi Antonio 1
Sanguineto, Tomasso 99
San Pietro, Girolamo 13
Schiltz, Katelijne xii, 14, 37
Schnoebelen, Anne 1
Schoenigij, Valentini 35
Schuster, Joseph 1
Senfl, Ludwig 89, 92-94
Sophocles 1, 309
Suave, Pablo 23

Index of Names

T
Theocritus 1, 309-310
Tigrini, Oratio 35
Tinctoris, Johannes 11
Toulmon, Botté de 3
Turini, Francesco 50

V
Vaet, Jacobus 23
Virgil 1, 93, 309

W
Wranitzky, Paul 1
Wuidar, Laurence 43

Z
Zacconi, Ludovico 86, 94
Zanotelli, Alberto 1-3
Zarlino, Gioseffo 11
Zuccari, Carlo 1
Zuccari, Francesco Maria 3